CAUSE

CAUSE

...and how it doesn't always equal effect

GREGORY SMITHSIMON

MELVILLE HOUSE
BROOKLYN · LONDON

CAUSE
Copyright © 2018 by Gregory Smithsimon

First Melville House Printing: January 2018

Melville House Publishing
46 John Street
Brooklyn, NY 11201
and
8 Blackstock Mews
Islington
London N4 2BT

Book design by Richard Oriolo

mhpbooks.com
facebook.com/mhpbooks
@melvillehouse

ISBN: 978-1-61219-676-3
eBook ISBN: 978-1-61219-677-0

Printed in the United States of America
10 9 8 7 6 5 4 3 2 1

A catalog record for this book is available from the Library of Congress

contents

introduction:
causality

The sociologist Emile Durkheim wrote that we explain social facts with other social facts. Why did the most recent recession occur? Because of housing speculation. Why did housing prices inflate in a bubble? Because mortgage funds were lent in risky ways. Why did that happen? Because financial regulations had been loosened, mortgages were chopped up, resold, overrated by rating agencies and insured in unsustainable insurance schemes, and waves of capital flowed into the mortgage market seeking what seemed to be guaranteed high returns. And so on.

But this kind of reasoning often misleads both sociologists and the general public. It examines only one form of causality—proximate human actions—as causes of significant events in human history.

The problem is not that social facts don't cause other social facts. The problem is that, in our hubris and because of the limitations of our cognition, we too often make decisions as if *only* social facts can explain other social facts.

It is tempting to say that sociologists simply make the same disciplinary error that most other professions make: to a carpenter everything looks like a nail, so to a psychologist every conflict seems to have a psychological explanation, to a geneticist every human fault has a genetic basis, to an economist every action has an economically rational explanation.

But it isn't just a shortcoming of social scientists, or even of professionals generally, to explain social facts with reference to the field they know best. Often, we mistake complex conflicts for purely social ones. Take the case of Andrew Speaker.[1] In May 2007, he was diagnosed with a difficult-to-treat form of tuberculosis. Health department officials in Georgia warned him not to travel, for fear it could infect others. But Speaker and his father—both lawyers—attended health department meetings. They pressed the department on whether they were *banning* him from traveling. And because officials did not know if they had authority to issue such a prohibition, they said no. Speaker took that admission as a victory, moved up the date of his departure, and flew to Europe. He spent time in Greece, Italy, the Czech Republic, and Canada. Of course, viruses operate unaware of such legalist arguments, and Speaker was eventually quarantined and had a section of his lung removed in the treatment of his disease. Sure, he won his social battle with the Georgia state health officials. But the real battle was with tuberculosis. Although there do not appear to have been any further cases in any of those four countries, Speaker should have made his choice based not on the first battle but on the second.

We often think like Speaker—at our peril.

Think of global warming and its widespread, devastating consequences. Climate change deniers often ignore the science behind the phenomenon. To them it's a political battle (between those who seek environmental regulation, and those who oppose it) not a scientific one. To the nonregulators, climate change has little to do with the nonhuman, nonsocial, empirical question of whether the Earth is actually getting warmer. Unfortunately, it is. But rather than accept this thoroughly nonsocial reality of the physical world (and then fight over the political question of what response would serve them best), climate deniers couch the debate in purely social terms: the presumed political biases of the climate scientists, the economic disadvantages of imposing restrictions on emissions, the way climate change policies fit into preexisting differences between political parties.

When prescientific people experienced a natural disaster—a drought, a flood, a hurricane, they asked *why* it had happened. To answer, they engaged in the same sort of exercise we do today, seeking to explain social facts with other social facts: people are starving during the drought, *so* it must be the result of people's behavior before the drought. Communities were destroyed during a hurricane, *so* the community must have done something sinful to attract that hurricane. The notion that human behavior has the power to rend the skies and shake the earth is meaningful enough to us that even some modern religious figures blame wayward human conduct for disasters, including the flooding of New Orleans, Hurricanes Sandy and Isaac in New York, and earthquakes from Japan to Haiti to Virginia. This kind of absurd social explanation reflects how particularly human, and specifically flawed, is the very question of *Why?* When we ask *why* we are not asking for the physical mechanism, which we can often determine, but a personal or moral justification, which is rarely available.

This use of *why* sends us down a dead end. When we explain *why* climate change is occurring, the ensuing argument is about the moral judgment implicit in the explanation that modern capitalism has ruined the planet. The fight is less about parts per million in the atmosphere than about an intangible sense of *why*.

Why is a question that we have the grammar to construct, but it is a question without an answer. This morning my daughter asked me where she could find her birth certificate. I told her it was in a bin in the basement. *Why?* she asked. How could I answer? Mechanistically, the certificate was sitting in a bin, which, when we moved, got put in the basement, and that particular bin, owing to its size and the fact that it contained nothing we needed very often, had not been moved upstairs. That, however, is a meaningless answer. What she meant, and what I understood was, *The basement is dirty so I was hoping my birth certificate was stored in a bedroom closet or a drawer; I'm frustrated and unhappy that I have to go down to that dirty, dusty basement to get it.* Why *are you making me go down there? It's your fault.* I could offer my sympathy that she had to do an unpleasant task; I could apologize for not bringing upstairs something that I might have foreseen she might need. But it was meaningless to explain why an inanimate object was sitting where it had been left. *Why*, like its existential and theological cousins, "Why are we here?" and "Why me?," are not questions to be investigated but shouts to the heavens. As we'll see, we want only certain kinds of answers, narrow answers, and what's missing from those answers shortchanges us in comprehension and overpays in frustration. Our mistaken answers to *why* repeatedly hobble our understandings of social and natural causation.

Throughout *Cause* I argue that we, as humans, misunderstand causality in several key ways, and that if we can recognize our limitations, we can also see that world more clearly.

One crucial limitation is that we often create causal stories under conditions of fear. That's because we're mortal and life is short; racing through life, trying to survive, to raise children, to care for those we love, to make the world a better place, to enjoy as many of its fruits as we have time to. It is as if life were lived rushing through a train station we had never been to before, trying to find our platform while also looking for a good meal, a nice drink, a close friend, and keeping sight of our children, our spouse, our friends and family also running through the crowd. Causal explanations are like the mental map we make of the train station as we race through it. The map would be provisional and incomplete, but it would help us get where we need to go. If we made it on time, we would feel that our mapmaking skills worked well enough.

But our on-the-fly impressions of the workings of those larger social and natural systems are not reality itself. And although we have no choice but to rush through, at our less-than-century-lifetime speed, we do have enough time to enhance our understanding of the world and its systems of cause and effect.

In addition to the existential fears that color our explanations, racial fears, terrorism, climate change, natural disasters, teen pregnancy, crime waves, and reactionary fears of women, people of color, the poor and working classes all factor into and distort the stories we tell to such a degree that we often embrace misleading ideas about who human beings are, and what we really need. Causal explanations and fear can feed off of one another to disastrous effect.

In the first section of the book, I consider who we are as people: deeply social creatures, for whom making up stories to explain the world is so instinctive that we are essentially narrative-making machines. Rather than ideal, rational actors, we are social animals who have evolved to have a particular set of social needs and understandings. Here I consider what race means to measure the power of social meaning: how what we collectively believe can shape what we do, and how a concept like race is a very powerful (and very misleading) story. Who we are is tied up with the kinds of stories we tell about the world; in the final chapter in this section, I look at those stories—from movie morals to murder alibis we hear in court—to see how, on closer inspection, our explanatory stories often make much less sense than we imagine. We have evolved to recognize certain kinds of explanations and causality, but are unable to see other kinds. Because certain causes matter to us and others don't, we often shape satisfactory explanations in our minds when real world facts don't actually support them. We are hardwired to ask *Why?*, but it often produces unhelpful answers.

In Part Two, I consider the kinds of explanations that we leave out when we focus on the low-hanging fruit of social causes. For instance, the space around us matters in ways we don't always recognize: how we build our communities, after all, influences who we bump into during the day, and who is segregated from whom. There are reasons that all of our twenty-first-century global cities are located on major waterways, after all, and reasons that, even in an Internet age, people still pay more to locate their homes and businesses in crowded city centers. Likewise, biology and social stress interact in ways we don't recognize. To take one example, medical researchers have attributed the rise in obesity to many causes—poor diet, lack of exercise, even the temperature of our homes. But we forget the role of social stress on our body: people are adapted to put on weight in periods of uncertainty about food supplies. Can economic uncertainty lead to physical health problems? Our bodies respond to social stresses in predictable, but rarely considered, ways. Our world is shaped not just by social causes, but by physical, biological, and spatial developments we attribute uneven significance to.

Finally, in part three, I build on these discussions of how humans (often wrongly) determine cause and effect to explain how we might become better at it, and therefore better equipped to handle the great problems of our time. Whether to consider climate change as a natural or social problem, how to confront terrorism, what to expect as US political parties undergo a seismic shift; a clearer understanding of causality can be applied to our most urgent contemporary problems.

I conclude by proposing that we embrace what I call *dynamic causality*. Dynamic causality recognizes the limitations of our own ability to explain situations: that we are social, that we over-emphasize social causes and social knowledge, and that we under-play physical, biological, and natural influences. Dynamic causality recognizes both the inherent uncertainty of the world in which we must make decisions and our ability to improve those decisions. It rejects simplistic explanations and lets us use insights from the social sciences to better understand how we can act on urgent issues like global warming, racism, healthcare, and community building. It moves us from a static understanding of how things are to a more useful understanding of how we can bring about change.

One advantage of dynamic causality is that it can help all of us recognize that simply identifying the rigid structural factors that make our political world the way it is does not tell us much about how such a structural situation can be changed. Outcomes are dynamic, involve many variables, and can go in unexpected directions. I aim to show that there are both more opportunities for change than we think, and more changes going on right now than we are aware of.

This book aims to tweak the formula of the how-to book: not to be a better employee, but a better political citizen, considering how we, as people, think, in order to make better decisions about the big political crises we all face together. We are entering a period of unprecedented political turmoil, when the political parties, traditions, and truisms that have served us for several decades no longer explain our world or our political options. We'll have to take sides and make decisions. To do so, we have to see a little more of the world as it is, and see through what people's stories make it out to be.

....

part one

WHO WE ARE AND THE

STORIES WE TELL: HOW WE

THINK ABOUT CAUSES

I.

individuals are not rational

L ots of people are afraid of driving past massive tractor trailers on the highway—perhaps for more reasons than they know. In one study, a truck driver described "traveling down a flat, straight stretch of roadway in the middle of the night in clear weather. Suddenly he 'saw' a calf standing in the road ahead. He swerved his vehicle sharply to the left, and it overturned in the roadway."[2] The driver admitted that in the past he had seen "things that are not there." The driver wrote off the hallucinations to being very sleepy. But there's another explanation: he was lonely.

There have been stories about truck drivers at the wheel when they're tired, or drugged, or delusional from methamphetamines. But there's a rarely recognized danger of being alone.

We hear similar stories of British and US Air Force pilots experiencing disorientation, anxiety, and a feeling of "detachment from reality" after flying for extended periods without other human contact. The disorientation was more likely to happen when flying at high altitudes, not because of the thinness of the atmosphere, but because pilots could not see the ground. In short, they were suffering from sensory deprivation.

We have learned more in the last decade about sensory deprivation thanks to the use of various forms of solitary confinement against people captured, imprisoned, tortured, and "extraordinarily rendered" as part of the so-called war on terror. US prisons, too, have radically increased the number of prisoners subjected to solitary confinement, often for extended periods of time.

To explore causality in this book—the ways we explain the world and how to do it better—we need to dispense with generic models of the human mind and recognize the way it actually operates. The experiences of people in isolation strip away some of our assumptions. For starters, we call humans *rational individuals* when really we're neither. We're not individuals because when we're taken out of the company of other people, even for relatively brief periods, we fall apart. We're not rational because our rationales are shaped by where we see ourselves in the social world, where our ancestors were in the natural order, and what social concepts we adopt to understand everything around us. It's clear that we don't think like some idealized computer. Like the trucker who hallucinated the calf, we see things that aren't there. Like the pilots in the stratosphere, we lose sight of things that really do exist. Our vision is selective and creative, and how we make sense of it all depends on what we learn from the social web of people around us. Isolation distorts our perception of the world, and we need to be more alert to its appearance than we are.

. . . .

We understand physical torture more viscerally than the torture of iso-lation. Certainly, most of us imagine that physical torture must be far worse than being left alone. But the horrors of solitary confinement are as unparalleled as they are unexpected. US Senator John McCain, who spent two years in solitary confinement after being shot down while bombing Hanoi as a Navy pilot in the Vietnam War, described soli-tary in unequivocal terms: "It's an awful thing, solitary. It crushes your spirit and weakens your resistance *more effectively than any other form of mistreatment.*"[3] This assessment is from a man whose escape from his crippled plane broke his right arm in three places, his knee, and his left arm, who then had his shoulder broken from a blow from a rifle butt, and was stabbed in the ankle and groin with a bayonet. His inju-ries were left unset and largely untreated for five years while he was a prisoner of war, where he suffered years of dysentery that reduced him to one hundred pounds, and was regularly subjected to physical torture to the point of losing consciousness. If solitary confinement is worse than that physical agony, then we must reevaluate how our minds really work.[4]

McCain's description of how crushing solitary is shows us some-thing about the brain we're working with. First and foremost, it's deeply social. Alone, the mind loses its resolve, loses its identity, and doesn't even know what it knows. We think in particular ways. (It would be impossible for us to think in every possible way.) The fact that social context influences what we know, that we notice social explanations and disregard others, gives us a preview into what we overemphasize and what we overlook.

In this chapter, the underappreciated effects of solitary confine-ment demonstrate how harmful the mistaken image of ourselves as rational individuals has been—not just to prisoners, but to everyday people from truck drivers to anyone who has been lonely in a crowd, and to the economic models (and Robinson Crusoe stories) we mistakenly think will predict how people will act. First we need a sharper sense of how being alone affects us.

Solitary confinement is used extensively in US prisons, in part because federal courts rarely acknowledge that it is torture. (Courts have said they will intervene only in cases of physical injury, not mental torture.[5]) This classification grossly underestimates the damage solitary confinement does to the human psyche. One prisoner who had a long history of offenses was sentenced to five years in solitary confinement when he was recaptured after escaping from prison. When he was brought into the thirteen-by-eight-foot cell, he thought, "This is going to be a piece of cake." He would have a radio and television and could read. But within a few months, he was pacing back and forth compulsively, then began having panic attacks and screaming for help. He hallucinated and became enraged by routine sounds, like the shutting of a nearby door. Soon he heard voices speaking directly from the television, which he hid under his bed.[6]

Solitary confinement can induce a predictable and terrifying array of symptoms. Examining a hundred years of research, journalist Brandon Keim found that:

> Consistent patterns emerge, centering around . . . extreme anxiety, anger, hallucinations, mood swings and flatness, and loss of impulse control. In the absence of stimuli, prisoners may also become hypersensitive to any stimuli at all. Often they obsess uncontrollably, as if their minds didn't belong to them, over tiny details or personal grievances. Panic attacks are routine, as is depression and loss of memory and cognitive function.[7]

Beyond prisoners, pilots, and truck drivers, who else might exhibit those symptoms—extreme anger, hallucinations, mood swings, hypersensitivity, panic attacks, depression, and loss of memory and cognitive function? Security guards? Cowboys? Suburban housewives? Kids stuck on social media? Video game junkies? Elderly people living alone? In a society where we take our rationality and individuality for granted, and make few explicit accommodations for our needs as social beings, the effects of solitary are more common than we acknowledge. These symptoms identify the outer bounds of how far humans can be from other people.

The changes brought on by solitary can be rapid. Psychiatrist Stuart Grassian, a former professor at Harvard Medical School, is one of the foremost experts in solitary confinement. At the outset of his research, he expected to conclude that the prisoners' claims of mental distress were self-serving exaggerations. But he found that the effects were far more severe than he imagined. Grassian noted that, "even a few days of solitary confinement will predictably shift the electroencephalogram (EEG) pattern toward an abnormal pattern characteristic of stupor and delirium." Victims often describe falling into a "fog" in which they cannot remain alert or concentrate. They are simultaneously deprived of external stimuli and unable to process what little stimuli they may experience, causing them to be hypersensitive to small noises or irritation by slight physical sensations.[8]

In 2009, three Americans were hiking on the border between Iraq and Iran when they were taken into custody by Iranian guards, and ultimately brought to the notorious Evin prison in Tehran. Unlike Iranian prisoners, they were kept in individual cells, and were not beaten like the inmates whose screams they could hear through the doors. But this diplomatic treatment turned out to be its own torture. Even though they saw their interrogator almost daily, got outside twice a day, saw the guards who brought them meals, and occasionally even whispered to a prisoner in the hall or a nearby cell, Josh Fattal, Sarah Shourd, and Shane Bauer began experiencing the effects of solitary confinement after just a few days.

Josh Fattal became so hypersensitive to the whirring sound of the fan in his cell that he hid in his bathroom, under the sink, to avoid the noise. More symptoms, like depression and loss of cognitive function, followed: "In the cell," Fattal wrote in the account all three contributed to, "the *blankness* is my enemy. I don't have a better word for it, but it's dulling my mind. It's a world where I can only reference myself in circular loops, where nothing makes sense."[9] His mind could no longer assemble logical explanations: hearing a helicopter, he became sure he was about to be rescued, and fixated on the thirtieth day of their captivity, certain that that arbitrary and insignificant date would bring about their release.

People in solitary confinement are often haunted by hyperviolent fantasies in response to tiny perceived slights from other people. Josh imagined he'd find a particular guard one day on the street: "I'll push him into an alleyway, get him on the ground, and kick him and watch him bleed amidst garbage and rats." What atrocity had the guard committed? "Bystanders will try to stop my rage," Josh went on, "then I'll explain to them that this guy took my books when I was in prison, and they'll cheer me on as I continue kicking him."

From his experiences, Shane Bauer described solitary confinement as "the slow erasure of who you thought you were." Each of them tried all sorts of mental gymnastics—working out endlessly, remembering the details of their life in sequence, singing songs, reading when they could get books, writing when they could find a contraband pen, but they felt themselves breaking apart.

Sarah Shourd's isolation was longer and more complete, so her symptoms became proportionally more extreme. Many days, Sarah wrote, she fumed for *every waking hour* over the thought that Josh and Shane were able to speak to each other while she was still alone. Hypersensitivity and hallucinations consumed her as her concentration deteriorated. Sarah wrote later, "Like an animal, I spend hours crouched by the slot at the bottom of my door listening for sounds. Sometimes I hear footsteps coming down the hall, race to the door, and realize they were imagined . . . These symptoms scare me. I'm certain solitary confinement is having an effect on my brain." She couldn't focus to read and became hyperpossessive about her stuff. She had violent fantasies, like Josh: "I will run up to the first man in a suit that I see and I will wrap my hands around his neck and I will squeeze. I will squeeze his neck and look into his eyes as he tries to scream." She heard screaming down the hall, and only when a group of guards rushed in did she realize it was she who was screaming, and that the wall was smeared with blood from her beating her fists against the wall. "I'm going crazy in here," she told a guard soon after, "I am not safe!" Mirroring the thinking of US prison guards, this guard didn't understand what the problem was: "We gave you a TV—doesn't that help?"

This quick descent into madness, triggered by nothing—triggered, in fact, by the absence of any trigger—tells us something important about ourselves. Once we realize that humans are so social that being alone, even briefly, is unnatural to the point of being dangerous, we see that being a lone individual is fundamentally at odds with being *human*.

Researchers now know that solitary confinement reprograms the brain. Research suggests solitary produces significant changes, like a smaller hippocampus region and impaired brain development.[10] The damage is often permanent. In the most extreme cases, people may experience psychosis and be permanently debilitated. At minimum, individuals who have been subjected to solitary confinement are often unable to socialize, have trouble speaking, suffer from panic, and fail to reintegrate into the social world.[11]

Few of us think of spending time alone as torture; many of us fantasize about taking just such a break. Probably because being solitary seems, to the uninitiated, so unobjectionable, research on the effects of solitary confinement tends to follow a predictable cycle of revelation, abhorrence, and collective amnesia: First, a powerful institution in society, typically government, will experiment with solitary confinement, imagining it will be harmless, even therapeutic, certainly not painful. After accounts of its true ferocity come to light, it is banished. After about fifty years, however, the culture has forgotten the effects of the last round of solitary, and the cycle begins again.

That cycle dates back to 1829 in the United States, when the Philadelphia Prison (or Eastern State Penitentiary) opened. It sought to be more humane and effective than earlier, intentionally punitive prisons. Eastern State aimed to be meditative, reforming, and enlightened. Prisoners would remain in solitary cells—in isolation from bad influences and distractions—where they could begin reflecting on their lives and reforming their ways.

The problem was that prisoners did not reform but went mad. Charles Dickens visited the prison in 1842, and reported in horror how one man "gazed about him and in the act of doing so fell into a strange state as if he had forgotten something . . . In another cell was a German, . . . a more dejected, broken-hearted, wretch creature, it would be difficult to imagine." Dickens saw yet another man "stare at his hands and pick the flesh open, upon the fingers."[12] Eventually researchers concluded that "[i]t was unnatural . . . to leave men in solitary, day after day, year after year; indeed, it was so unnatural that it bred insanity."[13]

In 1890 a landmark Supreme Court case demonstrated how damaging the justices recognized solitary confinement to be. Colorado had passed a law requiring condemned prisoners be kept in solitary for a month before execution. A man murdered his wife before the law took effect, but was still sentenced to solitary. The court found that the month he was to be isolated before his execution was so severe that it constituted an additional punishment beyond what could be imposed. They let him go. As the court wrote,

> This matter of solitary confinement is not . . . a mere unimportant regulation as to the safe-keeping of the prisoner . . . experience [with the penitentiary system of solitary confinement] demonstrated that there were serious objections to it. A considerable number of the prisoners fell, after even a short confinement, into a semi-fatuous condition, from which it was next to impossible to arouse them, and others became violently insane; others, still, committed suicide; while those who stood the ordeal better were not generally reformed, and in most cases did not recover sufficient mental activity to be of any subsequent service to the community.[14]

After the 1890 decision, solitary confinement fell out of favor for some time. Research was resurrected in the 1950s and '60s by the US military, stirred by the fears of "brainwashing"—the concern that US servicemen captured in Korea and other wars could be converted to communism through the use of solitary confinement during their incarceration as prisoners of war. In some of that research, college students and other participants in psychological tests were subjected to solitary confinement. Though projects often anticipated subjecting people to such conditions for over a month, their rapid deterioration often led to the research being curtailed after just a week. That research on solitary confinement served as a warning, not an instruction manual, until it was blithely ignored by the Bush administration, which, half a century later, sought to use solitary confinement and other forms of torture against people picked up in Iraq, Afghanistan, and elsewhere who were presumed to be terrorists.

Our conception of human beings as individuals runs counter to the reality of our existence. The model of the "rational individual" is fundamentally flawed at its most basic assumption: *Individuals* are not rational. Individuals are not even individual. We are social, and we need social contact nearly as frequently as we need water to survive. If there is any human rationality, it is socially produced, not individually exercised. Where did we get this utterly inaccurate fiction that we could survive on our own?

Perhaps that fiction came, indeed, from fiction. Daniel Defoe's novel *Robinson Crusoe*, regarded (perhaps erroneously, as it turns out) as the first work of realistic fiction in English, imagined what it would be like for an industrious man, armed with all the knowledge that a highly developed early industrial society had bestowed on him, and most of the products of that society, which he extracted from a wrecked ship, to be alone on a resource-rich island. The book reads like a catalogue of weekend to-do projects: "I went to work to make me a little Tent with the Sail and some Poles . . . (where I lay with all my Wealth about me very secure) . . . I ptch'd two Rows of strong Stakes . . . When I had done this, I began to work my Way into the rock . . . In the interval . . . I went out once at least every Day with my Gun . . . to see if I could kill any thing fit for Food . . . Having now fix'd my Habitation, I found it absolutely necessary to provide a place to make a Fire . . ."[15]

Crusoe was a rational actor par excellence, and he has been cited time and again as the conservative economist's ideal of the economic man. Crusoe's explanatory value in the field of economics has been criticized for many reasons, from perspectives that consider gender, colonialism, and critical economics.[16] But as an illustration of the individual separated from society, there is one important criticism: the story as told is impossible. Crusoe goes right to work and suffers very little loneliness. This narrative contradicts the stories of the many sailors who were actually shipwrecked in Defoe's day. Shipwreck meant solitary confinement, and solitary confinement carries a cost. As Grassian noted nearly three hundred years later in discussing isolation's effects on solo sailors and long voyages, "Anecdotal reports of shipwrecked sailors and individuals accomplishing long solo sea voyages have generally described 'disturbances in attention and in organization of thought, labile and extreme affect, hallucinations and delusions.'"[17]

Indeed, the sailor whose shipwreck is most commonly taken to be the inspiration for Defoe's novel did experience some of the classic symptoms of isolation. Andrew Selkirk spent four years and four months on an island in the South Pacific. An account by the captain who rescued Selkirk explained that, according to the castaway, the greatest challenge had not been physical survival, but mental survival. The captain reported that Selkirk said he had "diverted and provided for himself as well as he could, but for the first eight months had much ado to bear up against Melancholy, and the Terror of being left alone in such a desolate place." Though he had gunpowder and could hunt the goats on the island, "at first he never eat any thing till Hunger constrain'd him, partly for grief . . . nor did he go to bed till he could watch no longer."[18] (We often imagine, when we stay up too late watching or scanning YouTube, that modern people stay up too late because of technology. Selkirk's experience suggests we stay up too late because we are lonely.)

Defoe's Crusoe feels briefly despondent, but makes up a list of the pros and cons for being on the island and, thankful to have had his life spared in the shipwreck, rationally decides he's better off and things could be worse. Demons, doubts, and depression dismissed.

Defoe may have missed Selkirk's difficulties of being alone because his model for Crusoe may not have been Selkirk at all. Recently, historian and writer Tim Severin concluded that Defoe based the iconic castaway on Henry Pitman.[19] Pitman's own account of being stranded on a deserted island had been published by the same family that published Defoe, and who Pitman had lived upstairs from. Pitman's story shows greater similarities to Crusoe's and, in considering the effects of isolation, critical differences from Selkirk's experiences. Henry Pitman was a surgeon and, like Daniel Defoe, participated in the Monmouth Rebellion that sought to overthrow King James II of England.[20] Hundreds of rebels were executed. Although Defoe was pardoned, Pitman and nearly a thousand other rebels were enslaved as punishment and sent to work in the British colonies of the West Indies. Pitman escaped with seven slaves and debtors from Barbados, who were shipwrecked on an island along with four pirates and an enslaved Native American. With thirteen people on the island, Pitman's detailed account makes no mention of loneliness. Indeed, his account, just like Crusoe's, reads like an ambitious home-improvement checklist: Pitman and his mates busied themselves building thatched houses, ingeniously forging knives out of sword fragments, constructing a boat, hunting sea turtles, salting and preserving meat, even making liquor by burying a bitter fruit stalk until it had softened, sweetened, and fermented. With a dozen people, the principal challenges were survival and creature comforts. Robinson Crusoe didn't battle isolation because his real-life inspiration was never isolated. The difference between the factual and fictional account may have seemed minor to Defoe, but it contributed to a very inaccurate image of human nature.

We can experience loneliness in our own lives, but fiction and culture—not only Defoe's Crusoe—seem ill-equipped to convey the emotions that isolation can evoke. Movies celebrate isolation: the action adventure hero lives alone, without family connections. A certain sedate genre of film revels in a scene of the protagonist going silently, and calmly, through a domestic routine, being at home, alone, in peaceful silence. It's fun to watch (especially if one's life is hectic and frantic), but the actors go through these motions so flatly that it looks as though they've studied robots to prepare for the scene. However, it's not how we, as people, actually respond.

Isolation does not have to be as profound as a desert island to have deleterious effects. Research shows that patients with heart problems who are placed on strict bed rest in the hospital often experience some of the psychological effects of solitary confinement, developing acute confusion, paranoia, and hallucinations, particularly at night.[21] As anyone who has spent time in a hospital can attest, patients are hardly alone—indeed, they may wish they were left alone, rather than being frequently awakened by nurses for tests, meals, and other requirements. Yet their separation from the regular intensity of social interactions, the extra hours staring at the ceiling, the walls, even the television, take a measurable toll.

Isolation doesn't have to mean *no* human company, just fewer people around. There are abundant studies on the heightened and severe interpersonal conflicts that can occur in places like Antarctic research stations, where groups of a few dozen people will spend a long winter confined to indoor research labs. During his Antarctic explorations, Admiral Byrd found it was most dangerous to have a unit staffed with just two people:

> [I]t doesn't take two men long to find each other out . . . even his [campmate's] unformed thoughts can be anticipated, his pet ideas become a meaningless drool, and the way he blows out a pressure lamp or drops his boots on the floor or eats his food

becomes a rasping annoyance . . . Men who have lived in the Canadian bush know well what happens to trappers paired off this way . . . During my first winter at Little America I walked for hours with a man who was on the verge of murder or suicide over imaginary persecutions by another man who had been his devoted friend.[22]

Even diminished social engagement, or the restriction of people's circle to a small, confined group of individuals, can have catastrophic effects. Sociologist Georg Simmel theorized that a "dyad" of two people was the smallest unit of social interaction, but Admiral Byrd's observations suggest that even a dyad cannot stay healthy outside a considerably larger network of connections among people.[23]

How broad could the effects be of a syndrome whose conditions are easy to create, but whose dangers are generally not recognized?

The Technologies of Solitude

We underappreciate the impact of some experiences and overestimate the effect of others. Few things have been more hyped in recent decades than the impact of the Internet. "When I say, 'The Internet changes everything,' I really mean everything," claimed Oracle CEO Larry Ellison in 1999.[24] This bit of hubris is so widely embraced it's hard to know who said it first; it could as well have been Bill Gates's declaration that "Here on the edge of the twenty-first century, a fundamental new rule of business is that the Internet changes everything."[25]

Claims that the Internet is the most important invention ever, or that it has changed business, or culture, or commerce more than any other technology, invite critical comparisons. The telephone, after all, must have been unbelievable when users first realized they could have a private conversation with someone nowhere near them. Until that moment in human history, if someone you knew walked farther away than you could yell, you could no longer speak to them in real time.

But even if computer CEOs overhype the Internet, inventions can change daily interaction so dramatically that we no longer know what life was like for our predecessors. The more technology changes our lives, the more it obliterates our sense that things were ever different. Histories of how people ate in centuries past often scoff at the bland brutality earlier diets expressed toward vegetables. Humorist Bill Bryson is typical in his wry remark that in the Pilgrims' diet, vegetables were "boiled without pity."[26]

Why on earth did people boil vegetables to a colorless pulp? Authors never really answer the question. The answer, however, is the same reason tourists avoid eating raw salad in Mexico, and it's not nearly so funny: eating uncooked vegetables grown on farms with manure fertilizer, unwashed, in places with poor sanitation and unclean water can get you killed. Nineteenth-century hygiene in the United States was far worse than it is in Mexico today. (A related question never gets answered: When people mention Montezuma's revenge, the general diarrhea tourists can be afflicted with, someone inevitably asks, "So what do people who live there do?" People conjecture an answer about stronger stomachs, or getting accustomed to the bacteria in the region. The answer, once again, is not funny. They die. But not everyone. Mostly babies die, and the elderly. The United States has an atrocious, scandalous infant mortality rate, at 5.4 deaths per 1,000, putting us at thirty-fourth in the world, in the company of Malta, Hungary, Poland, and Slovakia, which have considerably fewer resources. But in Mexico, 16 babies out of 1,000 die in their first year of life, ranking our neighbor eighty-second in the world.[27]) As a society we have forgotten how dependably uncooked dirty vegetables make you sick because we have good septic systems and clean running water, food regulation, and refrigeration.

Just as we don't remember what life was like before we could eat raw vegetables (or what life was like when malaria was still prevalent in large parts of the United States), the arrival of the Internet is dwarfed by the collective introduction of the television and radio, especially if partnered with the air conditioner, window screen, and record player. These technologies of solitude changed the human experience in ways we overlook.

If we assume ourselves to be individual, rational actors, the impact of these technologies seems less significant. But remember, we aren't. Think of the phonograph for a moment. Before the phonograph, music was always a social experience and no one had ever listened to music alone. It took a group of people, with musical instruments, to play a song, and they'd play it for a group who made up the audience. Humans have only been able to turn on a radio—in the car, while doing dishes—for less than one hundred years. The radio completely reversed the traditional experience of hearing music, transforming it from an act of coming together with people to retreating away.[28]

The preeminent historian Kenneth Jackson's account of life before modern suburban conveniences is a useful reminder of what life was like before the technologies of solitude.

> A century and more ago . . . a house was a place of toil, a scene
> of production, the locus of food preparation and of laundering
> and of personal hygiene. During free hours, it was a place to get
> out of. The ventilation, heat, and lighting were atrocious; it was
> hot in summer and cold in winter. Window screening, which
> one observer termed 'the most humane contribution the 19th

Century made to the preservation of sanity and good temper.'
was not introduced until the late 1880s; before that time swarms
of gnats, mosquitoes, June-bugs, and beetles moved at will
through domestic quarters. The result . . . was an enthusiasm
for the commonality of neighborhood life. To be within the four
walls of a house was to be away from the action. Among its few
pleasures were reading and making love.[29]

Not only did air conditioning and window screens make indoors a
pleasant place to be, television and radio were technologies that, like
scuba gear, allowed us to dive into the abyss of being alone for longer
times without risking the hazards associated with even brief periods of
isolation. Television and radio temporarily fool the brain into thinking
that we are not alone.

And it works, for a little while. A successful radio DJ makes people
feel as though he or she is talking directly to them. An event like New
Year's Eve is almost more important on television than in person: there's
a party going on on television and we want, somewhat desperately, to
be part of it. Traditionally, the later at night and the lonelier it got, the
more television programs mimicked a party, so that live audiences and
laughing late night variety show hosts, from Jack Parr to Johnny Carson
to Joan Rivers to David Letterman to Conan O'Brien to Arsenio Hall to
Jon Stewart to Stephen Colbert, continued the genre on late-night television long after the variety show had disappeared from other hours.
(The daytime variety show with a live audience was also a popular
format on television when large numbers of women were home alone
during the day, but more about that later.) Viewers needed television
to convince us we were not alone; today, a flow of social media video
clips and images soothe the same late-night anxiety that shipwrecked
Andrew Selkirk could not calm.

Occasionally something interrupts our wired lives: a summer blackout, for instance. What happens when the power goes out reveals a lot about the technologies of solitude: everyone comes outside. They sit on their porches; they talk to neighbors. And they *stay* outside. They stay past dark; the kids stay out late. In such situations if someone has to go inside for something—to search for more flashlight batteries, perhaps—the journey into the house is quick and furtive, as if the house is about to collapse: go in, get what is needed, and hurry outside again, to rejoin the crowd.

But technological aids to isolation work only temporarily. As prisoners in isolation found, eventually the mind realizes the television broadcast is not a real conversation, and the brain begins constructing conversations of its own. Imaginary voices coming out of televisions, not the ones actually broadcast, take over a person's consciousness.

Radio in particular had another profound role—it made modern commuting possible. Being in a car is a profoundly isolating experience. Most Americans drive alone, and many do so for hours a day. So-called "extreme commuters" log ninety minutes or more each direction on their way to and from work. Imagine what it would be like to drive that distance in silence, with no radio, day after day. Three hours round-trip in an empty car? Every day? Those three hours alone would feel like torture. And where do Americans arrive at the end of these radio-enabled commutes? In many cases, the single-family home.

Suburbia has been subject to many criticisms; one of the earliest and most influential of these was Betty Friedan's book, *The Feminine Mystique*. In it, she argued that postwar suburban wives and mothers suffered from "the problem that has no name."

What, exactly, is the problem with no name? Friedan interviewed educated, physically comfortable women who had moved out to the suburbs to be wives and mothers, and felt a vague but profound unease and unhappiness. "Sometimes," Friedan wrote of a suburban woman, "she went to a doctor with symptoms she could hardly describe: 'A tired feeling . . . I get so angry with the children it scares me . . . I feel like crying without any reason.'" A woman told Friedan that "sometimes the feeling gets so strong she runs out of the house and walks through the streets. Or she stays inside her house and cries." A mother of four said, "I'm desperate. I begin to feel I have no personality."[30]

Friedan explicitly stated that the problem with no name began in 1945, at the end of World War II. Many things changed in the post-war period. Certainly there had been changes in education—the rate of women who graduated from college roughly doubled from 1930 to 1950, from about 8 percent to 17 percent. But because Friedan was considering only college-educated women, college graduation rates would not have created postwar dissatisfaction, only enlarged the pool.[31]

The bigger change was the mass migration to classic suburban developments. And Friedan wrote about women who adopted this new domestic setting. The women themselves are clear that the anxiety and unhappiness they face is linked to the suburbs, and that they didn't feel this way when they lived in the city, even in much more primitive housing. One "young wife" living on Long Island explained her symptoms and contrasted urban and suburban life: "I sleep so much. I don't know why I should be so tired. The house isn't nearly so hard to clean as the cold-water flat we had when I was working. The children are at school all day. It's not the work. I just don't feel alive." A cold-water flat—an apartment with no hot water coming out of the faucet—is not an easy place to live, to say nothing of trying to clean dishes, floors, babies, and bodies with only ice cold water and water heated on an old stove. The young woman didn't exactly remember the flat fondly, but she knew her emotional problems didn't exist in that old city neighborhood. Something had changed when she had moved.

The women Friedan interviewed described the symptoms of the problem that has no name as depression, lack of energy, mood swings and easy anger, and the loss of a sense of self. The symptoms Friedan chronicled can be called by many names. Nothing socially significant has a single cause, and the headline-grabbing explanations—the lack of professional and sexual fulfillment Friedan identified in her interviews—were real. But the "problem that has no name" does have a name. That name is solitary confinement.

Friedan's subjects had moved out to the suburbs in an era when the average suburban household had only one car, which the husband drove to work. The wife was isolated at home, perhaps with a young child or children, who were physically present (and charming and lovable, one hopes) but not intellectual, conversational, or emotional equals. Reports from the day describe an astonishing level of isolation. In one account, when a mother's baby stopped breathing, none of her neighbors had a car to drive to the hospital. There was no way to get help in time. All one mother could do in the end was baptize the baby in the kitchen sink. Hot running water was cold comfort in the isolated new suburbs.

In his landmark study of the suburbs, *The Levittowners*, Herbert J. Gans tried to deflect elite critics' disapproval of the suburbs. No, he insisted, most residents there were happy. Gans is one of the most sensitive, insightful, and provocative researchers the field of sociology has ever had. But here, close attention to his own data tells a different story from the argument he sought to make. Men there were happy, but they drove to work in the city and spent few waking hours in the suburbs. By his own account, the suburbs were *unhappy* for women, children over six, the elderly, the lower class, and the upper class. More to the point, Gans reports that women in Levittown felt torn away from the urban communities they had lived in before, where they were close to their mothers, siblings, school friends, and neighbors. Gans observed that the working class, who made up the lion's share of Levittown residents, had a close circle composed of family members—like cousins and siblings—and friends from childhood but did not make new friends easily. These women now lived in the suburbs where a call back to their old home was a long-distance call whose cost made frequent contact, even by phone much less in person, prohibitive.[32] In a survey, 57 percent of suburban women missed the old neighborhood.[33]

The suburbs do not have a monopoly on isolation and alienation. Much of the worst urban design of the last one hundred years—the massive urban renewal projects that produced barren plazas, isolated towers on vacant windswept expanses, urban housing projects on green lawns that can't be played on socially, but were expected to be appreciated passively and individually—is the product of the mistaken impression that designs should maximize privacy and individual space, rather than encourage sociability. William H. Whyte, an iconoclastic magazine journalist who specialized in challenging people's thinking about how we interact in cities, characteristically exposed the absurdity of this assumption. His research in the 1970s about why some urban plazas were popular but most were cold, empty, unloved, and unused came to a conclusion that was contrary to the prevailing wisdom of urban planning at the time. "What attracts people most is other people," he deadpanned. "Many urban spaces are being designed as though the opposite were true and what people like best are places they stay away from."[34]

Beginning in the mid-twentieth century, we organized our lives along the principles of the big bang: a hot, dense city exploding outward, each member of a network of people becoming an individual who sped out into increasingly empty space. Why did we speed away from community, from a belief in society itself?

Certainly suburban tract houses were the product of a housing policy that was driven by profit, not the needs or preferences of customers. (William Levitt of Levittown, for instance, did no customer research to determine the design of his houses; their design was determined by the most efficient means of production.) Levitt may have been insensitive to the social needs of people, but he was not hostile to them. As for homeowners, people moved out to the suburbs for more space, or to escape ethnic change (or restrictive ethnic ties) in their old neighborhoods, but not to inflict the injuries of solitary confinement on themselves or their family members. We did not recognize the isolation we were subjecting ourselves to, and we did not in part because of the ascendant belief that people were individuals, and that they could be ripped—as the suburban generation was—out of their communities with no harm done.

This suburban experiment took place during the historic shift known as the Great Migration, when African Americans moved out of the rural South and into the urban North in unprecedented numbers. Some of the more anodyne explanations for the explosion of American suburbs focus on the mechanical: that because we built highways we moved out to the suburbs. But why would highways make us move out? And why, if we didn't want to move out, did we decide to build the highways?

The cause, in this case, is more human than technological. People wanted space. They needed new homes after a decade and a half of Depression and war-induced shortages of housing and everything else. Other suburbanites moved out of the cities to a very significant degree because people who were Black were moving in. Observers call the process "white flight."

The hysteria of white flight is another phenomenon that we rarely appreciate in its full impact. In a few short decades, US cities went from centers of commerce, population, and capital to disinvested shells. By the early 1960s, after a few decades of the Great Migration and the opening of the suburbs, more than one writer described New York as "a paved jungle where muggers, rapists and gangs roam poorly lit streets, assaults, beatings and sex crimes sweep the city."[35] When African Americans moved in, whole blocks of white residents would put their homes on the market and move, sometimes within months or even weeks.

As whites ran away from Blacks, they ran away from each other as well, and isolation increased: families retreated to the suburbs, locked the doors, stopped trick-or-treating in public. Later, children stopped playing on suburban streets and were kept indoors. They rode buses (or drove cars) to schools built on suburban scales, which were too far to walk to from home. The public spaces of the city were suspect, and the public spaces of small-scale downtowns wilted under competition from privately owned (and thus more carefully surveilled and controlled) shopping malls. White flight's hysteria accelerated that suburban big bang, propelling Americans even faster into empty space that left them far from sites of frequent, face-to-face social contact. In the Great Migration, white Americans ran away from American society rather than integrating it—to our detriment. Eventually, Black and Latino Americans were able to break the color line and join the suburban exodus out of underinvested urban areas. Today, half of all African Americans in the one-hundred largest metro areas live in suburbs, not center cities. My research on African American suburbs indicates no reason to think that the effects of that isolation know any color line. Most of America had driven away to the solitary confinement of automobile-dependent suburbs.

Without ongoing, meaningful social contact, we are no longer rational beings. We lose our identity and have a disembodied sense that we don't know who we are. Because people are social, and only exist, properly speaking, in a web of social networks, it doesn't require malicious action to hurt people, only inattention.

Certainly, men direct hostility toward women, and that patronizing disregard was all the more evident in the early postwar period Betty Friedan wrote about. But a failure to maintain concern about the well-being of another person—an invisible man or an invisible woman—is just as dangerous. Yet whole swaths of the population are touched by isolation in their homes, their jobs, or their hospital rooms.

The point is not that we've forgotten what social life is supposed to be like; we forget earlier forms of life all the time. Life before radio and television is a life I never knew. Life before cell phones and the Internet is one my children will never know. After technological changes substantially reorganize our daily lives, we have no way of experiencing what life was like before, and certainly no way of reconstructing the different experiences of various races, classes, and genders. We also reorient our understanding of human nature: marrying technological change and the exigencies of market-based ideologies, we imagine we are not people, but isolates.

Despite this collective amnesia about life before the latest gadgets, we can draw one clear conclusion: people cannot live isolated from others, and avoid doing so even for short periods. Even partial isolation is dangerous, and sometimes permanently damaging, to a substantial proportion of people. Paradoxically, technology simultaneously mitigates the effects of isolation by mimicking social interaction and leads us deeper into isolation.

We understand the world not as objective individuals but as groups of people with shared ways of making sense of it. The stories we tell and the explanations we make up cannot be those of an individual, rational mind, but develop only as the product of a collective mind with particular evolutionary, biological, and social needs. Social contact and participation in making sense of things are needs that real estate developers disregarded in the postwar suburbs, that software developers toy with in social media, and that employers disregard when creating isolated jobs. As the next chapter shows, as we move away from that social context, whether because of isolation, the passage of time, or cultural difference, even everyday stories make less and less sense.

When we treat people as rational individuals or an invisible person, we deny them their very specific, distinctly social humanity. It's time we understand socially who we are, how we think, and how to do it better.

2.

we are narrative-making machines

How many times have you been disappointed by a classic? A friend says you must watch a particular movie, or someone from your parents' generation recommends a great novel. You sit down with it, but it falls flat. Often the story itself just doesn't make sense.

The film *Barefoot in the Park* is just such a classic. One of the longest-running nonmusical plays in Broadway history, the story, by Neil Simon, was made into a popular film in 1967 featuring two great stars of the era, Robert Redford and Jane Fonda. It captured a generation's imagination with the story of a fun-loving young woman, Corie, who married a reliable but somewhat stiff lawyer, Paul. They move into Greenwich Village, but he's not feeling the bohemian vibe. Corie accuses Paul of being too "proper and dignified"; she bristles against people who are "so stuffy" and wants him to be more fun loving and carefree:

> CORIE: You have absolutely no sense of the ridiculous. Like last Thursday night. You wouldn't walk barefoot with me in Washington Square Park. Why not?
> PAUL: Simple answer, it was 17 degrees.
> CORIE: Exactly. It's very logical, it's very sensible, and it's no fun.

The story reaches its resolution in the last scene. The rules of Hollywood plotlines require that the square loosen up and learn to enjoy life. But when I watched the film decades after its release, the climax hardly made sense: Corie and Paul fight, and Paul moves out. In the morning Corie finds him slouched behind a wall in the park, very drunk. He is vaguely hostile. He stumbles about with a bottle in his hand, barefoot. She observes, flatly, that he's drunk. He throws a half-full trash can on his head, dances around, tries to jump over a park bench, falls, and briefly passes out. He next tells Corie that he shouldn't move out of the apartment, she should. Apparently, viewers in 1967 (my parents included, who enjoyed the movie very much) took this behavior to be a sign not that Paul *had* a problem, but that he had *solved* his problem.[36] I didn't get it. He hadn't become more attuned to beauty and fun. If before Paul had been uptight (and secretly unhappy with his buttoned-down life), now he was also showing signs of a drinking problem and hostility toward his unfortunate new wife.

The audience in 1967 saw a happy ending. Enough alcohol liberated Paul to walk "barefoot in the park" while it was freezing out, and he was finally free of social norms that had required him to be buttoned down, sober, or polite to his wife.

Sometimes stories just don't make sense. But we cannot understand the world without them. So tightly do we cling to the stories we tell that they can be nonsensical and still make sense to us. Our causal stories are strange creatures, emotionally satisfying tales that make us feel like we've answered the all-important question *why* when we've done no such thing. We imagine they reflect our world. But far from being reflections of reality, causal stories are the (often imperfect) creations of our (often imperfect) human minds, fascinating for how they use particular, well-worn paths of our primate brains to string together events, beliefs, and objects into what appears to be a causal chain with a moral message.

The constructed nature of causality becomes clearer over time: because a causal account is generally embedded with assumptions specific to the time and place of the storyteller, to the extent that other people share the assumptions of that time and place, the story makes sense. The more removed we are from the telling, the fewer assumptions we share with the speaker about human nature, for instance, and the more odd and inexplicable the story. Accounts from our own society about the origins of the universe, the nature of the world, or the meaning of natural objects seem part of the fabric of nature itself, but after the passage of many years, those accounts stop making sense. The assumptions that supported them have been replaced with others.

Causal stories normally include a moral component, suggesting not only that people can influence events, but also, if they try to do so in socially acceptable ways, morality will help swing the odds in their favor: to win a war one must fight harder and smarter than their opponent, but the implicit suggestion in most stories we tell about war is that being on the moral side of the war helps us win.

Causal accounts, these imperfect concoctions, strung together timelines with a dubious moral motor driving the whole thing, are successful if they tell a story that adequately explains how to act in the world, or convinces others to see the world the way we do.

The sociologist Charles Tilly took a stab at distinguishing different kinds of stories and the purpose they serve. For Tilly, whose scholarly productivity over a fifty-year career averaged a book a year and a scholarly article every month,[37] taking a stab meant a book and at least three articles explicitly on the topic. In his book *Why?*, Tilly outlined the different types of explanatory accounts people use, organized by whether they were disseminated by specialists or everyday people, and whether they tried to provide cause-and-effect explanations of events, or merely formulaic justifications for an event.[38] A fourfold table of these kinds of stories would look like this:

TILLY'S TYPES OF EXPLANATIONS

	POPULAR ACCOUNTS	SPECIALISTS' ACCOUNTS
FORMULAS	Conventions "The train was running late"	Codes *Legal or Religious formulas:* A marriage or inheritance is proper if done correctly, irrespective of whether it "should" be done by other measures.
CAUSE-EFFECT	Stories How she saved her son from a wild boar in the woods	Technical Accounts Engineers' descriptions of why a bridge collapsed

The "formulas" in Tilly's typology are less important for our purposes; formulas are substitutes for causal accounts; they abdicate the responsibility to explain why things happened, and provide a cookie-cutter explanation that lets us skip consideration of the morality or righteousness of what happened.

The causal accounts I focus on in this book fit largely into Tilly's category of "Stories." He argued that stories do several things. First, they *simplify* social processes so they can be easily communicated. They truncate cause-and-effect, calling up a limited number of people whose disposition and actions, in a relatively limited time and space, cause the actions under discussion: Kennedy ended the Cuban Missile Crisis, Gorbachev ended the Cold War, Osama bin Laden attacked America, Putin challenged the West. Second, stories describe not just a mechanical process, but "include strong imputations of responsibility, and thus lend themselves to moral evaluations."[39] People change their stories depending on their audience: a football player tells a different story of the lost game to a journalist than to a teammate. Because our stories explain outcomes as the intentions of actors, Tilly pointed out, we inevitably minimize or ignore the role of errors, unanticipated consequences, and a host of other influences statisticians recognize but lay storytellers rarely do.[40] Instead, stories have a strong moral component, give "pride of place" to human actions, and often personify nonhuman actors—whether an animal, a storm, or a bureaucratic organization— with human qualities and behaviors. Most of our understanding of people, politics, our own lives, and the world are captured not in technical accounts but in popular stories, so most of our understanding in these areas is limited by our story types.

Stories also manage and reinforce our interpersonal relationships. For instance, when your spouse tells a story of an argument with the dry cleaner, they are asking you to take their side against the dry cleaner, maintaining your domestic alliance against the demands of the outside world.

Tilly considered how people used stories in social settings that are inevitably knocked lopsided by power and inequality. Stories exist within a relationship between people. As a paymaster during the

Korean War before his career as a sociologist, Tilly could approve or deny a request for advanced pay by creating a story about what the rules allowed. But he had a hard time saying no to a request from the commanding officer, who could reject his story. People are likely to disagree over stories and explanations when they disagree about the nature of their relationship to each other: if a business owner treats someone as a customer when that person feels they are a friend, the friend may find the explanation ("business is business") unsatisfactory. Elites can often use their authority to give explanations without being challenged.

Stories simplify. They pare down the number of actors, reduce the account to proximate causes, and elide complex or distant causality. The limitations of human storytelling require this simplification: we speak about one hundred words per minute, and in a friendly conversation we have only a few minutes to tell a story.

The more fabricated a story is, the more evident are the processes of narrative streamlining, and the more likely it is to conform to the conventions of a story (of individuals acting with identifiable moral purposes, and little ambiguous action or clutter). Early in the 2016 presidential election campaign, Donald Trump claimed that on September 11, thousands of Middle Eastern Muslims in northern New Jersey publicly celebrated the collapse of the World Trade Center towers.[41] The story is false. But many news accounts investigating the myth traced it back to a complex set of less narratively coherent events that had scattered on the ground the raw materials from which Trump constructed his contorted tale.

On September 11, 2001, a woman in her New Jersey apartment looked out her window at the burning towers with binoculars. In her parking lot, she saw three men on the roof of a white moving van labeled

"Urban Moving Systems." They were taking pictures of the burning Trade Center. The woman, who wished to be identified in news reports only as Maria, found their composure strange. "They were like happy, you know . . . They didn't look shocked to me. I thought it was very strange."[42] She found the behavior remarkable enough that she wrote down the van's license plate number and reported it to the police. The men left, but were pulled over near the George Washington Bridge later on September 11.

From this limited information, reporters tried to make sense of what happened, stringing pieces into a narrative like points in the sky connected into a meaningful constellation. The story spread broadly in the twenty-four-hour media coverage after the attacks.

The first accounts reported that the men were Middle Easterners who were spotted celebrating on September 11 as the towers burned, and were arrested and deported. The *New York Post* reported that an unnamed source said men had been "cheering" and "jumping up and down" on September 11. "The men, described as illegal immigrants from the Middle East," were facing deportation.[43] At the time, law enforcement officials declined to identify the nationality of those arrested, and the anonymous tip that they were Middle Eastern was no doubt taken by many readers to mean that they were Arab and Muslim like the terrorists.

As investigators soon found out, they were not Arab or Muslim, but Jewish Israeli citizens. They were working for a moving company, but were in the United States as tourists without authorization to work.

The need to construct stories was not limited to the press or the public. Once the men were arrested, the FBI began interrogating them. Investigators, and the public, needed a new narrative.

A second story developed that the men were in fact Israeli security agents, whose cover was that they were working for the moving company. Some speculated in print that they had been gathering intelligence about the fundraising of radical Islamic groups in northern New Jersey. Stopping in surprise to look at the burning towers led, almost by chance, to their being observed and misidentified by a resident, and then pulled over and arrested. The espionage story appears to have been based entirely on an anonymous source claiming to be a high-ranking US intelligence official with knowledge of the interrogation, but no corroborating evidence exists.[44] News sources quoted former law enforcement officials who accepted and amplified this explanation.[45]

Narratives have to be functional. In Israel, the most functional narrative was that the young men had gone to the United States to travel as many did after their required military service, had made some money working as movers, had no connection to the security services, and were unfortunately caught up in the post–September 11 dragnet that was searching for anyone who might be connected. Among the thousands of men detained and deported as part of this investigation were "dozens" of other Israelis.[46]

The possible narratives constructed from these basic pieces of information spiraled infinitely outward. Constructing the narratives inadvertently created new narrative elements to string together; some people interpreted poorly worded news reports as suggesting the men had set up cameras to film the towers before they were struck (although no evidence suggested they had). Mixed in with ambient conspiratorial anti-Semitism, this misinterpretation bore fruit such as a line in poet Amiri Baraka's poem "Somebody Blew Up America" imagining that Israelis had advanced knowledge of the attacks.

Two of Tilly's characteristics of stories show up here: first, storytelling simplifies causality by including fewer actors and discarding facts incongruous with that narrative. Second, the story one chooses likely conforms to beliefs already held. Whether one comes to the story already suspicious of Arabs, Israelis, the press, the FBI, or Amiri Baraka will influence which narratives a person embraces. With the three accounts in front of you, don't you gravitate toward the one consistent with who and what you already trust? Stories are neat. Reality is not.

Taken together, the fact that we need to draw people into our stories and do so quickly means we will nest our stories in conventions: we make the story recognizable by employing stock characters, attitudes, and agreed-upon rationales for people's behavior. These prefabricated components must be shared by our audience; therefore, although some may seem timeless elements of the human experience (love, rivalry, the villain, or the fearless), many components are particular to a society in a specific time and place. When we revisit a novel, a movie, or other story years later and are disappointed to find that it has "not aged well," we refer to the fact that the passage of time can unwind social conventions.

If conventions can be either more general (and therefore more timeless) or more culturally specific, then works that rely more on the former will age better and retain popularity. Works by Charles Dickens and William Shakespeare, which have survived so well for so long, rely on basic motivations like love, rivalry, ambition, hope, fear, loyalty, and duplicity. In contrast, for instance, Shakespeare's contemporary Christopher Marlowe's plays relied more heavily on contemporary issues and themes, such as the St. Bartholomew's Day massacre of Protestants in *The Massacre in Paris*. Marlowe's play *Edward II* benefits from an audience that knows some of the history, unlike *Macbeth*, a drama for which no history is required, which also has aged more favorably than Shakespeare's historical drama *Henry V*.

If culturally local causal components lead a fictional narrative to become less relevant over time, a similar effect happens with ostensibly nonfiction accounts. The further from our reality explanatory accounts (myths are one example of this) are, the more dubious their wisdom sounds. We can no longer conceive of the sky as being held up by Atlas not only because we don't believe in Greek Titans, but because we don't even conceive of the sky as a physical object that can be held up.

The shift of explanatory components from shared beliefs to dated notions can be rapid. The result can unravel contested narrative accounts whose truth previously seemed difficult to ascertain. I still recall, though I must have been only eleven years old, a *60 Minutes* report on the case of Jeffrey MacDonald, a surgeon with the US military. In 1970, MacDonald's wife and two daughters were killed in their home, and MacDonald survived after being hit in the head and stabbed with an ice pick that collapsed one lung. Beyond its horror, the drama of the story hinged on conflicting explanations: initially, police sought the attackers MacDonald described as having violently invaded his home; later, MacDonald himself was accused and convicted of murdering his own family, inflicting injuries on himself and fabricating the story.

Judges had disagreed: a military court dismissed the case against MacDonald for lack of evidence, and MacDonald continued his medical practice. But a civilian criminal court later convicted MacDonald and sent him to prison. That two courts could reach two different verdicts made determining which story was accurate very difficult but no less urgent: either MacDonald had suffered the double loss of his family and his liberty, or a man depraved enough to kill his own family might walk free.

The story inhabited the recesses of my mind for years, as it did many others: the journalist Joe McGinniss began writing a book intending to exonerate MacDonald, only to conclude he was guilty; a television miniseries was based on that book. Forty years after the

murder, documentary filmmaker Errol Morris, who had risen to prom-
inence for a film about a man wrongfully convicted of murder, wrote
a book arguing MacDonald had spent most of his life in prison never
having received a fair trial.[47]

Years later, as an adult, I was walking through a museum when I
passed a pop art canvas. On it was a silkscreen of a newspaper article
about the MacDonald case, in which it earnestly retold MacDonald's
version of events: hippies had come into the house, including a "woman
in a floppy hat" who held a candle while chanting "Acid is groovy. Kill
the pigs." Suddenly the old story came back to me, but with a very
different cast. Acid is groovy? At 11, it seemed entirely believable to
me that hippies would take drugs that would lead them to murder a
family; to my adult self it sounded absurd. The story hinged on what a
straight-arrow army captain in 1970 *thought* hippies did. I stared at the
newspaper story, and the account fell apart.

Over a protracted investigation and several legal hearings, the
investigators developed a narrative of the night's events that closely fit
the physical evidence. That account has held up well over the last forty
years: that MacDonald had worked a twenty-four-hour shift, that when
he went to bed he found his wife asleep next to his five-year-old daughter, who had once again wet his side of the bed. An argument ensued
between the couple, which became violent. MacDonald hit his wife
with a piece of wood but in the process also hit his daughter and injured
her badly (deduced from her blood found in the master bedroom) and
then, to cover up his misdeeds, ensured that the whole family was dead
and that he had a hastily constructed story to direct attention toward
outside invaders.

Wade Smith, a lawyer who was on MacDonald's defense team,
sought to explain, in 2012, why the account of chanting hippies had
once been believable. "It's hard to imagine now, but in the late 1960s

and early '70s there were spooky, weird people on acid—back then it was believable." Indeed, on the army base of a Southern town at the tail end of the Vietnam War and its associated social conflict, the story rang true for many people, but it sounds distinctly less so now.

MacDonald's story sounded less plausible the farther it got from a 1970s military base, whereas the prosecutors' story of interpersonal conflict, rage, and cover up feels more timeless—MacDonald's story is more of a Marlowe, the prosecutors' story is more of a Shakespeare. The reason the prosecutors' account is more likely accurate is that it provides more believable motivations for all parties. Imagine the scenario from the point of view of each of the individuals, and their actions are easy to make sense of. Consider the floppy hat hippie story, and the behavior of almost no one makes sense, from the inexplicable violence of the attackers and the passive encouragement of the woman, to the doomed family members whose calls illustrate the scene like a Greek chorus. In that case, only the actions of MacDonald, the creator of the story himself, have the plausible motivations of a person acting under his own steam.

Stories are how we make sense of the world, but over time so many of them fall apart. The story of *Barefoot in the Park* is that a woman embracing the sixties' unconventional attitudes can save a straight-laced man's life. Only three years after *Barefoot*'s release, MacDonald's supporters believed such a woman could be a mortal threat. Neither of those accounts turned out to be helpful: the Hollywood story ignored the real social revolution in men's and women's roles that was brewing and endorsed the convention of alcohol and a supportive young wife as the solution to a businessman's problems; MacDonald's story was embraced by a public ready to believe that that social revolution threatened decent families everywhere. On closer inspection, both revealed powerful stereotypes that distorted our understanding of conflicts, and neither adequately explained the problems they sought to account for.

Our stories rely on categories that seem obvious to us but are locked into particular places and times; as we recede from the moment in which our story is set, those categories blur and break down, making the narratives unintelligible. Hippie, businessman, family man. Muslim, terrorist, spy. Doctor, patriot, killer. As the next chapter shows, the same breakdown of categories in stories from thirty or forty years ago can happen when we try to look thirty or forty years into the future using categories from today. When we try to make predictions about tomorrow using categories from today, those predictions falter like Jeffrey MacDonald's alibi.

As *Barefoot in the Park* demonstrates, we won't always be reasonable, but we can understand the implicit meaning and assumptions of a story better if we keep inspecting the ground our bare feet are standing on. That ground—the assumptions and categories our stories are built on—is less stable than we imagine, but that doesn't mean we can't tell stories. We just need to ask questions about what will change and what will remain the same.

3.

what race will the white minority be?

In the previous chapter we learned that the stories and categories we use to understand our world often don't age very well, which doesn't keep us from believing that some of the categories through which we see our world have existed since the beginning of time. We take them for granted, thinking they are natural distinctions rather than concepts we've constructed.

Perhaps the category most often mistaken for natural law—and to the most harmful effect—is race. Recognizing how much categories like Black and white can change over time reveals how we create our causal stories assuming, incorrectly, that what we perceive is fixed and unchanging rather than socially constructed and adaptive. When we look for causality, we don't see with our eyes alone. What race a group is, even what races we can *see*, is changed by social conventions. In comparison, racial inequality is considerably more tenacious. Expecting, as the US Census does, that whites will make up less than 50 percent of the United States by 2043 implies that races are more coherent, and racial inequality more feeble, than either is. This is a perfect example of how our assumptions about what is fixed and what is changing shape predictions and stories we make about the future.

Does society really construct different skin colors? Can't we *see* race with our own eyes? The answer is no. Race is a social reality that we only *think* we can see. That reality has only a mediated relationship to our physical bodies. Race is so shaped by social perception that it manifests itself as physically real. But it is not simply about skin color, of course. To get ahead of my argument, whether immigrants in the United States today make it a majority nonwhite nation, or instead become defined as white themselves, depends less on the color of their skin and more on whether, for instance, Latin American and African countries get an atom bomb. Bear with me.

What Is Race?

In our everyday lives, race looks real. We see different skin colors and cultures, and people often define race, informally, as having something to do with people's origins.

Social scientists define race differently. Race is not color. Race is commonly understood to be about power relations. As sociologists focusing on the social construction of race, Michael Omi and Howard Winant define race as "a concept that signifies and symbolize social conflicts and interests by referring to different types of human bodies."[48] This definition is at once specific about what race represents (conflict and power inequalities) and vague about what it is physically (conflicts that are rendered onto perceptions of human bodies, but how?).

The key is that groups designated as racially different have different access to power. What are the power relations that each of our racial categories define?

Looking at early racial categorizations, and how they have changed over time, helps us understand the constructedness of race. The US Constitution provides one of the most fruitful examples, as it outlines three primary racial groups in the United States, while hardly using any direct references to race at all. Tellingly, the Constitution establishes racial categories with reference not to skin or origin, but to political power:

> Representatives and direct Taxes shall be apportioned among the several States which may be included within this Union, according to their respective Numbers, which shall be determined by adding to the whole Number of **free Persons**, including those bound to Service for a Term of Years, and **excluding Indians not taxed, three fifths of all other Persons.**

The language is oblique but can be parsed. The only group identified by names are American Indians. There are others: "three fifths of all other Persons" refers to the notorious Three-Fifths Compromise, in which enslaved African Americans couldn't vote, but their white slave masters enjoyed representation in Congress not only for themselves but for three-fifths the number of enslaved people in their state. The "other persons" in this phrase are African Americans. "Free persons" refers implicitly to whites.

So there are three groups, which we might today call Native American, Black, and white. But as the language in the US Constitution makes clear, these are not primarily color categories. They are political categories that place people in distinct and different relations to the government, taxation, representation, and power. Instead of Native American, Black and white, it seems more revealing to describe these groups in terms of their relation to power. Race makes these political inequalities "durable inequalities" that can last for someone's entire life, and be handed down to future generations and whole communities.[49]

The original racial categories could be defined by their relative power and their location inside or outside the boundaries of the state. People inside the boundaries of the United States who had relatively more power were designated as "white." The white group was not guaranteed citizenship (they could be indentured or recent immigrants), but was eligible for citizenship. Most of the members of this group are not ruling elites, but it is from this group that ruling elites are drawn. Members of this group are clearly subject to classic capitalist style exploitation as workers who sell their labor to capitalists and are crisscrossed by sex and gender inequality and exploitation in other forms. White men were eligible for citizenship, and citizenship meant voting, running for office, serving on juries, testifying in court, acting as police, and otherwise establishing and enforcing laws.

We don't normally define whiteness in terms of citizenship, but the relationship between the two has been rendered explicit often enough. For most of US history, racial categories have been citizenship categories. Three years after the Constitutional Convention, the Naturalization Act of 1790 explicitly limited eligibility for citizenship to "free white persons." The Supreme Court was periodically called on to define who was white, for the purposes of defining who could be a citizen. In 1923, for instance, the Court ruled against immigrants from India who said that they were Aryan and therefore white. It found that they were not white, and therefore could not become citizens.[50]

Notwithstanding changes like the Fourteenth Amendment that recognized citizenship for Blacks born in the United States, "whiteness"
was a prerequisite for citizenship for immigrants according to various
federal laws through the 1920s and until at least 1946.[51] Whiteness and
citizenship were similarly allied in the racist anti-civil rights organizations called "White Citizens Councils." Historically, and in the minds
of the members of such a group, "white citizen" was redundant, and in
some cases, white organizations that sought to segregate Blacks from
their neighborhoods took names like Atlanta's "Southwest Citizens
Organization."[52] If "citizen" were not a racialized term, what about the
name would have indicated that Black integrationists shouldn't join
this neighborhood organization? But race is deeply linked to citizenship, and in the organization's name, "citizen" meant "white."

Other people who were inside the United States but were not eligible for citizenship could be called "Black." While members of the white
group could be targets of capitalist exploitation of their labor and property, the second, Black, group could be subjected to *hyper*exploitation:
work in the harshest conditions, forced labor, unpaid labor, slavery,
sexual violence, and terrorist violence. Denied the rights of full citizenship, members of this group had no reliable recourse to courts, politicians, or political office to mitigate these threats. As Craig Wilder points
out in his history of Blacks in Brooklyn, slaves were not initially Black.
Some were enslaved or temporarily indentured people from Europe as
well as the rest of the world. When the Duke of York imposed official
restrictions on the enslavement of Christians soon after taking control
of what had been Dutch New Amsterdam ("No Christian shall be kept
in bond slavery" without official authorization), early slaves came to
be defined religiously, not racially. The people who were eligible for
enslavement and hyperexploitation were non-Christians, including
Native Americans and Blacks. The colonial legislature emancipated a

group of "Christian Indians" in 1687 on these grounds and another group of "Spanish Indian slaves professing Christianity." But slave owners became concerned that conversion to Christianity could make slaves suddenly ineligible for slavery. So in 1706 the Legislature reassured slave owners by dismissing "the groundless opinion that hath spread itself in this colony, that by the baptizing of such negro, Indian, or mulatto slave, they would become free, and ought to be set at liberty."[53] From then on, subjection to hyperexploitation would increasingly be determined by race, not religion or contract.

White and Black were within the country. Outside its borders were the "Other." Often, "Other" is used in surveys to designate people who don't choose one of the conventional boxes of African American, white, Asian, and so on. "Other" reflects Edward Said's work on Orientalism. To the white American and European imagination, the Orient has been the mirror image of the West, a foil against which Western whites could imagine the West to try to understand themselves and colonize others.[54] To Europeans, the Orient—from the Middle East, through India, China, Japan, and the rest of Asia—was the geographical location of early colonization and colonial exploitation. To justify colonization, the Oriental Other was imagined as fundamentally different from Europeans, always in ways that justified and rationalized subjugation. The Other was indolent and slothful. The Other was feminine, so that it invited masculine domination (a trope that continues to be reflected in the sexualized, feminized representation of Asian-ness). Unlike the rational Western male, the Orientalized Other was imagined as spiritual, timeless, feminine.

In the US case, particularly in the seventeen and early eighteen hundreds before the United States had colonized areas further afield, the Oriental Other was the American Indian. The parallels between the racialized images of Asians and Native Americans remain evident, such as the superior spirituality attributed to both groups, that explains everything from the popularity in the United States of Asian yoga and Buddhism to Native American sweat lodges, medicine men, and dream catchers. Native Americans who were "not taxed" were outside the polity of the nation, and have been subject to a prolonged campaign of expropriation of property (more than they were subjected to colonial-style labor exploitation) and attempted extermination.

Seen this way, the racial categories in the US Constitution that spelled out the bedrock of US racial classification in most parts of the country[55] for the next two hundred years could fit into a table that identifies racial categories by political power and their location inside and outside the United States.

	INSIDE THE UNITED STATES	OUTSIDE THE UNITED STATES
MORE POWERFUL	Eligible for citizenship (Designated as white) *Can also be exploited.*	Seen as a threat to the nation. Rarely a distinct race, or subsumed under white: England until War of 1812, USSR until 1989, China and ISIS today.
LESS POWERFUL	Subject to hyperexploitation (Designated as Black)	Subject to colonization and/or genocide (Designated as Indian, Asian, or the Orientalist "Other.")

FIGURE 3A: Classic US racial categories identified by their social relation to power and their physical relation to the state.

Before we go any further: just to be clear, the fact that race has historical roots doesn't mean it's natural, and it's certainly not behind us. Racial inequality is measurable and real today, and is not just "the way things are." African Americans earn about two-thirds of what whites do. Asian Americans in New York have higher median incomes *and* higher poverty rates than the city as a whole. Although African Americans want to live in mixed, 50-50 Black-white neighborhoods, almost all Black Americans live in segregated neighborhoods that are virtually all Black. (This is unique for white and Black Americans; ethnic enclaves rarely contain more than 30 percent of a single ethnic group.) Police shootings disproportionately target Hispanic and Black men. Wealth gaps persist and grow. These injustices are not holdovers in our own nonracist present from some earlier racist time. We continue to actively segregate communities, schools, criminal justice systems, and workplaces today. History is useful to us here because it demonstrates what the durable mechanisms are by which racial categories are created and reproduced generation after generation—and the surprising reality that they can change dramatically.

Changing Powers, Changing Races

Eligibility for citizenship—painted as whiteness—has remained a category since its inscription in the Constitution, but those eligible for membership in that group has changed since then. Studies of race have most often used the changing racial categorization of immigrants as evidence of the changing definition of whiteness. Groups like Germans, Irish, Italians, and Jews were popularly defined as noncitizens and nonwhite when they first arrived, and then became white. Certainly, this process is revealing. But in addition to the domestic influences on the boundaries of whiteness, international relations have also altered racial categories.

Figure 3A demonstrates that there is, logically, a racial category about which the US Constitution is silent. There are powerful and less-powerful people inside the United States, and less-powerful people outside the United States, but what about more-powerful people outside the United States? This is the kind of telling omission that psychologists call a "deception clue," an absence that hints at an important, concealed presence.[56] This empty category merits a brief detour to recognize its existence and understand its exorcism.

After fifty years as a self-proclaimed "superpower," Americans may not viscerally recognize what it feels like to have other states be more powerful and able to threaten one's nation and self. But the United States in the era of the writing of the US Constitution knew this vulnerability well. Several countries were almost certainly more powerful than the United States, particularly England, which, despite having just lost the American Revolutionary War, was unquestionably stronger on land and on sea than the United States, wealthier, and had a navy that already dominated the oceans, and, Americans recognized, could threaten the United States.

Americans were understandably preoccupied by the presence of this more-powerful state. The United States fought a war driven to a large degree by the anxiety about the presence of this fourth, implicit racial category. This was the War of 1812. Remembered today as the war during which Francis Scott Key wrote the *Star Spangled Banner* in Baltimore Harbor, it is hard to understand the causes of the war without considering it an effort by Americans to resolve the relationship between the United States and Great Britain. Historians seeking to explain the causes of the War of 1812 find that proponents of the war were "primarily concerned with the honor and integrity of the nation" or "national honor."[57] Historians have called it a "second war of independence." President Andrew Jackson's advocacy for the war nearly echoed the very definition of whiteness, calling the war a defense of that now-racialized category, the American citizen:

> Who are we? And for what are we going to fight? We are the
> free-born sons of America . . . and the only people on Earth

who possess rights, liberties, and property which they dare to call their own . . . We are going to fight for the reestablishment of our national character.[58]

Americans felt threatened because the British had attacked American ships at sea, impressed American sailors, and blockaded trade with France, with whom Britain was at war. They also believed Britain was threatening the United States by supporting Native American opposition to the United States.

The War of 1812 is curious. In the United States, it is assumed to be a "good war" like all others, and the fact that the British burned the White House adds to the sense that the British were the aggressors. In England, the war is a minor footnote, largely overshadowed by the Napoleonic Wars of the same era. In contrast, Canadians recall the war as one in which the Americans were the aggressors, having tried to seize part of Canada. For one side, the war was almost meaningless. For the other, it was the source of our national anthem. The War of 1812 was defining to Americans in some important way.

The war was the last burst of hostility between the United States and England. Afterward, Americans no longer felt threatened by England, though they could not dominate England (an important distinction for the purposes of the racialization of international conflicts). Confusion today about the genesis of the War of 1812 seems the result of the fact that the motivation—an acute American fear of inferiority to the British and the readiness with which Americans took offense—seems hard to grasp today. But it resolved the identity of the racial group in that fourth category. American whites no longer feared Europeans as a threat, and they were rendered white.

One-hundred-thirty years later, the United States was confronted with another anxiety of the fourth-box variety. The Cold War with the Soviet Union posited the USSR might—just might—be the kind of existential threat the British had been. The Cold War turned the Soviets more white (one of the many shades comprising any such vast, multiethnic society) and simultaneously stirred up a racialized anxiety about that fourth box. Historians of pop culture talk about 1950s sci-fi movies representing Cold War anxiety, and indeed those pulp fiction films about a "superior race of beings" from another planet gave an emotional outlet for the concerns Americans had, in the midst of air raid drills, that a superior race could invade at any moment.

The fourth category is the one that we are most uncomfortable with, and most often unaware of.[59] It is a shifting category occupied by different nations and groups at different moments in history, and a group's passage through the fourth category (into a fellow "whitened" ally or, surprisingly less often, a defeated nonwhite Other) is one of the unnoticed mechanisms of category change in the brutal system of racial classification in the United States.

If whiteness is a power relationship, then groups that are more powerful are likely to be classified as white, and less-powerful groups as nonwhite. As the power of a group changes, it should become more white or less white. This is not only true in respect to assimilation of immigrant groups but, like the War of 1812, as a reflection of changing military and economic power relations between the United States and other countries. Most often, we recognize how during war, racist characterizations of the putative enemy are used to dehumanize people from opposing countries. But often war has had the paradoxical effect of making people more white in America. For instance, during the West Coast gold rush of the 1800s, Chinese workers had clearly been Others, imported for hard labor in highly exploitative conditions. As the need for Chinese labor declined, the 1882 Chinese Exclusion Act prohibitied Chinese citizens from emigrating to the United States.

Asian eligibility for citizenship—whiteness—was at an all-time low in the United States.

Seeming to add insult to injury, during World War II, the Korean War, and the Vietnam War, Japanese, Korean, and Vietnamese soldiers and civilians were dehumanized with a slew of derogatory racial terms. In 1943, when the United States and China allied against the Japanese, the Chinese Exclusion Act was replaced by a law that allowed a symbolic number of Chinese nationals to naturalize as citizens, although it retained prohibitions on property ownership.

There was a dramatic reversal of these exclusionary laws in 1965. After twenty years of near-constant war with Asian nations, and amid the long buildup of the Vietnam War, the United States passed an immigration bill eliminating all specific bans on Asian immigration and citizenship eligibility. Today, students (particularly Black and Latino students) regularly ask me how it is that Asians can assimilate as white more quickly than Blacks and Latinos. (As is evident in the differing receptions Chinese immigrants have received, it has little to do with skin color and nothing to do with culture.) How was it that the dehumanizing efforts of wartime racial stereotypes were followed by improving the eligibility for citizenship of the same people? Somehow, a war replete with racial vilification paradoxically began integrating the Other into the nation as a citizen.

The case of Mexicans and Mexican Americans offers some indication of how war brought greater whiteness. The racial classification of Mexicans and Mexican Americans has been one of the most unstable racial projects in the United States. At times white, at times Native American, and at times part of a distinct "Hispanic" race, these shifts have not been at random. Mexicans have been most white when Mexico was a powerful threat, least white when Mexico has been least powerful.

Given the recent hostility of elected Texas officials toward Mexican immigrants, it is noteworthy that in the mid-1930s, Texas law (and federal law) made clear that Mexicans were white.[60] Mexicans in Texas could vote in whites-only primary elections. This was only eighty years after the conclusion of the Mexican-American War of 1846–1848. When the California Constitution was written a year later, even the proslavery framers felt compelled by the treaty with Mexico to expand voting rights to "white citizens" of both California and Mexico.[61] In World War II, as historian Nell Irvin Painter points out, Blacks and Asians were segregated in the US military; Latinos served in white units.[62]

Although the Treaty of Guadalupe Hidalgo that ended the Mexican-American War is still in force, its attendant racial project that rendered Mexicans white has ebbed and flowed. As Mexico receded as a powerful threat, subsequent state laws excluded Mexican children as nonwhite. (In one pointed exception, in 1931 California courts reversed a local Jim Crow ordinance and required that Mexican-American children be allowed to attend the new white school, because California law explicitly allowed for discrimination against Native Americans, Orientals, and Negroes. But Mexicans, the court concluded, were Caucasian and could not legally be barred from a school.[63]) Later in the twentieth century, as Mexico itself became less of an adversary and more of a one-party state under US influence, Mexicans became less white in America.

Power conveyed whiteness. The initially paradoxical case of war in Asia occurring simultaneously with the racial project of whitening Asians follows a similar pattern: when Asian nations were colonized, their people were nonwhite and subject to domination. When Asian nations were serious threats to the United States, Asians came closer to occupying the same position that the British had occupied at the time the Constitution was written: outsiders who were powerful enough to pose a threat.

If military and economic power categorically require the bestowal of whiteness, then there is a correlation between increasing military and economic power and increasing whiteness, on the one hand, and decreasing power and increasing categorization of the people of those nations as an Oriental Other, on the other hand.

Whiteness and Nuclear Weapons

Consider countries that boast a nuclear arsenal. White people have nuclear weapons, right? Not particularly. Only a minority of nuclear powers are US-based or European; the list includes China, India, Pakistan, as well as North Korea, and Israel (which is believed to have nuclear weapons but has made no official declaration).

How strong is the conceptual association of race and military power? Intriguingly, one country in history has disarmed the nuclear arsenal they developed: South Africa. While it was ruled by a white minority, South Africa undertook a nuclear program and developed a small nuclear capability. Before recognizing Black majority rule, the white apartheid government dismantled and destroyed its nuclear stockpile, foreclosing the possibility that South Africa would be the first majority-Black government to have an atom bomb. This unique story can be viewed from an incredible number of perspectives—in terms of foreign relations, as a victory by antiproliferation negotiations and the antinuclear movement, as Cold War calculations and post–Cold War realpolitik. But if race is about power, then this changing racial power and nuclear power intersect.

What influence did the fact that the white government knew

Blacks would soon accede to power in South Africa have on its decision to destroy South Africa's nuclear program? As our examination of dynamic causality will show throughout the book, any major social structural development or institution has multiple causes. A number of different factors led to South Africa's unique decision to disarm itself, factors that challenge many of the assumptions we have used for decades to tell our geopolitical causal stories.

One explanation focuses on international relations. In a paper presented to the US military, Lieutenant Colonel Roy Horton presented the view that South Africa had simply adjusted to the shifting winds of international relations.[64] Today, histories of the program suggest the purpose of creating a nuclear weapon in South Africa was to deter attacks from communist-leaning (and antiapartheid) African states. In the event of threats to attack, South Africa's plan was to announce their nuclear capability to the world, demonstrate a test detonation if necessary, and hope this would induce the United States to offer protection to South Africa to prevent nuclear escalation. By 1989, conflicts between South Africa, Namibia, Angola, and Cuban forces in Angola were settled with a three-way peace treaty. The change reduced South Africa's immediate sense of a need for nuclear deterrence. A few years before dismantling apartheid and creating a democratic government that led to the election of Black African leadership, the white South African regime dismantled their existing nuclear weapons and ended their nuclear program. Although a nuclear program seemed like an advantageous foreign policy in earlier decades, international displeasure at a new nuclear power was contributing to South Africa's isolation and support for sanctions. Dismantling the program now served the same goals (of international recognition) that developing nuclear weapons previously had.

That analysis seems reasonable enough. But the racial implications of South Africa's nuclear decision are inescapable. Part of the reason white South Africans developed a nuclear weapons program was to defend themselves from states that opposed the racist apartheid system itself. More critically, the end of the nuclear program and the end of apartheid came hand in hand. South African President P. W. Botha met the still-imprisoned African National Congress freedom fighter Nelson Mandela for tea in 1989. Botha suffered a stroke six weeks later and was replaced by President F. W. de Klerk. De Klerk believed that apartheid was unsustainable, and almost immediately took two actions: In February 1990 he released Nelson Mandela and lifted the ban on the African National Congress. That same month, he sent written instruction to start dismantling the six nuclear weapons South African had in its stockpile.[65] In April 1993, the final rounds of negotiations that would establish a postapartheid democracy began between antiapartheid groups and the white government. The next month, the South African Parliament ratified the Non-Proliferation Treaty.[66] A year later, in April 1994, South Africa held its first free elections.

Even some analysts who focus on international negotiations and state security explanations for South Africa's disarmament recognize the role of race in the decision. Lieutenant Colonel Horton cites concerns that the ANC would have given nuclear technology to states that had aided their struggle, many of which were not US allies. Changes in nuclear power and racial power had to go hand in hand, Horton concluded in his presentation to the US Air Force Academy. For de Klerk, "The solution, therefore, was to conduct the two activities in parallel."[67]

High-ranking apartheid-era South African officials support the view that the two decisions were linked. As a South African diplomat said, his country's disarmament was "motivated by concern that it didn't want any undeclared nuclear material or infrastructure falling into the hands of Nelson Mandela."[68] As Frans Cronje of the South African Institute of Race Relations in Johannesburg noted, disarmament remains a counterintuitive choice for states in the world today, which is why more states have not followed South Africa's lead:

> "A nuclear African state would be taken more seriously and would have a stronger leadership role—it forces people to take you seriously. In leadership terms, renouncing nuclear weapons does the opposite—it reduces your influence in foreign affairs and international politics. If renouncing nuclear weapons grows your influence, others would be falling over themselves to surrender their nuclear arsenals."[69]

Commentator Mawuna Koutonin remarked that "While a racist, violent, and brutal oppression white apartheid regime was trusted to have and manage nuclear weapons, a Black and democratically elected regime was not trusted to manage them."[70]

Although disarmament is an important and laudable goal, the correlation of nuclear power status and whiteness is striking. It is a historical oddity that South African disarmament should be little more than a footnote in the antinuclear movement rather than a cause célèbre. But the achievement for antinuclear and antiproliferation forces is mediated by the context in which it happened, a context not only of foreign policy calculations, but calculations by the white South African government about the meaning of race and power.

In the South African case, changes in military power developed in concert with changes in the racial political order. The process follows a similar pattern in the United States: a group's gain in power may lead to them being vilified, but it is often followed by a racial reclassification that "whitens" the group. More generally, because race is about power, race is susceptible to the influence of military, political, and economic international relations, not only the power of domestic activism and civil rights jurisprudence.

Invisible Races

If large groups of people's assignment to racial categories can change, even though we think we see actual physical evidence of race in people's skin, faces, and hair, then as groups move from nonwhite to white, from one race to another, or as one group that was formerly a separate race joins into a larger group, could racial characteristics disappear?

The paradoxical expansion of whiteness during US wars in Asia leaves important distinctions overlooked. During World War II, China was an ally, but Japan was an enemy. The US military found it necessary, then, to identify racial differences between the Chinese and Japanese. In a series of cartoon illustrations that have been widely reproduced as examples of grotesque ethnic stereotyping, a flier tried to educate American soldiers about what to look for—what to *see*—to distinguish a Japanese solider who might be trying to blend in among the Chinese population.

Today the leaflets titled "How to Spot a Jap" are an offensive novelty, used either to illustrate the history of US racist stereotyping or sold on postcards as ironic curiosities. But they can be examined in another way. The sociological theorist Norbert Elias looked at European Renaissance manners books to understand the process of the creation of what he called *habitus*. Manners that we see as utterly natural and inevitable today—like not blowing one's nose at the table, or eating off the serving spoon, or belching or farting in public—are, in fact, socially constructed and learned behaviors. At the historical moment that they were introduced into adult society for the first time, manners books were required to teach what is today utterly obvious to adults. The books make for incredible reading. In his chapter "On Blowing One's Nose," for instance, he quotes a "precept for gentlemen" that matter-of-factly explains that "When you blow your nose or cough, turn round so that nothing falls on the table." "Do not blow your nose with the same hand that you use to hold the meat." "It is unseemly to blow your nose into the tablecloth." Some of the recommendations are as poetic as they are graphic. "Nor is it seemly, after wiping your nose, to spread out your handkerchief and peer into it as if pearls and rubies might have fallen out of your head."[71] The point is that actions that seem utterly natural to us—we can't recall being taught not to do these things; they seem utterly natural despite being, evidently, learned behaviors—had to be taught explicitly in ways that both disturb us and reveal that something that seems natural was in fact socially constructed.

The "How to Spot a Jap" flyers were printed to serve much the same function as the manners books Elias studied. Today we hardly need pamphlets telling us what to look for when trying to decide if someone is white or Black. If the distinction between Japanese and Chinese had remained as salient today in the United States as it was to US soldiers during World War II, we would probably see it as self-evident. "How to Spot a Jap" sought to create and implant a racial habitus that distinguished Japanese from Chinese. People who view the document today dismiss as offensive and outrageous the idea that the government was trying to ingrain in soldiers the idea that Chinese and Japanese people looked racially different, and those viewers do not worry that they're suggesting that "Asians all look alike" when they do so.

But what does this say about the racialized differences we see and don't see? It was not only Chinese and Japanese differences that needed to be inculcated in this way. After all, what we think we know about race has to be learned, and what people "know" and "see" as self-evident changes over time. As proof, other racial characteristics seemed perfectly obvious to people at one time but have virtually disappeared today.

Thomas Nast's cartoons are notorious in this regard. His caricatures of Irishmen and Blacks are particularly shocking because they are a type we no longer see today. Working-class Irishmen are represented as chimpanzees in crumpled top hats and curled-up shoes. Their faces had a large dome-shaped upper lip surrounded by bushy sideburns.

At times, Nast partnered the Irishman with an equally offensive image of a Black American, with big sambo-style lips, and perhaps a large rump and clunky bare feet. Today, few Americans have an image in their mind of what an Irish American should look like. Unless, perhaps, someone meets a man named O'Connor with red hair, an American today rarely thinks to themselves, "Of course! They look Irish." But Nast was not only nastily caricaturing Irishmen, but needed to do so in a way that would appear believable to his audience. In a similar example of invisible ethnicity, 15 percent of Americans today report German heritage. This ethnic group is widespread and numerous. So I pose a simple question: What do German Americans look like? One in seven Americans are German American; how many of the German Americans you meet have you identified that way? Even more so than later immigrant groups like Italian, Irish, and Jewish, German is invisible.

Have you ever seen an American-born person and thought, "They clearly look German," or "They look French"? Probably not, and certainly not on a daily basis, despite the frequency with which one would find people of German, French, or Irish heritage in a group of white people.

But you could say that. It's not the case that all white people look the same. My parents are both of predominantly Irish heritage. One summer, my family was traveling and had a layover in Ireland long enough for us to see the city of Dublin for the first time. As we walked through the airport and observed the people around me, I had a thought, but I kept it to myself. Yet we had not even walked out the door to leave the airport before my seven-year-old son said what I was thinking: "Everybody here looks like grandma and grandpa!" My family, according to my seven-year-old, looked like people from Ireland.

In contrast, a few years later I was to meet a French colleague at a busy Paris train station at rush hour, but neither of us knew what the other one looked like, and there were hundreds of people milling about. I tried to guess which of the women entering, exiting, waiting, smoking, and texting was the person I was to meet, but to no avail. Then I turned, and from a block away, through a crowd of hundreds, a woman waved directly at me. She had picked *me* out. I had been vaguely aware, before then, that no matter how familiar I got with Paris, I stood out on the subway: I might feel perfectly French riding the train, reading the advertisements in French and understanding the conductor, but when I got home and looked in the mirror I knew my face was different from the diverse visages I saw in public.

Later I asked my colleague, and she said she knew I wasn't French. How so? I asked. She considered me. Scrutinized me. "La mâchoire." It was your jaw, she said with a satisfied smile. Until that day I never knew there was such a thing as an Irish chin, but I had one. And no doubt, if Thomas Nast ever met my earliest US ancestors on the street, he knew they looked Irish too. We don't *see* Irish anymore, we don't recognize it, we no longer caricature it. But we could.

That brings us back to the "Spot a Jap" poster. It is offensive—crude, reductionist, insulting. We think it is ridiculous, which it is. We think that recognizing that ridiculousness makes us less racist than the people who made it. It doesn't. It merely means that we have different racial categories than in 1942. Chinese and Japanese people look neither the "same" nor "different" any more than Irish Americans and French Americans do. Americans cannot distinguish a white American of Irish versus French citizenship walking down the street. But that evidently does not mean there are not differences. Nor do on-the-street racial distinctions have to be perfect; people often don't recognize the author Malcolm Gladwell as Black, though he is; other times whites are mistaken for Blacks. But no American thinks Black and white can't be real. There are large groups of people of Celtic ancestry in Ireland and France. For the purposes of making or unmaking a racial difference, that genetic inheritance and diversity doesn't matter. We can believe we see or don't see "typical types" among Chinese civilians and Japanese soldiers. What we actually, literally see is shaped by politics. That is, the same two groups can be visibly different racially *or* indistinguishable racially, depending on the political context and power relations that categorize them racially.

Francis Galton was a pioneer in modern statistics. But he was also a eugenicist, and made notorious photos that purported to reveal the "Jewish type." People believed Irish, Jewish, Japanese, Chinese, or German denoted races. When Jews were a race, people believed that they could tell who was Jewish by looking at them. Today, Jewish people often recoil at the idea that there is a Jewish "race," and find the suggestion that there is a Jewish "look" inherently racist. The point, for these purposes, is that at times, the US Army, Thomas Nast, and the father of the statistical method of regression analysis all believed there were visually distinct and observable races that Americans today would be generally unable to identify—certainly not with the level of certainty they feel on a daily basis with racial categories such as Caucasian, African American, Latino, or Asian.

Given the paradox between the sense people have that today's racial categories are visible, but that categories that are no longer in current use cannot generally be seen (and *should* not be seen), I suspect that a visitor from a planet without race would have a very difficult time categorizing anyone on Earth into the racial categories we use today. If they were asked to group people visually, there is no statistical possibility that they would use the same set of arbitrary categories that we use today, but even if the categories we use were described for them (perhaps with a set of Francis Galton's ideal type photographs), they would probably not sort actual people into the same categories that Americans would.

To understand race, we must accept this paradox: that fundamentally, race makes power relations visible by assigning them to physical bodies. In this way we *see* race. Yet despite the evidence right before our eyes, that evidence is *not* visual evidence of a physical reality but social perception. Our racialization of people means both that we see races that don't exist as much as we cannot recognize things that do exist. Perception of the physical world of race is so shaped by social conditioning that we cannot see reality without it.

Recognizing and Resisting Our Categories

In terms of who we are and the stories we tell, the undeniable, observable reality of a socially constructed convention like race reveals the third eye through which we see the world. We can't help but see through these categories, and their effects are undeniably real, yet any closer examination reveals the dimensions along which they are unstable and mutable. We base our causal stories on categories that we think are solid but are not. Recognizing the ways these categories do and don't shift doesn't paralyze our ability to tell stories, it reveals that the answer to questions like "What future will immigrants of color build in

America?" involve not just changes that transpire between one group and another, but changes to the membership of those groups and their symbolic meaning. In response to demographic shifts, the position of whites may change, the dominance of Republicans may change. But there is even more dynamism at play: the very boundaries of whiteness may shift, the political meaning of the party may change shape, occupying a different collection of positions on the political spectrum.

Historian Nell Irvin Painter argues that there have been four historic enlargements of whiteness. First, formerly suspect non-Protestants—prominent among them the Irish—definitively gained whiteness in the late 1800s, contrary to a Protestant and Saxon mythology promoted even by Ralph Waldo Emerson. For Painter, the social upheaval and physical relocation during World War II—both for servicemen and migrating industrial workers—stirred up the next great expansion of whiteness, as formerly ethnic groups including Italians, Jews, and Mexicans experienced upward economic mobility in the war economy and sought to present themselves as allied with Anglo-Saxon beauty ideals (the only Jewish Miss America was crowned in 1945) and were recast as white. The narrative of *white* inclusivity continued from the Roosevelt era into the postwar period. Finally, the racial differentiations within whiteness devolved into ethnicities, as few white Americans could claim a single national race (Swedish, German, French) with any confidence; races no longer could be imagined within the color category of white, while intermarriage across contemporary racial boundaries further altered previous notions of racial boundaries. For Painter, this most recent change in racial structure has dismissed any scientific basis for race, done away with national origins as racial categories (which were still part of racial discourse earlier in the twentieth century), and made the United States a country where people are much more mixed, in the old racial terms, than ever before.[72]

One can only hope that Painter is right, and America is finally warming to a multiracial identity—something that is global but particularly evident in the New World. But if that is indeed happening, it is not because of where people are from, but what antiracist activists have accomplished. If America is majority nonwhite it is not because of where people were born, or where their ancestors came from, but because of the challenges to racism and racial segregation that activists, particularly activists who were classified as nonwhite, have made.

The movements for racial justice promoted by people of color can grow not because of demographic shifts (since, if history is any precedent, many people of color are more likely to become white than become activists), but because of the challenges to racial categories, privileges, and inequality that, when called out and accounted for explicitly, are unable to justify themselves in the face of an organized alternative. Lots of countries have been minority white and held onto whiteness; to the extent whiteness meant citizenship, these were states that were ruled by a small minority and oversaw the hyperexploitation or genocide of a much larger part of the country. Being majority nonwhite by 2050 could just mean being apartheid-era South Africa, or Brazil, or Guatemala, where a small light-skinned group has enjoyed privileges at the expense of many more who are excluded. The route to improvement is to continue challenging the prerogative to put people into categories that justify their exploitation or colonization. Avoiding that path means recognizing and challenging what racial categories stand for. It's not multicultural color, it's power, and power is too wily for us to expect it to stand still and be overtaken by demographic change. We need to confront the power of racial privilege no matter who the inhabitants of the privileged caste are at any given moment, not imagine that our innate human diversity will render the system powerless.

Nell Irvin Painter's outline of the expansions of whiteness shows the census shift toward majority nonwhiteness for what it is: not destiny, but an opportunity for America. Any specific system of racial hierarchy is built on specific assumptions: if the ruling racial group is the majority it can embrace formal democracy and maintain power, whereas a minority ruling racial group (as in South Africa) will not. A system with a shortage of racial elites may enlist the aid of mixed race people, granting them specific prerogatives; in the United States where there are more whites than elite spots to be filled, mixed race people are given little more in the way of rights than those categorized as Black.

Painter notes that when external conditions change, the racial hierarchy can be upended as well; there is room to challenge the old prescriptions. The geographical and social remixing of World War II cooked down the diverse European identities in the United States into a single racial category of "white." Likewise, Asian immigrants occupied one role when Asian immigration was largely working class, West Coast, limited in numbers, and male, at the end of the nineteenth century. The racial constraints on Asian Americans are different when immigration law explicitly favors professionals, and brings middle- and working-class people, women and men, in larger numbers than before, to more US cities.

For African Americans, the end of labor-intensive agriculture in the United States and its attendant systems of sharecropping and slavery created an opening regarding what role African Americans could occupy next. Since then, deindustrialization has posed the question again: if African Americans are no longer constrained to the realm of often less-well-paid industrial wage labor, what economic position might they gain? The fraying of the social safety net and falling wages for whites means there is less correlation between "whiteness" and "economic stability" than in the mid-twentieth century, and a larger Black middle class than before.

Changes like these create opportunities to disrupt, to redefine, to resist, to break out. Changes in demographics, employment, or political power don't lead automatically to ruptures in the racial structure; people have always invested considerable effort in challenging the old racial structures. We can look at the intersection of demographic change and social activism to see ways that, as in the history that Painter describes, historical sea changes and activist pressure can reconfigure racial identities and inequality, positively or negatively. A host of such changes underway could imperil communities or provide openings for activists.

The Black Lives Matter movement seeks to take away the police's prerogative to use violence against African Americans with no legal sanctions; succeeding would undermine an important means of maintaining racial segregation and inequality. What if we made every neighborhood in the United States safe and hospitable for African Americans to live in?

The wage gap remains frustratingly stable. But the education gap has narrowed: 71 percent of African Americans graduate from high school today (versus 86.6 percent of whites); the percentage of African Americans with four-year college degrees nearly doubled in twenty years.[73] These statistics are not cause for celebration but strategic reflection. If African American women, for instance, have a 46 percent graduation rate and, with a bachelor's, earn 80 percent of what college-educated white women do, what opportunities are there?[74] Black women's higher college enrollment rates and higher graduation rates mean that the gap between them and Black men, who have lower levels of college degrees, is likely to widen. That may create difficulties and opportunities. What will it do for Ronald Reagan's racist stereotype of the welfare queen?

What will the end of the draconian sentences from the war on drugs, which could reduce the incarceration rate of Black men, mean?

Will it be an opportunity to integrate more Black men into society, or will it lead to the alienation of a generation of men marked by criminal records and younger cohorts' continued segregation from the labor market?

What would it mean to frankly acknowledge our nation's racial past, and think about what reparations would set us on a path to greater prosperity? What would it mean, once and for all, to bury the shameful, misplaced pride some white people have for the South's role in the Civil War and acknowledge the irredeemable mistakes of their forefathers?

What would it mean for South Africa or Kenya to have a nuclear weapon?

Using shifting social situations to destabilize racial hierarchy may not just be about challenging racism, but challenging race itself. Challenging race does not mean the conservative, disingenuous denial of race when racism still very much exists, but a collective challenge to its right to determine our lives. Race is not something we inevitably see, but a way that we perceive power. We cannot wish it away, but there are opportunities to upend aspects of race from both directions, by taking advantage of the instability in what we see, and in redistributing the power that perpetuates race.

What would it take for the United States to be majority nonwhite in 2043? The United States has been squeezing its shimmering diversity of immigrants and citizens into the same categories—Black, white, Native American—in the same percentages for hundreds of years, redefining the imagined "races," all while insisting that races are visible realities.

Whether immigrants today will be classified as white or not has no more to do with their skin color than it has for previous generations of Irish, Italians, Russians, Kazaks, Mexican-American schoolchildren, mixed-race African Americans, and Native Americans who pay taxes, which is to say something, but relatively little. More pertinent to the question of whether today's immigrant will be Black or white is whether India's economy surpasses ours, China's navy succeeds in controlling the Pacific Ocean, Mexico's economy grows as fast as Brazil's, or South Africa unlocks its cabinet of nuclear secrets.

Challenging racism requires clarity about the nature of the enemy. The way to defeat white supremacy is to destroy it. The United States will no longer be "majority white" when white is no longer the privileged citizenship category, when white is no more meaningful than Octoroon or Irish. This is not to discount the anxiety about cultural loss conjured by talk of an imagined colorblind future, but to recognize the inextricability of racial identities and power inequality. With work, perhaps the fifth expansion of whiteness will be into oblivion.

One question left unanswered is why, if racial privilege has been so central to the American order for five hundred years, we see race much more than we acknowledge power. Privileged people most of all deny privilege. There is something uncomfortable about identifying with power, and some virtue sought in denying it altogether. The next chapter suggests our contradictory relationship to power, seeking but disavowing it, is intimately tied up in the contradictory nature of who we are, and the ability of our causal stories to accommodate those contradictions.

4.

victor and victim

W e contradict ourselves. That's not a weakness. Holding contradictory ideas is a reflection of the complex social and physical reality we live in, an inevitable result of having imperfect information, and a feature we should embrace in our causal stories. It's an inevitable outcome of using a bunch of different local categories and frameworks to explain things at a small scale: we can announce that all politicians are crooks while still being supporters of one political party over another. Crooks and patriots can be the same person.

Our ability to embrace contradiction in our understanding of the world comes from an early moment in human evolution. The social sciences quite wisely avoid considerations of how biology shapes our role in the social world. Every once-influential claim that biology was social destiny (or justified social inequality) has proved to be junk science in the service of prejudice: eugenics, Nazism, social Darwinism, phrenology, mid-twentieth century research on homosexuality, centuries of patriarchal arrogance. Biology does not determine social order, because social orders have been so variable. But our primate minds did evolve under certain evolutionary pressures and not others. We tell stories about those origins that are typically full of bluster and short on fact. We claim our ancestors were smarter and fiercer than the competition. That narrative shapes ideas of who we are and what we should be. The reality is much more complex and contradictory. How we think is intimately tied up with who we are.

In her most fascinating and undernoticed book, *Blood Rites*, the social critic Barbara Ehrenreich explores our dual identification with predator and prey. Ehrenreich began the book—a study of mankind's relationship to war—with a deceptively simple mission: asked to write the introduction for a book on the German military elite, she thought that, as someone who was against war, she should have an understanding of why we fight. Researching our reasons for fighting led her to the central symbolic importance of violence in human societies.

In the section that gives the book its title, Ehrenreich looked at how animal slaughter has regularly been ritualized.[75] What could be the mundane, practical task of processing protein and calories has often been imbued with cosmic, religious significance: from sacrificing a calf at the top of an altar, to the ritualistic rules that religions like Islam and Judaism apply to the work of butchers. Blood rites also appear in the disturbingly long history of human sacrifice. Why is such ritualistic importance accorded to both animal slaughter, a sustaining practice, and human sacrifice, a destructive one?

Ehrenreich suggests that our fascination with blood rites comes from our own conflicted consciousness: we are both predators *and* prey. Against our claim to be predators—"man the hunter" in a typically misleading version of the archetype—she points out that *homo sapiens* have spent far more of our evolutionary history as prey than as predator. Most of the human condition has been running away from other creatures that ate us. Only in the relative blink of an eye has our slow-running, small-toothed, dull-clawed, weak-muscled species developed the weapons that allowed us to turn the tables. Evolutionarily, we are lunch.

When we see an animal killed we have a strong dual identification: a human is doing the killing, and we thrill at the power of that killing and the nutritious outcome. But we also feel a terrifying horror at the slaughter, the blood, the mercilessness, which for most of human existence was directed *at* us. Ehrenreich notes that wolves—actual wolves—were predators of people's children in recent, written European history; fairy tales of scary wolves were not fairy tales, nor were city walls and gates merely to keep out human invaders.

That we are more prey than predator explains a range of human behaviors. Why, when children play tag, do few children want to be "it"? That is the power position, of course, the predator in a game where everyone else is prey. One imagines that if baby wolves play tag, *everyone* wants to be it; no one wants to play the rabbit. But we connect with the experience of being prey so strongly that kids want to experience it again and again; to do so the game requires a predator, but that role is merely a social obligation necessary to make the real action happen, like a designated driver. The role is either so terrifying or so outside human experience that kids don't even have a word for that role—not hunter, not wolf, not predator, but "it."[76]

The centrality of being prey in this duality even extends to our most predatory relationship, that of war. Ehrenreich pieces together tantalizing evidence that suggests that the psychological trauma of battle less likely results from the imminent, terrifying fear of dying than the horrible, unhuman experience of killing. Her theory lacks more concrete evidence in part because, as she finds, although the army collects detailed post-battle accounts from every soldier leaving duty, which record not only whether they were shot or wounded, or shot at, but even whether they witnessed shooting where no one was injured—that is, all of the most minor variations of being prey—the exit interview does not ask whether the soldier killed anyone. It would be unseemly in the extreme to ask that question, but it is worth noting that killing people is the singular job description and objective of front-line soldiers in battle; there is no assessment of whether soldiers carry out this horrible assignment. Studies of earlier wars suggest many do not; even in battle, historically only perhaps 15 to 20 percent of soldiers even fired their gun.[77]

When soldiers reintegrate into society after war, they reveal how we feel about inhabiting the role of the predator: they don't talk about it. Most important, soldiers don't talk about killing people, at least, never in public. Research by a student of mine suggests the conversations at the bar of the neighborhood Veterans of Foreign Wars hall might turn to the topic of having killed in war. But only children ask war vets, "Did you kill anybody?" and even the most frank response I have heard sidestepped discussing individual people. Killing someone is so fundamental a transgression of the human condition that even in the most socially sanctioned situation soldiers avoid admitting to it.

Nonetheless, we continue to construct our political narratives as if we are the aggressor, even when we are clearly caught up in the dual existence of victim and aggressor. I was living in France during the November 2015 terrorist attacks by gunmen and suicide bombers that killed 130 people in and around nightclubs, restaurants, cafes, and a stadium. French President Francois Hollande responded with "France is at war," reversing the position from victim to aggressor. A state of emergency imposed that dual experience, predator and prey, on the already-shaken populace.

As an American, the state of emergency quickly became, for me, as unbelievable as the terrorist attacks themselves. I like to think myself a critic of my own government—of its wars, its corruption, its opportunism, its inequality—as I hope anyone would be of theirs. But inevitably, one's own government—from which we learn so many of our own mythologies and values—has a legitimacy in one's mind that another government simply cannot. The United States has no established state of emergency. In France, a law predating the attacks enabled the declaration of a state of emergency that grants the government sweeping powers in times of crisis. Those powers supersede basic individual rights—those rights Americans call inalienable precisely to indicate that they cannot be suspended. The French president, invoking the state of emergency (which the constitution authorized for up to twelve days but was immediately extended, by near unanimous parliamentary acclaim, to three months, later to six months, then indefinitely) eliminated the right to assemble and prohibited all protests. Searches without warrants suddenly became permissible, and the police executed over 170 in the first weekend alone. Police conducted 3,397 warrantless searches in the first three months, but in only 5 cases were the results deemed worthy of sharing with terrorism investigators. In the ultimate nightmare for gun-toters in the United States, the state of emergency gave France the right to confiscate people's guns (and give them a receipt in exchange). The government closed over twenty mosques that it deemed too radical.[78] Two-hundred seventy-four people were placed under house arrest, including twenty-seven environmental activists in the days before a climate change conference in Paris.[79] Later that spring, several dozen more activists were placed under house arrest without trial, not because they were terrorists, but because they were protesting the government's new labor law. As is so often the case, extraordinary powers were extraordinarily abused, with little or no antiterror progress to show for them.

Americans envision this level of suspension of civil rights in dystopian fictions about police states, dictatorships, Cold War–era Soviet invasion, or the behavior of the British toward American colonies that justified revolution and independence. Yet in the first week of the state of emergency, I was startled that among a wide collection of French citizens with whom I spoke, both European born and not, all understood the state of emergency to be necessary.

Meanwhile, and crucial to our consideration of individual identifications with predator and prey, the state of emergency insinuated itself into the minutiae of daily life in surreal ways that emphasized this dual consciousness. Ever more patrols of soldiers, now not only groups of three, but six or twelve, slowly walked the streets, in full camouflage and flak jackets, carrying heavy, black steel machineguns, a show of aggressive force close enough to touch but so intimidating no one would dare. They walked spread out from each other in a defensive formation that made their already bulky bodies literally occupy the streets. In contrast, because all events could take place only with approval from the prefecture of police, the talent show at my son's public school was summarily canceled; the fate of the school's Christmas market was left in doubt pending a police decision. Police sirens screamed down a major street like the rue Beaubourg, while the permanent exhibit of sculptures by Brancusi just off that street was closed indefinitely—for reasons of security. Police patrolled subway cars, and train lines were unexpectedly shut down "for reasons of security." On the first day of the state of emergency, the government closed parks, pools, museums, and movie theaters; department stores and other large venues followed suit, some reopening with more restricted hours or policies. My daughter's high school began checking IDs and preferred sending kids home with an absence from class rather than allowing a student to enter school without an ID card. A small online journal of urbanism, the editorial board of which I was a member, had been planning a cocktail party for its fifth anniversary and was told they would now need to hire a *third* security guard to look through the bags of everyone coming to the party. French bombing runs against Syria intensified.

The constellation of responses submitted the public to a dizzying dual sensation of predator and prey. The soldiers, the rifles, the police, the bombing, the claim that the state would go to war with those responsible—believed to be the Islamic State, then based in Syria and Iraq—all clearly conveyed the message that France was a powerful predator, pursuing and defeating its prey. But at the same moment, a web of daily experiences—prohibitions against gathering in large groups that could be targets for attackers, security looking into visitors' bags in every shopping mall, government building, office building, and even supermarkets—reminded us that people were targets for another gunman, another suicide vest.

As is always the case, so many of the efforts seemed patently useless. I don't believe I am furnishing terrorists or violent, unstable people with ideas that have not occurred to them by pointing out that prohibiting protest marches and inspecting bags at shopping malls does little to reduce the accessibility of targets for terrorism.

But what the actions of the state of emergency lacked in efficacy they retained in symbolic power. For six months, the state of emergency renewed the public's daily experience of fear. In fact,

some people who in the days immediately after the attacks defi-
antly demonstrated a business-as-usual resolve—going out to dinner
the weekend after the attacks, frequenting cafes, and going to the
movies—over time came to feel the gnawing worry of the state of
emergency. France's declarations of strength against a threat engen-
dered an equal and opposite perception of being threatened.

For their part, even the terrorists, unbelievably, experience the
duality of predator and prey. As they machine-gunned unarmed
people—an act not only of brutality, but of a putrid cowardice, tar-
geting the unarmed with heavy weapons in a way that betrayed the
lies of their own self-image as brave fighters—the terrorists justified
their acts by imagining themselves to be *victims*: victims of the state
they were taking their revenge against, victims of Western aggression
in Syria that they were avenging, victims of degrading, profane treatment by a society they were now attacking.[80]

The patrolling soldiers embodied this duality of fear and aggression. The most arresting parts of their appearance were their machine
guns' barrels and their bulletproof vests, the first potent and dangerous, the second reminders that standing in front of the Museum of
Jewish Art and History made them presumed targets themselves.

At the outer extremities of our experiences, that dualism manifests itself in ways that are difficult to explain. Consider my observation in chapter two that in the United States, wars that involved
racially dehumanizing an enemy (such as the Japanese or Vietnamese) were followed, paradoxically, by greater integration of that group
into the citizenry. Time and again, a comparable dynamic appears in
France's relationship to Muslim fundamentalism, to which the current wave of terrorism is attributed. In a rejection of such religious
fundamentalism, France passed a law in 2004 that, despite its vague
wording banning "ostentatious religious displays" was understood,

and applied, to prohibit Muslim girls from wearing headscarves to school. There were even cases of girls being sent home for wearing skirts that were "too long"; the implication that a proper French woman must wear a suitably short skirt captures the absurd affront to liberty and dignity of such a law. Likewise, many French people saw the wearing of the body-covering "burkini" at the beach instead of an appropriately skimpy French bikini as an unmistakable sign of dangerous proterrorist radicalization.

A public school teacher I interviewed said that when the law was passed she supported it, believing it freed girls from an oppressive tradition. But as she heard more Muslim girls argue that although they were eager to fight against oppression, the burka was not the battle they chose, she began rethinking her position. She recalled that her grandmother, who lived in a provincial village, had herself worn a headscarf whenever she went out, as did the other women in the village. They also, of course, made sure their heads were covered when they went into a church, as required by religious dictate. Was her grandmother's headscarf religious or cultural? Both, as much as the Muslim headscarf is. Today, France opposes, as inconsistent with French values, a practice that was itself French within living memory.

A more startling example is French attitudes toward the independence of women: French opponents of Islam will point out that women in (some) Muslim countries have so little freedom that they are not allowed to go outside without being escorted by a male family member. But the author McKenzie Wark—researching the 1950s Paris-based Situationists' artistic movement—found that one reason white, French bohemians got married to each other so young was that only if the women in those artistic circles had husbands could they avoid police harassment or arrest for being out in public without their fathers present.[81] In France, women could open checking accounts or pursue professions without their husbands' permission only after 1965 and 1966, respectively.[82] That is, many people in today's France condemn ideas as incompatible with French ideology, which France evolved beyond only fifty years ago.

How different is the imagined other? Thomas Guénolé, in his provocatively named book, *Do the Youth of the Banlieue Eat Babies?*, interrogates negative stereotypes about the immigrant youth of the French suburbs. He notes that, although there is evidence to back up the claim that French Muslim teens are anti-Semitic, surveys show that 37 percent of *all* French people imagine Jewish people "have too much power in France," 56 percent guess that Israel means more than France to their Jewish neighbors, and a whopping 63 percent believe people who are Jewish have "a special rapport with money."[83] In brief, anti-Semitism among French Muslims reflects their being French, not just their being Muslim.

The dualistic embrace of the enemy's symbols extends to the ultimate French symbol, the croissant, which is actually modeled after a Muslim crescent. Perhaps it is not worth asking why American hipsters started wearing long beards and short pants while the United States was at war with Wahhabi Islamic terrorists, who wear long beards and short pants. Historian Richard Hofstadter argued that secret organizations are particularly prone to adopting their enemies' styles; he went so far as to conclude that the Ku Klux Klan expressed their rabid anti-Catholic prejudice by "donning priestly vestments" when they put on white robes.[84] The general pattern holds: the other becomes ourselves, predator is also prey.

We not only can, but most often *do* believe multiple contradictory things at once. These contradictions are not just a Freudian tendency to deny the forbidden and desired. We embrace both locally and broader valid explanations: at a local scale I may be a victim, but at a national scale I can be an aggressor, oppressed on one side and oppressing on another. I find the biggest handicaps of social theorists are that they try to make the models of society they construct *consistent*, contrary to what field research regularly finds about people's embrace of contradictory positions.

The problem with identifying as both predator and prey is not that it's irrational—we are so genuinely both at once that it calls for a redefinition of "rational" to more easily embrace duality. More damage comes from a one-dimensional self-image of ourselves—man the hunter, rational actor, defenders of liberty—that is at odds with our actual situation. If we acknowledge that duality for a moment it either appears to be a weak understanding of things—the dreaded on-the-one-hand-on-the-other-hand—or a contradiction that needs to be immediately resolved: We have been hurt but we will fight back! As George Bush put it, quite understandably, "This enemy attacked not just our people, but all freedom-loving people everywhere in the world . . . But make no mistake about it: we will win." Isn't that response only human? Yes. But does it work? A better understanding of a nation's position, particularly in moments of crisis, accepts the complexity (we have been hurt by a small number of terrorists, we have a military designed to wage war against whole nations) that better explains both the conditions that brought us to such a moment and the options, limitations, uncertainties, mistakes, and outcomes of what we might do.

The insistence that we should respond to crises with aggression and dominance confuses our naturally dualistic thinking. In part two of the book, we'll see how reasoning from fear impairs our ability to understand causality. In part three, we'll see how, in the case of a problem like terrorism, the predator archetype (and the reality of our dual consciousness as predator and prey) spirals us into unproductive responses. Biology is not destiny, nor is there a way for us to reason except with our evolutionarily produced social brains. Being alert to the allure of narratives that paint victor over victim puts a spotlight on crisis responses driven more by brave stories we wish were true than the evidence around us.

5.

egocentric causality

Conducting a study of the first wave of growth of African American suburbs, I was struck by an odd feature of white residents' explanations for why Black residents moved into suburban neighborhoods around the country in the postwar years. When whites were upset by integration, they imagined that Black families moved in *to make them upset*. One real estate broker in the 1960s told a researcher that

> There is a certain period of fear. It seems like a calculated procedure that's followed by the colored people before they break into a neighborhood—such things as shopping in the target neighborhood. Yes, Negroes come in deliberately to shop in the

stores. They also drive up and down the streets for no apparent reason. They'll also utilize some of the public playgrounds on a limited scale once in a while.

The realtor couldn't imagine why Black people would go to the store, bring their kids to the park, or drive down the street. Weren't those normal, everyday behaviors? But to this broker, Blacks' actions seemed carefully planned, done with the purpose of frightening white people. That is, he presumed that the *effect* he observed—he and other whites being uneasy—was the same as the *intent* of the actor—frightening white residents—which is a key fallacy of our causal stories.

The presumption that the effect actions had on white residents must be the intent of Black people was widely held. One woman recounted for me the tale, retold by her family for decades, of why they had been forced to move out of their neighborhood: Black people tried to burn down her family's house. Blacks had been moving into the neighborhood, the story went, but this white family demonstrated their tolerance and disbelieved white stereotypes about the danger of new Black neighbors. Then one day they found three birthday candles stuck to the back door, not burning. Of course, she told me, her family had to move.

Why? I asked, genuinely confused.

They tried to burn our house down, she explained to me. They were trying to commit arson, and it scared us out of the neighborhood. We had no choice.

I asked what kind of arsonist would use birthday candles to send a menacing message, when there's a filling station at every major intersection that sells gasoline by the gallon. She was stumped: Was I suggesting that malicious Black arsonists had not tried to burn her family out of their home?

I don't know what the birthday candles were doing there. It sounds distinctly like something a kid might do because candles were left over from someone's birthday, because kids play with fire, or for one of the inscrutable motivations of childhood. It is possible, but to me less likely, that a child planted them there to intimidate someone. (Wouldn't a threat be accompanied by an aggravated message scrawled next to it?) The least likely possibility is that they represented the best effort by an adult or teenager to scare someone or set a house on fire. The candles didn't make symbolic sense but demanded an explanation; ultimately in their dissonance they symbolized disorder.

Stories of Black people intentionally and maliciously disrupting the tranquility of white neighborhoods became institutionalized, told and retold in the stories we urban social scientists teach about racial change in residential neighborhoods. The most well-known version is of the blockbuster, a profiteering real estate agent who, it is said, paid Blacks to act disruptively in white neighborhoods, thereby scaring whites into selling their homes to the blockbusting agent for a loss, so that he could sell or rent them to Blacks—who were otherwise stuck in overpriced, badly maintained buildings run by negligent landlords—at extortionate rates.

The original account seemed to come from a reliable source: a first-hand confessional by an actual real estate agent, under the pseudonym Norris Vitchek. "We speculators and brokers . . . really went to work. One paid several Negroes with noisy cars to begin driving up and down the street a few times a day. He also paid a Negro mother who drew aid-to-dependent-children payments to walk the block regularly with her youngsters. Another arranged to have phone calls made in the block for such people as 'Johnnie Mae.'"[85]

The story had traction: Vitchek's article, called "Confessions of a Blockbuster," is quoted in at least a half dozen major works on neighborhood change from 1969 to the present, even though it was not widely available: one author would cite the article's work in a second author's book, who themselves would have only an incomplete citation with no date, as if it had been photocopied and passed on from author to author.[86]

"Confessions of a Blockbuster" enjoyed a half-century as the go-to reference on blockbusting, despite, problematically, not having been written by a blockbuster. It was credited as "told to" a magazine editor who, although he talked to real estate brokers in Chicago, took more of his talking points from Mark Satter, an early, pioneering civil rights lawyer who fought *against* housing scams that cheated Black home-owners.[87] The article bore little relation to how actual real estate brokers talked about their work, even anonymously, sounding much more like an indictment than a confession. A great article for making white readers think about integration, it was not an accurate portrait of how racial transition happened.

This article from a weekend magazine had such an exceptionally long life because the confession was too good to resist. Another piece *also* called "Confessions of a Blockbuster" was nearly as influential and also had a longer afterlife than its original source warranted: historian Andrew Wiese quoted a section he found in a book by Rosalyn Baxandall and Elizabeth Ewen, who in turn were quoting it from a book by Lawrence Harmon and Hillel Levine. Harmon and Levine were the only authors to see the article, and they no longer have a copy of it, nor does any library. As best we can tell, this much-cited authority on "panic peddling" was an unsigned letter published in a Boston-area real estate trade publication that went out of business two years later.[88] As the most-cited descriptions of blockbusting in the literature on urban neighborhoods, these two articles by unnamed authors make an unexpected pair.

The articles did important work. They distilled the sprawling US housing market's systematic exclusion, exploitation, and abandonment of Black buyers into one actor called the blockbuster. The character of the blockbuster is typically blamed for the rapid transition of neighborhoods from all white to all Black, a process that was common in US cities in the mid-twentieth century as the Great Migration from the rural South to the urban North entered its last years. It's a typical causal story in that it simplifies a constellation of causes to one simple cause and reduces the multiple players and forces into a few moral archetypes.

In fact, neighborhoods switched from white to Black not because of one blockbuster, not even because existing white residents on a block sold and moved out. My research on a typical neighborhood that transitioned from white to Black made it clear that the change happened because whites throughout the metro area stopped buying houses in neighborhoods near Blacks. That is, it wasn't one blockbuster, or twenty families. It was the thousands of white families around the city and suburbs who avoided racially mixed neighborhoods when they were looking to buy a house. Black families were still willing to buy in such a racially mixed neighborhood, and did.

As I heard stories like the birthday candles and the "calculated procedure" of shopping in local stores, I came to recognize that people were conflating cause and effect. They imagined that events were *caused* by the *effect* they had on the observer. I call this *egocentric causality*: the white realtor imagined African Americans must walk down the street *to make him uneasy*—not to get where they were going; the on-edge family was frightened by the candles on their back door meant someone must have put them there with the intention of frightening them. We practice this thinking everyday: if my ex brought a date to a party, they must have done it to upset me—not because they wanted to bring a date.

Whenever someone says, "they did it just to annoy me," they're practicing egocentric causality. No, someone probably didn't act specifically to annoy someone else. More likely, they didn't care how someone else felt as much as they worried about their own pressures (the boss's rules, their own pocketbook, a need for status within their social group) that led them to do something others were annoyed by.

A guard at San Quentin once explained to my sister on a visit that prisoners in solitary confinement—some of whom have been there for thirty years—will do pushups and other exercises together, calling out their counts across the cells—one, two, three—even though they can't see each other. "See," the guard said, "even in solitary, they're trying to show that they have some power over us guards. That they're in control." My sister thought that was ridiculous. It seemed obvious to her that the prisoners were grasping at any opportunity to connect to each other, however remotely. Egocentric causality meant that the guard was sure this was not about them, it was about him.

Classic stories of good and evil rely heavily on egocentric causality: the villain acts to be villainous. The *cause* of the villain's actions, as posited by the author, is the *effect* it has on the hero or the people the hero pledges to defend: The Devil acts to be devilish; James Bond's nemeses demonstrate gratuitous cruelty for Bond's benefit. Dr. Evil perfectly caricatures the type of villain who has no purpose other than being evil.

As with any satisfying good-versus-evil story, egocentric causality distills a vast array of complex causes into a concentrated personification of wrongdoing. When local residents told stories about blockbusters, it allowed white homeowners to disavow any involvement in segregation: they and their neighbors would not have sold their homes and moved out at the site of the first Black man; evil blockbusters had staged scenes that sowed anxiety and frightened them away.

We've discussed the period-specific causal details in Jeffrey Mac-Donald's fabricated account of the hippies he claimed killed his family in 1970s. Unsurprisingly, it is also a prime example of egocentric causality. According to MacDonald's testimony he had been sleeping on the couch, and woke up surrounded by a woman in a "floppy hat," a long blond wig, and boots, holding a candle, who chanted "Acid is groovy. Kill the pigs." Three men with her, one Black and two white, began beating him. In the background he could hear his daughter calling "Daddy, daddy, daddy," and his wife asking, "Jeff, why are they doing this to me." The attackers stuck him in the chest with an ice pick, and he passed out.

Note the efficiency of MacDonald's account, in which the only observations he was able to make about the alleged attackers were useful character details in his simple morality story: Who were they? Occult hippies, thanks to the floppy hat and candle. Why were they doing it? They were on drugs and hated law and order, as conveniently repeated in the woman's chant.

But the narrative lacks anything demonstrating that they acted with a motive other than clarifying things for the benefit of Jeffrey MacDonald. None of the three men who were trying to beat him said anything. Expressions like "Get him!," "I'll hold him," "Watch out!" would seem inevitable to coordinate a group assault. People tripping on acid might say other less rational things that wouldn't fit into the narrative at all. In this telling, the attackers speak only to provide a motive and justification for their acts, not to coordinate the attack they allegedly undertook.

Likewise, the family shouts for MacDonald, but what about their motivation? Why, for instance, would the girl cry for her father and not her mother (or just cry)? His wife didn't scream "Help!" Why would she ask "Why are they doing this to me?"—the very question MacDonald would have to invent an answer to in order to stage a home invasion as a cover-up for the murders he had committed. Their actions make no sense: the family was brutally and suddenly murdered. Either they would have already been killed (thus unable to call to him), or they would still be alive (and would have acted more desperately than asking for his help).

Finally, even the crime scene pointed to an egocentric story of causality. The only bloody prints come from the bodies of the victims, and Jeffrey MacDonald himself, including his bloody bare footprint. The four alleged attackers had apparently entered, fought with a Green Beret doctor, killed three other people, and left no footprints, no clothing fibers, and no blood. In fact, the only trace in the whole house attributable to the killers (the crime scene was too compromised by police and paramedics for there to be a meaningful search for fingerprints) was the word "Pig" written in blood above the master bedroom, a detail that seemed to exist not as something that served as a motive of the killers, but as supporting evidence of Jeffrey MacDonald's account of killer hippies. After all, only six months earlier, the followers of Charles Manson had committed a horrifying murder and written "Pig" in blood on the wall of his victims' house—a fact that Jeffrey MacDonald had read about in the magazine sitting in his living room.

A criminal defendant is not required to say what *did* happen in a case, merely to establish doubt that they committed the crime. But we so readily accept egocentric causality that for twenty years courts have been considering and reconsidering MacDonald's guilt, though his story—the only alternative to the prosecution's case—seems impossible to enact.

We rely too heavily on egocentric causality to explain evil like terrorist attacks—confusing the effect (a perceived threat to our entire way of life) with the cause (the full motive of the attackers). In fact, common egocentric explanations activate our predator and prey duality: if our values are under attack, we must fight back. After the Paris attacks, Parisians concluded that the terrorists—many of whom were French-born citizens—fired at crowds in cafes, restaurants, a music venue, and a

soccer stadium to attack the "French way of life" and "French values."
In the days immediately afterward, residents pointed out that, since its
origins, the Bataclan concert venue had been a place that young people
of all religious and ethnic groups mixed. This was presumed to offend
the orthodox religiosity of the Muslim attackers, and the Islamic State,
which was believed to have sponsored the attacks. The attacks trans-
formed quotidian parts of urbane Parisian life—the café, the restaurant,
the concert venue—into sites of fear, anxiety, and sadness for French
people.

But this does not mean that the attackers' purpose and the public's interpretation were the same. One of the hostages released after the
Bataclan attack reported that the shooters "explained to us that it was
the bombing of Syria that drove them to be there to show to us West-
erners what the airstrikes are like over there."[89]

The terrorists are not the only ones who can define the purpose of
their acts. Plenty of analysis has suggested that their marginalized position in French society was part of the motivation, and this can be true
even if the attackers might not admit to resenting exclusion from a society they claimed to reject. Nonetheless, there is an inherent weakness
in trying to understand the motivation of actions by working from the
perspective of the public who was targeted rather than the attackers. It is
akin to the platitudinous "They hate our freedoms," cited among President George W. Bush's explanations for the terrorist attacks on September 11, 2001. (To his credit, in that State of the Union Address, Bush
pointed out that the terrorists had other goals, such as overthrowing
regimes in Saudi Arabia, Jordan, and Egypt, and destroying Israel.[90])

Egocentric causality is an acute expression of our general instinct to
tell stories that prioritize the forces closest and most meaningful to us and
omit the more significant influences about which we're less preoccupied.

Detecting egocentric causality in the stories people tell can help us question the explanatory value of those stories. MacDonald's account starts to smell fake. Tales of terrorists who hate our freedom are simplistic enough to send us down the wrong path. Retelling tales of scheming Black homeowners creates a boogeyman where there is none. In the rest of the book, we'll look at how we might tell more complicated stories, making room for messier motivations and bringing in a little of what we normally leave out. Egocentric causality reinforces the moral component of an explanatory story. (Someone harmed me on purpose, so they're in the wrong.) We get further in understanding what happens in the world by recognizing that the motivations of people—neighborhood newcomers, terrorists, crime suspects—are often more common than the malevolent scheming proffered by egocentric causality. We can also start to recognize that large-scale social changes can happen for reasons other than proximate, intentional human actions. The next section moves away from expecting everything can be explained by such actions and recognizes important influences we often overlook.

Egocentric causality suggests that we can't stay out of the spotlight. Think of those pre-Copernican medieval astronomers who believed that Earth was the center of the universe.[91] How far have we moved out of the center? The sun may be the center of the solar system, but we are still at the center of the universe. Cosmologists say that from every position, including our own, all objects appear to be moving away from the observer, so that it appears that Earth is the center of the universe. We may know that we're not the center of the universe. It's just that every time we open our eyes it looks like we are.

part two

THE CAUSES WE DON'T SEE

6.

beyond social facts: space

Part one of this book explored how society, evolution, history, and the types of stories we tell (including their deficiencies) have shaped who we are. In this section we'll consider some of the factors we overlook when constructing stories about cause and effect, and our world more generally.

Perhaps the most glaringly overlooked factor that influences our lives is right beneath our feet: the space we all occupy. Our interactions with people, our proximity to hazards and benefits, our ability to group together or keep our distance all stem from where we are located and how the environment around us is constructed. Even in the age of ubiquitous communication networks, space plays a much larger role in organizing our lives than we recognize. As becomes painfully clear in isolation, people are not abstractions. We exist in physical bodies and on physical landscapes, which interact with the social and natural conflicts that shape our lives.

In an epoch when rising seas and changing climates are reclaiming land that we thought was ours, upending carefully knit communities and spilling them inland into already-occupied spaces, it's critical to understand how physical space obstructs or fosters our efforts to group and regroup socially, to be together or apart, to be protected or vulnerable.

In this chapter I address how places where I've done research—the neighborhoods around the World Trade Center after September 11, 2001, a generation of protests including Occupy Wall Street that later swept from country to country, and the threat that displacement from climate change poses for urban communities—allow us to better understand both unappreciated causes and effects of political and climate-caused threats to our communities. If we explain the world through stories, we must also recognize that stories happen not just to people, but in places.

In the years after September 11, 2001, nearly everything in the neighborhood surrounding the World Trade Center had to be rebuilt. The neighborhood I was studying, Battery Park City, was right across the street from the Trade Center site at the southwestern edge of the island of Manhattan. Battery Park City was surrounded on three sides by water; on the fourth side, it was separated from the rest of Manhattan by an intimidating ten-lane highway with the deceptively quaint name of West Street. (It had been the elevated West Side Highway until the 1970s when, typical of the era of neglected infrastructure, a section collapsed sending a truck and several cars crashing down from the highway to the streets below. Rather than fix the problem, the city dismantled the whole elevated highway and retrofitted it to become a surface-level street.)

Battery Park City residents' lifeline to the rest of Manhattan had been a pedestrian bridge from their neighborhood into the lobby of one of the World Trade Center towers; they used it to get to work, to school, and everywhere else. When the towers were destroyed, the residents lost that connection, and the state started planning to replace the bridge with an underground passage.

Locals worried about how their neighborhood was going to be rebuilt, and attended the public planning meetings in large numbers. I attended one such meeting at which plans for the new pedestrian tunnel under West Street were unveiled. Many in the audience had questions, usually indicating their own favored solution to the West Street problem: move the tunnel to another location, put the cars in a tunnel and let the people cross a park instead. One man raised his hand with a more specific question. Looking at the big cross-sectional drawing of the tunnel, he asked why a pedestrian had to walk down three steps at the start of the passageway, then up three steps at the end. That seemed crazy. New construction should be handicap-accessible, he argued. Why not just make the tunnel straight across?

The state planner nodded sympathetically, then pointed to the drawing. Beneath West Street, above and below the pedestrian passageway, the illustration was filled with pipes, tubes, and cables. There were so many underground conduits beneath West Street that the planners had just six inches of "wiggle room" in placing the tunnel.

I have often used that discussion to define what a city is: a place where moving six inches knocks into someone else's interests. The conventional sociological definition of a city comes from researchers at the University of Chicago. In the process of staking their claim as the birthplace of urban sociology (or, as they saw it, all sociology in the United States), the Chicago school proposed three defining features of cities: size, density, and heterogeneity. In other words, cities are big and full of diverse people.[92] Those characteristics are often taken to mean that the quantitative difference in cities—more people, more variety—produce a qualitative difference. The Chicago school's definition acknowledged that cities were different from one another based on these three factors. But the early-twentieth-century Chicago researchers imagined the different types of spaces within each city occurred almost *naturally*—any city would have a poor district, a Black ghetto, an immigrant enclave, a wealthy waterfront redoubt. That kind of determinism eventually distracted researchers from studying spatial dynamics and made them focus on statistical models, which imagined that cities' poverty, segregation, or level of community organization could be measured by surveys and existed with no relationship to the hills, highway walls, or neighborhood streets that shape the landscape we stand on.

The ethnic and racial enclaves the Chicago schools studied only look inevitable. And how those spaces turn around and shape us requires a more delicate understanding. We *create* ghettos, enclaves, and suburbs, and then those places shape who we are—in a process so pervasive, it can almost feel natural.

After years of neglect, one of the most exciting developments in urban sociology has been the renewed, more sophisticated attention given to the ways in which spaces define our cities. Starting around the year 2000, researchers who studied conflicts in cities—community battles over development projects, racial inequality, gentrification, and crime—began focusing on the neighborhoods, buildings, and streets they took place in.

Without attention to space, social research can give the false impression that people are virtual nodes, who can be connected to groups, or other individuals, or larger networks in any way that status or shared interest might dictate. Even before the Internet made us feel connected

beyond social facts: space   101

to each other irrespective of distance, social science researchers had long neglected how distance, physical obstacles, and spatial arrangements of people influenced our social connections.

Attention to space helps us get a sense of how to integrate outside information that will push beyond explaining social facts by referring just to other social facts. Space is both a social and a nonsocial influence on developments in our societies. Space is social in the sense that people organize and argue over how to reshape it, reclaim it, build it, map it, delineate it, and make it meaningful. Yet unlike laws, institutions, or taboos, space remains nonsocial in that it has a physical reality that endures and influences us all on its own.

Like Odysseus's crew sailing between the mythical sirens and the whirlpool, these efforts to create a more sophisticated story of what drives us demand that we navigate between twin risks of explaining all human action via other human actions, or a crude mechanical determinism that explains human action as the outcome of external forces. ("The growth of highways created American suburbs" is an example of mechanical determinism; other countries that could build highways didn't grow American-style suburbs.) This chapter, then, will chart a course that departs from solely social explanations, but avoids sinking itself on the shoals of an overly confident belief that people are mere pawns, driven to act by forces outside their control. We navigate this same territory in our everyday lives, between our ability to make choices and our subjection to forces that constrain our choices.

Occupying Public Space

Because space influences all of our social relations, it plays a crucial role in social movements. I studied a community group that communicated mostly online. Their first ever in-person meeting took place in a small oval park in the neighborhood. After that meeting, the members who lived in the building that faced the park became the de facto leaders. Their spatial proximity to the meeting made them seem like hosts and gave them authority. Whether groups form, dissolve, persevere, win, or lose often depends on the space they can claim.

Occupy Wall Street used space to tremendous effect. Groups have spoken out against income inequality and corporate malfeasance forever. But Occupy Wall Street captured the public's attention—and much public sympathy—when they claimed Zuccotti Park, in the heart of Manhattan's financial district, as their own. Similar protests took hold around the world, from the Puerta del Sol in Madrid to public squares commandeered for protest in Cairo during the Arab Spring, or the Maidan Nezalezhnosti in Kiev during protests in Ukraine that toppled the elected government there. Groups that didn't occupy space did not generate the press attention or public sympathy. Likewise, after Occupy Wall Street was displaced from the park, public attention quickly waned. A sit-in, an occupation, a sit-down strike, an encampment, a shantytown, a squat, all temporarily take over spatial control from the government and maintain it in opposition to the state's wishes, and get attention in a way few other actions do.

The rare locations where protesters take over a space and actually exclude the police, even for a little while, can be called a Temporary Autonomous Zone, or TAZ, to use the term of anarchist theorist Hakim Bey.[93] A TAZ offers a preview of what an anarchist future might be like: a space free of state and police control, overseen collectively by the users of the space. When students take over a college administration building, when a rave party occurs in an otherwise abandoned and isolated space, when a protest gets so large that the police cannot enter or control it, there is a visceral excitement tinged with danger. Even as a researcher, I know I'm in a TAZ by my gut. What comes next could be revolutionary freedom or repressive violence. Anarchist theorists may embrace TAZs for their taste of the revolution, but they're just as useful for recognizing government control and police authority (through its absence), whose otherwise constant presence makes their full effect hard to precisely define.

Space matters in understanding social movements in ways we often don't appreciate. Consider four major protests in four world capitals: Occupy Wall Street, in New York in 2011; the *Indignados* occupation of Madrid's Puerta del Sol in May 2011; the movement called la nuit debout in Paris in April 2016; and Occupy London in 2011. I spent a considerable amount of time at Occupy Wall Street, spoke to protesters at a satellite protest for Los Indignados in Spain, and interviewed dozens of people over several days at La Nuit Debout. As social movements, they shared similar origins, goals, and methods. All four were physical occupations of public spaces begun by young activists, acting outside of political parties, begun as protests over economic crises that were poorly managed (or even precipitated) by politicians. These protests over recession, bank corruption, and regressive labor laws evolved into to a broader challenge to politicians who had grown disconnected from the people they ostensibly represented, and culminated in calls for greater public political involvement and a deeper, more active and direct democracy. Activists in each campaign organized in an anarchist-inspired, nonhierarchical organization and held public meetings (called General Assemblies) to make decisions. Protesters adopted hand gestures so that participants could express noiseless agreement with a speaker at large meetings by using "twinkle" fingers, in which they raised their hands and wiggled their fingers.

Finding one's self in a TAZ is a shock: it is a rare moment that we are in a space outside the control of any police, or any government.

That anarchy transcends mere symbolism: when the police leave such a space, the occupants have to figure out how to govern it on their own. What do they want to do about people using drugs there? How do they resolve disputes or prevent violence? Visitors feel both the dangerous thrill of being in a space, and the acute absence of established law and order. As a result, occupying space—a city plaza, federal lands, the entrance to an Native American reservation—garners a grudging respect from onlookers. But in New York, London, Paris, and Madrid, occupying these spaces did more than telegraph to viewers at home that these were movements to take note of.

Every one of these protests arrived in the wake of major terrorist attacks and established their camps on or near the site of the attacks. Occupy Wall Street's encampment in Zuccotti Park sat across the street from the site of the World Trade Center attacks. Spain's Indignados set up in Puerta del Sol, not far from the Atocha Station, the epicenter of that city's March 11, 2004, bombing, and where Spanish presidents have attended annual commemoration ceremonies.[94] Parisians established La Nuit Debout in Place de la République, where people had only recently turned the central statue into a memorial with photos, signs, flowers, and candles; the place was just down the street from Bataclan, the cafe-theater where the largest number of people were killed in the November 13, 2015, terrorist attacks, and not far from the restaurants attacked that day, and the offices of Charlie Hebdo, where terrorists had struck the previous January. Occupy London first claimed St. Paul's Cathedral (where there had been a public memorial event after London's July 7, 2005, terrorist attacks) and then took over another site in Finsbury Square, just past the site of the Liverpool Street station bombing.

Protest can be an integral step in the mourning process and the construction of a collective memory of a traumatic event. All of the protests articulated a set of liberal values—popular democracy, citizen participation, and tolerance—all of which political leaders had highlighted as values the terrorists attacked. Protesters also manifest discontent with their leaders, who had demonstrably failed to keep them safe. Unprotected by the established political order, protesters organized outside the umbrella of existing political parties.

A student of mine, Remy Monteko, conducted a study of graffiti murals painted in New York as memorials to people who had died. She spent time with the family of Sean Bell, an unarmed man shot to death by police, while they maintained a twenty-four hour a day vigil in a trailer parked near where he was killed. The emotions there were still raw and immediate. When a memorial mural was unveiled, Monteko detected a shift in the stages of mourning that she compared to the unveiling of the headstone, in Jewish funeral rites, a year after burial. Both events marked a shift from active mourning to commemoration, a transition from the immediate grief of recent loss to the memorializing and ritual that continues in the years to come and allows a return to normal life.

The protests, which had concrete effects like the reinstatement of a millionaires' tax in New York and the victory of a new political party in Spain, also reaffirmed citizen participation, a liberal value of democracy that political leaders had argued the terrorists opposed. Particularly for young people, who were often the ones most moved by the attacks, protests were a moment of powerful solidarity, togetherness, and collective security. In traditional New Orleans funerals, the music played on the way to the cemetery is somber and mournful, the music leading away after the burial animates the joyous celebration of the "second line." The protests represented a kind of second line after the terrorist attacks.

In making sense of La Nuit Debout (which can translate as "Up All Night" or, more literally, "Standing All Night"), sociologist Sarah

Gensburger wrote that "'Standing All Night' comes first of all from a desire to be together, at night in République, in this place and in this time that were those of the attacks. To be 'Standing' after all is to not be dead as were so many that famous Friday the 13th."[95] The name in Spain similarly reflected the terrorist events; the March 11 bombings being referred to as 11M, and the protests several years later taking the name 15M.

Direct action protests existed in conflict with terrorism. Activists in New York and elsewhere had just been gearing up for direct action occupation and disruption in Washington, DC during the World Bank meetings when the Pentagon and World Trade Center were attacked in 2001. (In a touching gesture, protesters sent their gas masks, which they had expected to use in confrontations with tear-gas–wielding police, to the Trade Center site in the hopes that they could be used by rescue workers to protect against the dangerous dust, gas, and chemicals spewing from the long-burning site.) Cancellation of the protests in Washington marked a long hiatus for such actions, because, in the aftermath of the terrorist attacks, no one had the appetite for disruptive, illegal protests that provoked confrontations with the police. Then, nearly a decade after the attacks, in May 2011, Osama bin Laden was killed, marking a symbolic end to a long period of tension within the United States. Four months later, on September 17, direct action reignited with Occupy Wall Street.

Protesters themselves did not describe the occupations as a second line of rejuvenation after terrorism, but the locations, timing, and larger themes linked their movement to the response to terrorism. New York protesters objected to the American government's massive and ongoing surveillance program. Some protesters in Paris argued that the government had overreacted to the terrorist attacks by declaring a state of emergency that banned political protests and other large gatherings. "We are protesting the state of emergency . . . The president said 'France is at war,' and they've also been at war with working people," said Girard, a man in his fifties.

The classic view in the study of disasters holds that such events unite people as they come together to help one another in a "community of comrades." This view contrasts with the work of sociologist Kai Erikson, whose decades studying disasters indicates that such events, particularly when man-made, divide people.[96] The protests I've studied did both: they united a self-declared public much like the public that traditional studies found would spontaneously assemble to rebuild after a tornado or flood, while cleaving off a portion of the polity, along what Erikson described as the fault lines that existed before the disaster.

The Uses of Community in Disasters

Spatial arrangements shape how a community will respond to a disaster, and different neighborhoods have strikingly different reactions. Consider our Battery Park City example, the neighborhood next to the heart of Manhattan but cut off by highways. That neighborhood boasted incomes in the top 1 percent for New York City, but it was not particularly white because one in five residents were Asian. In most households, at least one member of the family walked to a high-paying job in the financial district. Not surprisingly, residents had a strong identification with the neighborhood. All of them delineated their neighborhood using the same spatial boundaries, and most who turned up to community meetings wanted to reinforce those boundaries.

People's worldviews are shaped by the spaces they live in—by their neighborhoods, by the boundaries of their country, and by the people living within and without those neighborhoods and nations. But the reverse is true as well, and people construct their spaces with particular social goals in mind: to exclude other people and to connect themselves to other people and places. People form boundaries and boundaries form people. The result of these two processes is what I call space's reciprocal relationship: space influences people, people then try to influence the space, and that new space, once re-formed, influences the behavior of future generations of people.

Battery Park City perfectly demonstrates this reciprocal relationship. The neighborhood started out as landfill dumped into the Hudson. The residents of the first few buildings, surrounded by vast vacant lots and construction sites, were, according to an early newspaper report, "feeling rather proprietary these days about the esplanade" along the waterfront.[97] They had staked their claim and felt that outsiders didn't belong. Life in Battery Park City was often inconvenient because of its isolation from the rest of the city—the early planners had misrepresented the distance to the subway in their presentations.

After September 11, the city offered plenty of money to rebuild, and (before the wiggle-room walkway) they proposed hiding a section of the roaring West Street underground, so that a park could make it easier for residents and others to move in and out of Battery Park City. Residents' reaction was quick and unified: they hated the idea. Publicly, they worried that the highway tunnel would cost too much or that it would require years of disruptive construction. Privately, however, in interviews and on anonymous online message boards, they said that they liked the fact that their neighborhood was isolated, and they worked to keep it that way: "I do not want West Street buried because I like the feeling of being separated from other parts of the city. This is, I know, a totally selfish reason," wrote one resident. The reciprocal relationship continued its cycle: the city had built a space that isolated residents, residents defined their community through that isolation, and then banded together to influence the redevelopment process, keeping their neighborhood cut off, to give a new generation a similar sense of isolation. There was nothing natural about the development of this community.

And yet, we so often accept the built environment as natural. Traffic planners know that a sign posting a low speed limit can infuriate drivers who feel it's an artificially imposed restriction, and they ignore it or lobby to change it. But a narrower road that must be navigated more slowly appears to drivers to be a natural feature of the landscape, and they accept it. In Battery Park City, the entire highway that separated the neighborhood from the rest of New York City was just another fact of life. One resident who was confined to a wheelchair had missed several community meetings owing to out-of-service elevators and pedestrian bridges that had trapped her on the wrong side of the highway. Yet she advocated for keeping it in place: "Well, personally, I don't see it's a barrier. It's *just an eight-lane highway* that we had to manage to get across one way or another." She also recalled a friend who was hit by a car trying to cross. Another community member noted that his own mother had trouble getting across the street to his neighborhood. Yet all of them denied that the highway presented a problem in need of fixing. They accepted it as a feature of the landscape.

It is easy to be critical of Battery Park City residents' desire to fend off outsiders, particularly in contrast to the generosity that the rest of the country had shown New York, Battery Park City included, after the terrorists attacks. But physical isolation can have benefits worth replicating in other areas.

Battery Park City's isolation has fostered a stronger sense of "community" than most neighborhoods in US cities. But as Iris Marion Young has pointed out, although Americans use "community" in a strictly positive sense, the term carries an inherent opposition: unity begets exclusion.[98] In fact, "communautarisme" is an insult in France. When I did research comparing US and French cities, I could tell people in the United States I was studying "communities," but I never used the term in France, where calling a group like Muslims, immigrants, or people of color a "community" is a way to charge that a group is intolerantly walling themselves off from society.

That comparatively tight-knit sense of community that developed from the neighborhood's isolation buoyed residents in the months after the terrorist attacks of September 11. People I spoke to had watched the buildings burn and collapse from their living room windows, and had fled for their lives in clouds of ash and darkness. They had been frightened, some convinced they and their families were about to die.

Most residents could return to their homes within a few weeks. In the months that followed, they used the abundant parks of the neighborhood as informal, open-air group therapy sessions. If residents felt lonely, they could always run an errand and pass through the park. A year after the disaster, one resident echoed the observations of others when she said, "Now, you'll talk for an hour if you're outside five minutes." Adults talked and reconnected in the playground while children played. Residents felt guilty for admitting that the attacks, the subsequent isolation of their neighborhood in the recovery period, the need to get to know neighbors to lobby their landlord, the city, or the state for rent reductions, reconstructions, or other assistance had all improved the community.

Compare the experiences of Battery Park City residents to those of people who lived through the 1972 Buffalo Creek Flood, in which a mine company dam burst and flooded over a dozen West Virginia towns, killing 125 and leaving almost all 5,000 residents homeless. Kai Erikson, who carefully studied the resulting human displacement, described residents' emergency housing as a "second disaster." People who had lived their entire lives in towns of friends and extended family were suddenly uprooted at a traumatic moment and left to live among strangers. As Erikson wrote, "In effect, then, the camps served to stabilize one of the worst forms of disorganization resulting from the disaster by catching people in a moment of extreme dislocation and freezing them there in a kind of holding pattern."[99]

The necessity of a physical community, where people live close to others they know and can turn to them for help, is often overlooked when we think about a disaster. Emergency housing in trailers provided by the Federal Emergency Management Agency (FEMA) often fails to keep displaced communities intact, although when possible the agency can install trailers on the property where a resident's damaged house sits, which keeps people in their neighborhoods. When residents of New Orleans were belatedly evacuated from the city after Hurricane Katrina in 2005, they had no way of knowing where the bus they got on was taking them, or whether family members were going in the same direction. Residents ended up in Houston, Atlanta, and beyond. Their accounts speak to the difficulty not only of displacement, which was unavoidable, but of isolation from friends and community, which was not.[100] Emergency housing can be assigned with attention to preserving, where possible, the socio-spatial networks people have (for instance, by assigning people from the same town or people traveling together as an extended family to housing in the same place). Likewise, aid agencies tend to lay out their emergency housing camps in rows. Although this configuration serves a utilitarian function, it does not create a physical space that reflects most people's previous community, nor does it encourage the development of meaningful social ties as found in a circle of houses facing each other, or with streets radiating from a central location.

On the rare occasions that we *do* pay attention to space, we imagine it to be all powerful. For decades, observers fretted over the state of public housing projects. Researcher Oscar Newman gave critics and supporters of public housing a scapegoat they could both point to: the design of modernist apartment complexes. The buildings, Newman argued, were too tall for parents to keep an eye on their children playing in the grassy areas below, and too anonymous for residents to feel ownership over the space. Instead, Newman advocated "defensible spaces," developments with a single entrance, lower buildings, and enclosed courtyards so that an outsider "perceives such a space as controlled by its residents, leaving . . . an intruder *easily recognized and dealt with*."[101] Reimagining these spaces would reduce crime.

Newman's designs took hold everywhere. The first complex in Battery Park City was built explicitly following Newman's recommendations; the sprawling 1,712-unit complex had a *single* entrance. In nearby Brooklyn, affordable housing was built with the kitchens in front in the hope that mothers at home would keep their "eyes on the street" and help police the space.[102]

In 1992, the federal government instituted a program called HOPE VI, on the premise that high-rise public housing apartment buildings were inherently conducive to crime, and that low-rise buildings like row houses created more stable communities by producing more intimate areas where residents could get to know each other and recognize outsiders. Studies measured some improvements: residents felt safer, crime rates seemed to be lower, and incomes were higher. But the data was misleading. Incomes rose because most sites combined low-income units with higher-rent housing, not because poor residents were doing better. Crime rates were unavailable for half the old units. Because the new housing developments had only half as many apartments for low-income families, whatever benefit those residents gained had to be measured against the half of former public housing residents who, in many cases, lost their homes.[103] When Sudhir Venkatesh followed residents of Chicago housing projects, he watched residents struggle and fail to find adequate housing. He saw people with physical and mental health problems torn away from the neighbors who had taken care of them.[104] Eventually, city agencies that had promised to help residents had to admit that they could not make good on those promises.

But do tall buildings really cause crime? Although the towering New York headquarters of investment banks like Goldman Sachs support the correlation between high rises and criminal behavior, the luxury residential towers of Manhattan's Upper East Side or Chicago's Gold Coast do not record high crime rates. After HOPE VI, it has been taken for granted that public housing design causes crime, and the assumption that redesigning the buildings will solve the problem—despite doing nothing to change people's social situations—is temptingly simple.

Space, as the first nonsocial cause we've explored, serves as an example of how to treat other casual factors more thoughtfully. The trick is to neither ignore the importance of where we stand, nor to be overly deterministic. Thinking about space's reciprocal relationship helps us understand how the relationship between cause and effect is perpetually in motion: space shapes people, even while people shape that space. To say that someone is either out in the sprawling exurbs, separated from their job by a long commute on the freeway, or stacked up in a high rise indicates how the landscape may shape their map of social connections. But it's not a static map, nor is it natural.

Building is not destiny: tall buildings or short ones can harbor crime, isolated communities can nurture or suffocate residents. That's precisely why we need to examine nonsocial causes when we're searching for answers, because we know they are likely to be influential, but need solid observations and adaptable models—not guesses or preconceived notions—to understand how they actually work in a given situation. Everyday life and historic community traumas don't play out in the abstract; our experience of them involves the ground we stand on, who we share it with, and who it connects us to. Because we are deeply social people who need social connections and shared stories to make sense of the world, recognizing, preserving, or grasping the possibility of such connections is vital to helping communities in crisis.

Public Space

One of the reasons social movements and communities work so hard to control space is that space is, in many ways, the perfect soldier. If someone hopes to separate two groups—Sunnis from Shiites in Iraq, a Black neighborhood from a white one, boys from girls in school—it is possible to achieve the segregation they seek solely by relegating the two groups to different spaces. But once that difference is put into the form of concrete, bricks, and mortar, it becomes difficult to upend.

When the American troops arrived in Baghdad, the US authorities quickly altered the legal statutes that had supported the power of President Saddam Hussein, but the concrete organization of power proved more durable: US headquarters, the "Green Zone," was located in the buildings of the former regime. Thus the location, arrangement, and proximity to other institutions were preserved. As the war became a civil war of Sunni against Shiite Muslims, residents had to move out of formerly mixed neighborhoods, and the US military constructed high concrete blast walls around neighborhoods to deter terrorist attacks. Towering concrete walls surrounding those neighborhoods contributed to social segregation after the United States declared the war over;

to demolish the walls, to reintegrate the populations, would be not only a significant social and legal undertaking, it would require the removal of tons and tons of concrete.

In the United States, space has a similar perseverance. Residential racial discrimination has been prohibited by federal law since 1968, but it persists. That persistence is not just a residue of previous prejudices, to be sure, but segregation is noticeably higher where existing spatial separations of Blacks and whites can maintain that separation than in places where it would have to be established anew. A highway built, as it was in Chicago, to separate white Mayor Richard Daley's neighborhood from nearby Blacks is impervious to the Fair Housing Act, and the two neighborhoods have remained separated.

My research on public space indicates that everyone who wanted a hand in the design of parks, plazas, even highways and transit lines believed that the design of the built environment could shape communities and induce people to act the way they wanted them to, and this accounted for the ferocity of many battles over public projects: spaces shape behavior, and at some level, *everybody knows it*. Architecture is politics by other means.

The persistent importance of space and proximity has preserved cities' relevance in the age of ubiquitous communication. Technology has reshuffled the spatial organization of activities, certainly, sending some to far-flung corners of the world but concentrating others. What goes where is not always immediately obvious; communication technology helps firms in Manhattan order clothing made in China, but garment factories remain in Manhattan at the same time to pick up quick turnaround work distant firms can't complete in time. Banks may move back office functions out of the city, but increasingly specialized managerial functions become more concentrated in a small number of global cities.

Climate Change

The devastating reality of climate change reveals the dramatic importance of space in our ability to act as communities. At every turn, climate change requires thinking about displacement.

From studying urban renewal, which uprooted tens of thousands of Americans (especially African Americans) in the 1950s and '60s, or earlier disasters, we know that the effects of displacement can lead to shortened life expectancy. Displacement separates people from those they care about and who care for them, from their daily routines, from the neighborhoods they know.

The cruel irony of climate change is that it will cause large-scale displacement whether we refuse to make any preparations or make the very best preparations. Remember, it cannot be explained away merely with social facts. Either people will be displaced when their communities are inundated by floods, or we will recognize the inescapable reality that sea-levels will continue to rise throughout the century no matter what we do—and displace people from at-risk, low-lying neighborhoods.

Storms like Katrina in New Orleans and Sandy on the East Coast, or droughts disrupting nations in North Africa and the Middle East have already displaced populations. Some vulnerable areas may be protected, but others will be relocated. Moklesur Mollah, a graduate student at Brooklyn College, interviewed 200 homeless people in Bangladesh. He found that 51 percent became homeless as a result of climate displacement: their villages flooded, or their water-navigating way of life was no longer possible. Climate displacement has already begun and will continue the rest of our lives and our children's lives.

Although predicting the scale of displacement is difficult, researchers expect climate change to displace millions of people over the coming century, with high estimates in the range of 50–200 million. Many will relocate locally, within the same country. Some will evacuate temporarily, then return home. Some will immigrate to other countries. A disproportionate number of those forced to evacuate will be poor, and as it presently stands, the international community's plans would leave most of the burden of displacement on poor countries.[105]

Whether poor people are displaced by storms or well-intentioned plans to limit storm damage (for instance new sand dunes or other searise protections), the degree to which their new communities preserve their social networks is a matter of life and death. Poor people need their local, spatial networks the most: they need nearby family members to watch the kids after school, they carpool more, they check-in on an elderly neighbor. Tear up that delicate social fabric, and the poor will suffer disproportionately. Not to mention the fact that in times of crisis like a hurricane, government mistreatment of people of color intensifies, and they are often maligned as dependent, policed as dangerous, or simply ignored in their moment of needs.

The Black-white wealth gap in America and a system that leaves rebuilding to individual homeowners means that homeowning Black residents in a place like the waterfront neighborhood of the Rockaways in New York City have less wealth to finance reconstruction than white neighbors on the same shore. The comparatively supportive experience of Battery Park City shows how effective recovery can be if communities can stay together. The experiences of many New Orleanians shows the opposite. Today, progressive cities are drawing up plans to adapt or mitigate climate change; in New York a boatload of Dutch hydroengineers have proposed sea walls, wetlands, clam beds, sand dunes, and storm drains, but none have discussed how communities displaced from some of these low-lying areas will be kept intact, or at least organized more durably, and they must.

A serious program to prepare for climate change must think about the impact of displacement. But the role of space, and the risk of displacement, goes even further. If we do nothing to reduce the burning of fossil fuels, climate change will happen more rapidly, seas will rise higher, and the amount of displacement will increase. This explains the urgency of environmentalists' calls to reduce the use of fossil fuels. Imagine, then, that we could replace all the coal mined in West Virginia with solar panels in a sunny desert in Arizona. It's a simplistic proposal, but in terms of the amount of energy generated, not inconceivable. Would that solve the problem by reducing displacement?

Not exactly. What, after all, would happen to the 74,000 people employed in the coal industry nationwide, or the 30,000 in West Virginia alone? Another 172,000 work in the oil and gas industry.[106] This does not mean that the coal, oil, and gas industries should be untouchable because they employ lots of people. But consider what losses to the auto industry did to cities like Detroit, and to the lives of people who lived there as it slipped from a city of 2 million to less than 700,000. Even ambitious, industry-altering plans to stall climate changes would themselves cause types of displacement. We can do nothing about fossil fuels, and people will be displaced by storms. Or we can overcome the political challenges and actually do something about fossil fuels, and fewer people will be displaced by storms, but tens of thousands will be displaced by the permanent shuttering of fuel industries. Many of those people, and their families and communities, would be displaced like auto workers, leaving in search of jobs elsewhere.

The old union invocation "Don't mourn—organize!" applies to social space as well. Whether the mourning follows terrorist attacks in New York, London, Madrid, or Paris, or the rising disasters of climate change, how we organize our social space—our permanent neighborhoods, our protests in public plazas, our temporary camps (of Occupy

Tents or FEMA trailers) will shape how that mourning can evolve into renewal. Everywhere we look, the lay of the land shapes what we can and can't do; yet, like the resident who couldn't get her wheelchair across the highway, our impulse is to accept the built environment as a fact of life, not something fabricated that we can (collectively) rebuild in a new image. Space is more than proximity, it's the organization of connections across space, and the shared history a place has that makes it meaningful to people. We are social beings, and the stories we tell give symbolic meaning to places like central squares, residential neighborhoods, or corporate high rises. We make space social, and space shapes how we can be social.

7.

allostasis or, does ronald reagan cause diabetes?

M y father had been suffering the truly awful effects of end-stage diabetes for years. Eventually, in and out of the hospital for a kidney transplant and foot infections, he stopped reading his beloved right-wing *New York Post*. I was concerned. His tax-cutting fiscal conservatism was as far to the right as I was to the left. Once so stalwartly conservative that he felt betrayed by the slightest liberal gestures by Ronald Reagan and Richard Nixon, he could no longer even get worked up about Obama's presidency.[107] Almost too tired to speak, he said, "Those Republican congressmen complain about what Obama's doing. Who cares?" In my family, a man who no longer cared about politics was a man who no longer cared about life.

He was transferred to a rehabilitation center, but he started refusing to do the exercises that were supposed to make him strong enough to walk again. The infection in his foot got worse. Doctors amputated his leg but it didn't heal. He refused to eat; the taste of food became repulsive. A week later, I spent the night in his hospice room. He took a breath only every ten seconds or so. I bedded down in a lounge chair. In the midst of my dreams I heard his breaths, much farther apart. A raspy breath. Twenty seconds. Another breath. The gaps between breaths jolted me out of the chair and to his bed side. I stood next to him and called my mother and sister to tell them to come right away. Then, as I looked at his face, my father took his last breath.

Why did my father die of diabetes? The disease does not have to lead to a gruesome end. With attention to diet, exercise, and weight management, the effects can be greatly reduced. And the effects—like vision loss, toe, foot, and finger amputation, kidney failure—should be gruesome enough to motivate someone to divert the course of the disease.

But so many people don't. For his part, my father stubbornly resisted doing anything sensible about diabetes. His ignorance was willful. My sister remembers a moment from her teenage years in which our father stood in front of an open refrigerator after being told he should cut down on sugar. "Does this have sugar in it?" he asked her, holding up a colorful cup of fruit-flavored yogurt. "Dad," she deadpanned, "Is it sweet?" "I don't know! Just tell me if it has sugar in it," he responded impatiently. Little surprise that diet modification never went anywhere for him.

No small part of my father's resistance was ideological: he was a dedicated defender of capitalism (though generations of downward mobility meant it had been more generous to his grandfather than to him) and if the invisible hands of private enterprise were the ideal means of distributing goods to fulfill people's needs and desires, then people who warned that the American diet was unhealthy were liberal meddlers with more faith in big government than the almighty free market. To my father, it was left-wing propaganda: Saying you had to watch what you ate was saying capitalism was not humanity's salvation but an evil menace. As an anticapitalist who watches his weight, I always figured he was right.

My mother told me about my father's shock at being told he had diabetes at sixty, when she remembered his doctor telling him he had it at *thirty*. Why had he ignored it for three decades? she asked in frustration. By that time I had worked on health research projects that involved interviewing more than a hundred diabetes patients and many doctors. It turns out, ignoring it was the norm. People would tell me the story of being diagnosed and given pills to take. They would try them for a while and then stop. They stopped because they felt fine and figured they didn't have diabetes. They stopped because they had seen their grandmother live with diabetes and were so scared of it that they wanted to deny they had it. They stopped because they had no health insurance and the more affordable option was to decide the medicine was unnecessary anyway. The lucky ones I interviewed had slipped into a diabetic coma, woke up in a hospital where they were told they were fortunate to be alive, and took advantage of the second chance to get the disease and their dietary habits under control. My father ignored diabetes because part of its maliciousness is that lots of people ignore diabetes until the damage is done.

My research on diabetes also revealed a vast missing link in the explanation of why so many people got diabetes in the first place. Unsurprisingly, it pointed to a number of factors we don't often account for in our causal stories.

The medical story of what causes diabetes was straightforward enough: though medicines can slow the progression of the disease, the best treatment is diet and exercise. Cut way down on sugar and starches—soda, juices, candy, potato chips, bread, pasta, potatoes, refined sugar, flour—in short, stop eating most of what occupies a modern supermarket, other than the little periphery running around the edge of the store made up of the produce aisle and the meat cooler. The mantra has been "diet and exercise." When the mantra hasn't worked, medical experts advocate more education for patients, like workshops on diet and nutrition. Like sex ed in the case of teen pregnancy, the presumption is that people who don't follow conventional wisdom must lack education.

But is education lacking? Anyone I interviewed could recite back diet and exercise to me, but few people had their diabetes controlled. The mantra of diet and exercise hasn't worked. The disease has grown to an epidemic in the last thirty years, and spreads wherever in the globe modern capitalism goes.

The conventional explanation of diabetes remains inside the world of medicine to explain how we might regulate our weight, our blood sugar, or other measures. But that story doesn't ask why some bodies raise those levels to dangerous heights, and thus it is insufficient for understanding diabetes as an epidemic. Our bodies respond—even anticipate—conditions in the social environment around us. The social causes are as important as they are overlooked. To clarify, the social factors extend beyond the mere availability of junk food and soda (commonly named culprits). The availability of junk food leads only to the question of why some people consume them (despite the known risks to their health) while others don't. Understanding the role of the social environment means recognizing that social insecurity drives some people, but not others, to seek out those foods. Treatment for the chronic diseases that are most common in the modern world will be inadequate until we look at the social conditions that cause them. A more complex story that weaves together medical and social causes can show us that recognizing how social and nonsocial factors interact gives us a route to effectively reduce the spread of the disease.

The Medical Model

Diabetes impairs the body's ability to process sugar. When we eat sugar, it is absorbed into our bloodstream. On command, our pancreas releases the hormone insulin, which individual cells need to take in the sugar and use it as a source of energy. In the more rare form of diabetes, type 1 diabetes, the pancreas stops producing insulin, and people must take insulin shots with each meal to allow them to process sugar into energy. Type 1 diabetes seems to be an autoimmune disorder, in which the body disrupts the ability of its own pancreas to make insulin.

The form of the disease that is epidemic is called type 2 diabetes, and typically appears in people who are overweight. The body can still produce insulin—sometimes lots of it—but the cells can't process it efficiently. The body is *insulin resistant.* There are pills patients can take to help process sugar, but as the disease gets worse, they may also need to take insulin to provide the quantity the body needs to process sugar.

The harm of diabetes comes from the devilishly simple matter of extra sugar circulating around in the blood. The sugar damages fine blood vessels, causing vision loss, damaging the circulation system so that fingers and toes don't get enough blood (and can't heal and thus are at risk of serious infection). The kidneys are overtaxed trying to clean the excess sugar out of the bloodstream, leading people to pee a lot and be frequently thirsty. (In a vicious cycle, drinking lots of soda provides the water the body craves, and the sugar that the cells still crave, but it only exacerbates the problem of excess sugar, making the kidneys filter out more sugar and demand more to drink.) After several decades with diabetes, the kidneys may fail, requiring dialysis, the mechanical filtering of the blood every other day. Even with treatment, diabetes increases the risk of heart attack and stroke.

Today, the disease afflicts nearly 10 percent of the population, but even that understates how widespread it is. Considering that 25 percent of people over 65 have type 2 diabetes, and the numbers have been rising, some researchers estimate a third of Americans will have diabetes. Although rates differ by race, it is a crisis in every demographic. While almost 8 percent of whites, 9 percent of Asians, and 13 percent of Latinos and African Americans have diabetes, the rates of people with elevated, "pre-diabetic," blood sugar levels is roughly the same for all groups, at least 35 percent.[108]

The rate of diabetes in the United States has grown explosively. Between 1990 and 2013, the rate in the United States increased by 71 percent.[109] In 1995, only three states had diabetes rates over 6 percent. By 2010, *every* state had rates above 6 percent.[110]

Rates are growing globally as well. Diabetes is now as common in China as it is in the United States, and rates have doubled worldwide since 1990.[111] As researchers in *Nature* said, "Diabetes mellitus, long considered a disease of minor significance to world health, is now taking its place as one of the main threats to human health in the twenty-first century. The past two decades have seen an explosive increase in the number of people diagnosed with diabetes worldwide."[112]

Allostasis

What explains this incredible spread of diabetes in the United States? The proximate cause is weight gain. Before the epidemic was recognized, researchers Earl Ford, David Williamson, and Simin Liu conducted a study finding that a weight gain of 11 pounds increased a patient's risk of diabetes by 27 percent.[113] Noting that the number of overweight and obese people had increased in the previous decade, the researchers predicted ominously that their findings "may portend an increase in the incidence of . . . diabetes . . . with important public health consequences in future years."

The researchers' prediction was remarkable. Yet the connection they found was to a *proximate cause*; weight gain caused diabetes. There remained a crucial question.

What caused the increase in *obesity*? The answer requires that we look beyond proximate causes.

In the 1960s, Peter Sterling straddled two worlds: one as a neuroscientist and one as an activist. Canvassing door-to-door in the poor Cleveland, Ohio neighborhood of Hough, he was struck by how many people who answered the door were partially paralyzed: one side of their face was sagging, or they limped to the door. He never encountered this phenomenon when knocking on doors in affluent Brookline, Massachusetts, and began wondering what in Hough's history had led to such high incidences of stroke.

The area had been through plenty. A poor, predominantly African American community, Hough had riots severe enough that the National Guard had been called in. Sterling later met researcher Joseph Eyer, who had assembled clear evidence that the rate of stroke and heart disease was correlated with social disruptions like migration, segregation, job loss, and divorce.[114] Sterling quickly became interested in understanding how social crises shape physical health. "Back then," explained Sterling, "standard medicine attributed essential hypertension and atherosclerosis to excessive consumption of salt and fat—as though what people chose to eat were unrelated to their internal physiological and mental states. So it was compelling to learn that the peripheral hormones that raise blood pressure, such as angiotensin, aldosterone, and cortisol, also modulate brain regions that stimulate hunger for sodium. Similarly, peripheral hormones that increase catabolism, such as cortisol, also modulate brain regions that stimulate hunger for energy rich substrates—fat and carbohydrates."[115] What Sterling meant was that, although medicine rightly attributed disease to things like diet, the real question was what changed people's diet. By looking at the role of hormones and the body's own effort to maintain a certain blood pressure, weight, and blood sugar level, Sterling found a domino effect: social stress raised hormones that triggered cravings for salty and sugary foods. Social pressures altered biological health.

From this insight, Sterling and others came to recognize a biological process they called "allostasis." It was a revolutionary moment in how we understand the body. Previously, medicine had assumed that our bodies have something like a row of mechanical gauges, and that the body tries to keep those gauges at the same level: body temperature at 98.6 degrees Fahrenheit, blood pressure below 120/80, fluid levels topped off, blood sugar levels moderate, and so on. This model, called homeostasis, assumes that if a level gets too high or low, the body tries to return to that original level, or setpoint: if you overheat, the body sweats to cool down; if a predator attacks, blood pressure rises to pump more blood and energy to muscles. If an argumentative relative attacks at Thanksgiving, blood pressure rises to send more blood to the brain to dispatch their misguided political arguments. After the tiger or the climate change argument has been dealt with, blood pressure returns to normal.

Those who proposed the new allostatic model concurred that after a brief event levels returned to the previous setpoint. But, they determined, if the stress lasted for prolonged periods, with no sign of abating, the elevated levels became the new normal. Proponents of the allostastic model point out that the body regulates these levels in anticipation of future needs: the pancreas releases insulin not after food enters the digestive tract, but as you sit down, in anticipation of a meal to be digested. If a situation is always stressful, the body may anticipate that a higher blood pressure is needed, and aim to keep blood pressure at that new, higher level. The shift from a vision of the body that has fixed points of reference to one where "normal" is relative to chronic stress is like the shift from Newtonian physics to Einsteinian relativity: there are no absolutes, only the experience of the individual observer in the world. Different bodies respond to different types of stress in their environment, and chart different courses to survival. Cardiologist Sandeep Jauhar takes this perspective, noting "Allostasis is attractive because it puts psychosocial factors front and center in how we think about health problems."[116]

Today, sociologists of health think of the body's response to the environment in terms of what they call *fundamental causes*: weight gain increases diabetes, but what external factors cause weight gain? In other words, instead of looking at the immediate risk factors, what increases the "risk of risks"?[117]

For medical conditions from workplace injuries to asthma to heart disease, research into "fundamental causes" find that, not surprisingly, being poor or otherwise disadvantaged puts people at risk of being at risk, for two reasons: First, poor people have less access to the information, medical technology, and specialists that could better treat their condition. Second, poor people have greater environmental risks, whether that includes polluted air that contributes to asthma, dangerous jobs that cause injuries, or cheap food that harms long-term health. If sociology's contribution of fundamental causes seems obvious, consider that it's still not a major part of how we treat diseases. Individual risk factors monopolize our attention in treatment, even if social factors underlie so much of what makes us sick. As German doctor and social critic Rudolf Virchow observed in 1848, "medicine is a social science, and politics nothing but medicine on a grand scale."[118]

But if the fundamental causes of disease—like economic and nutritional insecurity—have existed forever, how do we explain the sudden epidemic of obesity and diabetes? The work on fundamental causes offers key insights.

Neoliberalism

A search for the causes of illness that stays inside the body has a limited opportunity to understand why bodies malfunction, or function in ways that hurt us. Even when an internal cause can be identified—a cell turned cancerous or a mutated gene—the inevitable next question is what caused that change. The search migrates outside the body, but that is terrain that microscopes and blood tests are poorly designed to explore. That's probably why, for instance, 95 percent of cases of high blood pressure are listed as "idiopathic"—without identified cause—which in turn hints at why, even with an armamentarium of over 200 blood-pressure reducing drugs on the market, 75 percent of cases of high blood pressure remain dangerous and uncontrolled.[119]

In the case of diabetes and obesity, there are no doubt multiple intermediate factors that aggravate the epidemic. Researchers have looked at unhealthy diet and lack of exercise, to be sure, and have also asked whether other contributing factors could be a more sedentary work life, genes shaped by environmental factors (called epigenetics), sleep deprivation, depression, a more climate-controlled existence, or the presence of synthetic hormones in the foods we eat.[120] Yet all of these are discreet variables that can be measured in isolation without understanding the risk of risks. Each time one of these factors is identified, it begs that we investigate how social structures shape health risks. How does the social organization of our world put us at risk for a disease like this? If we recognized that how we organize society—things like job security, the types of jobs we do, the family structures we live in, the anxiety of being unable to afford better food at the grocery store—shapes our health on a massive scale, what changes would we make?

In the case of diabetes and obesity, we must ask why people gain weight. We eat differently when we're worried, and research even shows that we do different things with calories, burning them or storing them, depending on our situation. In conditions of uncertainty, our bodies focus on obtaining and storing calories. That's a useful reflex to have when winter is coming, burning them off as needed through the barren months, and emerging, thin, in late spring ready to gather another bounty. But when the stress is not seasonal but continuous, that weight gain can lead to chronic obesity and to diabetes and related health effects.

America started gaining weight in the 1980s. As researchers wrote in the *Journal of the American Medical Association*, "Over the period 1960–1980 (covered by the earliest NHANES surveys and the National Health Examination Survey), obesity prevalence was relatively stable, but then it showed striking increases in the 1980s and 1990s."[121]

The 1980s did indeed stoke insecurity. After the social progress of the 1960s, the 1970s saw economic stagnation and a flat rate of corporate profits. Unemployment skyrocketed to levels unseen since before World War II. Even with high unemployment, inflation continued and prices of everything from food to housing continued to rise. Despite rising prices, corporations feared that the postwar Golden Years that married high wages to high productivity and high profitability were near an end. Elites worried about the working class power of unions, the demands of civil rights first from African Americans but also, as the '70s progressed, from Native Americans, Chicanos, and a second wave of the twentieth-century women's movement. Around the world, liberation movements challenged both European colonialism and the prerogatives of American corporations to dominate the extraction of natural resources. In Iran, a rebellion against the US-supported dictator led to a revolution and a protest that overran the US embassy and held embassy staff and others hostage for over a year. It was an anxious time to be a rich white American man with a shriveling stock portfolio.

In 1980, Ronald Reagan ran for president on a promise to end that anxiety of the elite. He was not only good looking but firm and hawkish. Iran released the US hostages within minutes of Reagan taking office. The Reagan administration was hostile to the civil rights movement, the women's movement, the environmental movement, and unions. Reagan argued that government programs needed to be cut, and that cutting taxes would give business more money to stimulate the economy.

Political scientists have taken to calling this right-wing response, which took various forms around the world, seemingly contemporaneously and independently, neoliberalism. Calling Reagan's policies neoliberal is confusing in the American context, because Reagan inveighed against liberals (that is, the political left). But so it goes with labels sometimes.

By any name, neoliberalism increased insecurity in the United States in a wide range of ways in the 1980s and '90s. Wages fell for middle- and low-income workers. Beginning in 1980, the minimum wage, which had been about $10 an hour in today's money, began a sharp and prolonged fall. Social assistance programs like welfare and unemployment were under attack. As unions were pushed out of work-places, employment became less secure.

Inequality between the rich and poor grew to levels not seen in living memory. As Richard Wilkinson and Kate Pickett show, in industrialized societies, a wide range of health indicators vary not in relation to how rich the country is, but in relation to the size of the gap between rich and poor. The greater the wealth gap, the greater the health gap. Countries with large differences in how much CEOs are paid compared to employees show higher rates of obesity and diabetes, and the United States has one of the highest inequality gaps.[122]

The allostatic model, with its consideration of social factors, also encourages restraint in passing judgment about other people's body types. In situations of uncertainty it is strategic, not maladaptive, for the body to store fat. While doctors, sociologists, and health professionals may feel secure about their economic prospects, the less advantaged may respond, consciously or not, to a condition of perceived insecurity. We should not assume that people are "wrong" for gaining weight. Rather than making radical interventions to insist that people lose weight (which might be ineffective, just as studies are showing that people who undergo liposuction surgery to remove fat gain back an equal amount of fat, but in new locations around their body), it would be worthwhile to attack the conditions of insecurity, and let people and their bodies adapt to the new conditions of security.

If politics can cause the problem, can politics solve the problem?

There are the faintest hints of reason for optimism. In 2010, President Obama passed his landmark health reform act, which insured over 11 million more people, reducing the amount of uninsured people to 8.6 percent of the population. Between 2009 and 2013, the rate of new diabetes diagnoses in the United States fell slightly for the first time (to 1.4 million per year).[123] People with diabetes began living longer, which researchers attributed to better health care.[124] This is far from solid evidence of a change in the direction of the epidemic—and with the recession and global economic slowdown, had the rate climbed rather than dropped, it would have been easy to attribute a growing diabetes rate to economic uncertainty.[125] But the first major extension of social welfare benefits in a generation has correlated with a significant drop in new diabetes cases. Future rounds of legislation that expand or reduce coverage could either perpetuate or curb the epidemic.

The causal story that limits an explanatory story about diabetes to diet and weight has poor prospects for turning around a growing global epidemic. That is a comfortable kind of causal story, because it avoids asking difficult questions about inequality. To do so, it draws a line down the middle of the situation, limiting our attention to medication that addresses the most proximate causal mechanisms—the functioning of insulin. That line exiles things that are more challenging to address, like economic uncertainty and social insecurity, to a realm beyond consideration. The conventional story does offer the kinds of social causes we prefer in our stories, but they're individual questions of diet, discipline, and exercise, not collective questions about why we create such perilous conditions for people that their bodies stockpile calories for an uncertain tomorrow, even at the expense of their long-term health.

The allostatic story of how external stress resets the body is a vital improvement in understanding causality. As with physical space in the last chapter, for too long we have overlooked an interplay between social and natural causes, in which society's problems create physical problems and vice versa. We ignore nonsocial causes, and therefore fail to understand the play between social and nonsocial causes. Even when we try to link behavior and biology, we do it in an individual, not a social, way: we know that how an individual eats affects their body. Or people do it in a nasty and inaccurate eugenicist way, imagining a biological/social link that lets observers redouble their contempt for the oppressed. A better understanding of causality asks how changes in society affect how people eat and what their body does with those calories. The diabetes epidemic isn't the result of a sudden loss of discipline by millions of Americans standing in front of the refrigerator. It reflects that worry so many of us feel about what's going to be in the fridge tomorrow or the next day. In a world of uncertain jobs, inadequate wages, and rising debt, we stock up and bulk up.

I remember as a child watching Reagan's inauguration with excitement—the first one I had seen—and sharing my father's eager anticipation of what this confident new leader would mean in the dawning of a new day in America. I can measure the ways Reagan didn't help my father or our family—decades of stagnant income, a blooming government debt we all have had to pay off, a loss of faith in the possibility of continued social progress, the validation of parochial racial prejudice in our mixed-race suburb, the relaunching of a religious social agenda my father and the rest of us had no interest in.

The neoliberal era of insecurity that Reagan introduced may have been most damaging to America's health. If shaky social welfare and the perpetual fear of falling can increase our stress and impair our health, then America's health epidemic points to two underlying epidemics: social stress and the politics that cause it.

This new, more social causal story can be liberating. Rather than worrying patronizingly over people we think are making the wrong choice, we can investigate why people make the choices they do. For many people, eating on the cheap and storing up calories for a rainy day may be the best of the bad options available to them. As the next chapter shows, when we think someone else is making the wrong choice, we often misunderstand the choices they have at hand.

8.

pregnant in philadelphia? don't worry

Despite the vast array of data we have marshaled to understand the causes of prominent social problems, there are a significant number of phenomena for which we don't have good, verifiable causal explanations. Teen pregnancy rates have risen and fallen in the last four decades. There has been plenty of public attention when rates rose, but little when they fell. In the last twenty years crime has dropped sharply across the United States. There are no shortage of explanations, each to match the political preferences of the person proffering it. But social scientists lack a satisfactory answer to the question of why crime declined, in so many places, across so many measures, for so long. The kinds of explanations we prefer for these stories, and the explanations we ignore, tell us something about fear and the need for familiar moral explanations, right or not.

Worrying about other people is a central activity in politics. Politicians worry about and pontificate about the poor, criminals, women, minorities, the rich, terrorists, immigrants, kids, teenagers, juvenile delinquents.

Social scientists have found, though, that when politicians theorize about the disadvantaged, they divide them into two imaginary groups, the "worthy" and the "unworthy" poor. A middle-class voter imagines that the "unworthy poor" waste their money drinking too much or doing drugs, having children they can't support, not saving carefully, not working when they should work. To some middle-class voters, these unworthy poor do not deserve assistance from society. The image of the unworthy poor has dominated United States discussions of poverty from Ronald Reagan's invocation of a mythical "welfare queen" who drove a Cadillac to the welfare office to pick up multiple checks under multiple names, through Bill Clinton's signing of the welfare reform act, which supporters argued was needed to prevent "abuse" of the welfare system, to the faith-based proposals of George Bush, Jr., and beyond.

The worthy poor, on the other hand, work hard, save their money, have children only later in life when they have some economic stability, and stay married to keep two incomes in the household. In other words, the worthy poor act like the middle class. So much so, in fact, that it's hard to believe how this imagined family isn't middle class themselves, working and saving, investing in their children's future, and carefully weighing each expense.

Conducting research in Baltimore from 2007 to 2014, I found the city blanketed in a billboard campaign borne of just such worry. A teenage girl stared at the viewer, looking stern with her arms crossed. "I'm not giving it up," the billboard read, "and I'm not giving in." The message seemed to be on a billboard or bus at every corner I passed. The campaign, by a local ad agency, targeted Baltimore's teen pregnancy rate, which was among the nation's highest. This girl wasn't going to be pressured into having sex. Somehow the billboard sounded frank and direct despite its slightly antiquated notion of female sexuality being about "giving it up." The billboard implied that conniving boyfriends influencing impressionable girls caused teen pregnancy and deprived the girls of the chance to pursue bigger and better things.

This kind of collective mythmaking has major consequences. The image of the duped teenaged girl, the intemperate laboring classes, or the spendthrift welfare recipient have worried voters out of supporting even those social welfare program that could help voters themselves—who, after all, might need unemployment payments, or disability assistance, at some point in their lives. These stories give the worried middle class a sense of moral superiority over the disadvantaged, but it doesn't give them any better understanding about why they act the way they do.

Sociology offers an antidote to this kind of public scapegoating. Who wouldn't worry about 17-year-old girls getting pregnant and 17-year-old boys running away from responsibility? The question is why people make different decisions. What are the root causes that lead to that decision? If other people make different decisions than you would have made, they likely did so because they had different options to choose from and different structural circumstances determining those options.

If everyone believes that education is a key strategy for getting ahead, why would a teenage girl decide to have a baby, when that would greatly hamper her ability to finish high school, let alone college? Furthermore, she should know that the statistics suggest that the baby's father won't stick around, and that she'll be raising the baby as a single mother, with less money to give the child what they need.

This worry, implicitly directed at the urban poor, fed into a general sense of cities as chaotic, broken places, an idea that has dominated American thinking in recent decades. A poster that the *Philadelphia Inquirer* published and republished captures the idea quite deftly. "Got a Problem?" it asked, above illustrations of every problem the paper thought readers might encounter in the city—drug dealing, prostitution, underage drinking, "belligerent homeless person," illegal dumping, or trash-strewn lots—and a number to call for each. The poster inadvertently illuminated how poorly the city's bureaucracy had adapted to addressing its urban ills: there was one number to call for "dead animal in your house," another for "dead animal in an abandoned building"; one number to call for "abandoned car," another for "abandoned car in river." Problems deemed common enough to appear on the poster may never have occurred to residents in well-maintained suburbs: who to call for a missing manhole cover, a damaged mailbox, a flooded intersection, a collapsed street, a payphone used by drug dealers, "cougars or other wild life," a broken alley light, street light, or red light (each a different number), or "public buildings that seem to be fire traps."[126]

The response was not always as comprehensive as the poster; in 1999 I saw a four-story, abandoned brick row house that had collapsed into the street, spilling its pile of bricks into the middle of the road. Someone had dutifully put yellow caution tape around the pile, and there it sat. The fact that most of the block was already vacant lots indicated what would eventually happen; perhaps after someone found the right number to call, the building would be bulldozed, and Philadelphia would have one less stately, nineteenth-century row house and one more vacant lot. There was plenty to worry about in Philadelphia.

For better or for worse, Philadelphia has attracted (perhaps because of all those evident problems) a great deal of research on social problems. The roster of researchers was nearly unprecedented in American cities. Before being a founding force behind the NAACP and numerous other organizations, W.E.B. Du Bois had undertaken one of the most thorough sociological examinations ever. In his book, *The Philadelphia Negro*, Du Bois sought to speak with every single Black person in the city—and nearly succeeded.

Continuing the tradition in the 1990s, sociologist Elijah Anderson wrote a series of studies about low-income African American neighborhoods in Philadelphia such as *Streetwise* and *Code of the Street*. Kathryn Edin and Maria Kefalas followed with *Promises I Can Keep*, and Alice Goffman continued the tradition with *On The Run*, to name only a few of the most prominent books that looked at social problems in Philly.

In *Streetwise*, his study of a poor African American neighborhood, Elijah Anderson detailed the promises and ploys an adolescent boy might use to get a girl to have sex and have his baby. Anderson wrote at the height of teenage pregnancy nationwide. As he observed, society viewed teenage pregnancy with distress, while many of the young fathers "congregate on street corners, boasting about their sexual exploits."[127] Anderson was clear about the cause of the problem: unwed mothers and street-corner fathers represented "interconnected realities . . . of the difficult socioeconomic situation in the local community." In decades gone by, young men barely out of high school could quickly find industrial jobs that allowed them to stay, and support, if the couple carefully economized, a growing family. As those jobs disappeared, the fathers could no longer make meaningful financial contributions to their families, and they disappeared.

What replaced the idyll of working-class life appeared to Anderson a cruel, intimate deception, a "sexual game" in which a young man would make "vague but convincing promises of love and marriage" until the girls found themselves "pregnant and abandoned."

Anderson described courtship as told to him by local residents. A young man might visit a girl's family, go to church with them, and do chores around the house, all to show he was an "upstanding young man." A new couple might stroll around downtown window-shopping for furniture, and the boy would promise the girl that he'd make enough money to buy a nice house in the suburbs, with new things for themselves and a baby. One twenty-three-year-old, who had become pregnant at seventeen, recalled, "Yeah, they'll take you out. Walk you down to Center City, movies, window shop. They point in the window, 'Yeah, I'm gonna get this. Would you like this? Look at that nice livin' room set.' Then they want to take you to his house, go to his room: 'Let's go over to my house, watch some TV.' Next thing you know your clothes is off and you in bed havin' sex, you know." The girl has reasons to want to believe her boyfriend's promises. Soon the girl is pregnant, but after the baby is born, the father is gone.

When I used Anderson's book in a race and ethnicity class at a suburban campus outside Philadelphia, my mostly white students were incredulous: How could the girl believe these promises? Why would she think someone who struggled to get a high school diploma was going to be her ticket out of her poor neighborhood? Why would anyone fall for the game?

I gave them a task: assume they were a 19-year-old young woman who wanted to move out of the tough, poor neighborhood she had grown up in. How would they do it? My only stipulation was that the girl was not a great student—she had dropped out of high school and didn't think she'd succeed if she went back or aimed for college. All other approaches were fair game.

The students brainstormed. Save your money, said one. But how could they save if they weren't making anything? They wanted to find a job, but what paid decently without a high school diploma? Asking friends and family for loans, or job leads, didn't seem promising given the straits neighbors were likely in themselves. Perhaps she could at least find a *rich* boyfriend, but how, with the city so segregated by class? Finally, a young man in a leather jacket looked around at his classmates, "Well, the girl could find a guy in the neighborhood who seemed like he had better prospects. He might say he was going to make lots of money, and I could hope he was going to succeed." Students paused. No one could think of a better strategy. Score one for Anderson's explanation of the structural constraints young women experienced in poor neighborhoods in Philadelphia.

I thought I had stumbled on a great exercise that explained just how overdetermined people's choices were by structural conditions.

But the answer was too simple.

That semester I was shuttling back and forth between the white suburban campus and a small class in Center City of almost all Black students. I posed the same question to the class of African Americans: imagining themselves as a 19-year-old girl in a poor Philadelphia neighborhood, what could they do to earn $20 an hour without a high school diploma?

This time hands went up.

"You could work in a restaurant. With tips plenty of restaurant jobs pay more than $20 an hour." There was general agreement from the class.

"Or a call center. They make $20 an hour. You don't need a diploma for that."

"Nail salon. You can make that much."

"Day care, at your house, if you're watching a bunch of kids."

We filled the board at the front of the room with a long list of jobs a 19-year-old could work to bring home a solid paycheck. This time Anderson and I were defeated; the students' responses suggested that our hypothetical teen didn't need to tie her dreams to a guy.

The lesson about structure was more complicated the second time around. The students in this class did not come from Philadelphia's poorest neighborhoods (though they might have known some people who did). They had grown up in working-class African American Philadelphia neighborhoods. Most worked during the day themselves, often in offices or city agencies, and were taking my class at night to complete their college degrees. Many had friends who had the jobs on the board. But unlike the teens in Anderson's study, these young people seemed upwardly mobile. Even if the restaurant or nail salon was hiring, it's not clear that our disadvantaged teen would be a competitive candidate. There weren't as many of these jobs in Philadelphia as there were people looking for jobs.

A common conservative response to unemployment is that people should be willing to "go work at McDonald's." But as Katherine Newman pointed out in her study, *No Shame in My Game*, McDonald's is always hiring, but that doesn't mean they're handing out jobs to anyone who comes by.[128] In low-income neighborhoods, McDonald's can be quite selective, hiring only applicants who a current employee will vouch for (so that the new worker is doubly obliged not to misbehave, for fear of getting their friend or family member in trouble too). Managers in Newman's study also knew the addresses of nearby housing projects and categorically dismissed applicants with those addresses on their applications. Even where jobs existed, they discriminated against people from the city's poorest neighborhoods.

During good economic times, unemployment among young Black men can be 50 percent—and unemployment statistics count only people who are actively looking for work. That means that half of all young men who are *trying* to work can't find a job. If for every person working there is another person looking for a job, then there are twice as many young men who want jobs as there are actual jobs. "Get a job" cruelly ignores the amount of people trying to do just that. The account now needed an extra turn in the road, an extra level of complication. And it is a turn in the road many people are unlikely to see.

Many white commentators invoke their experiences in high school jobs to understand the low-skilled labor market. Like me, they entered the labor market in a suburban area where low-end service jobs seemed abundant and easy to obtain. The fact is that these early experiences with easy-to-find jobs that young people do after school or over the summer actually *impair*, not improve, our understanding of the low-wage labor market, because for many people such jobs are neither common nor easy to obtain. (The only generalizable trait my high school friends and I learned about such work is that no one, ourselves included, wanted to stay in such a job for very long.) The students in my downtown Philadelphia class were right that jobs that paid better than minimum wage existed even in troubled Philadelphia, and that some of their friends had found such jobs, but few employers hired the poorest job applicants. Service sector jobs in particular are more accessible for people with dress, speech, contacts, and culture that reflected a higher social class. My students had some of those advantages, the poorer teens in Anderson's study rarely did.

Anderson perceptively described how bleak economic times shaped people's decisions to start a family. Although cautioning that the people he was writing about are only 15- to 20-years old, inexperienced, and perhaps naïve, he still recognized the influence of the larger economic situation on their decisions. "The dreams of a middle-class life-style nurtured by young inner-city women are thwarted by the harsh socioeconomic realities of the ghetto," Anderson wrote. Meanwhile "the lack of gainful employment . . . deprives young men of the traditional American way of proving their manhood—supporting a family. They must prove themselves in other ways." Although he detailed behaviors—the "game" young men played—that might add to the public worry about teen pregnancy, he explained how they were a product of the constraining structure of poor job opportunities.

Several years after Anderson's study, Kathy Edin and Maria Kefalas embarked on an ambitious plan to interview low-income, young, single moms in Philadelphia. The result of their interviews with 162 white, Black, and Latino mothers upended many of the central myths about single moms and demonstrated that the public worry was misplaced.

The first myth about single mothers was that they were indeed single. Edin and Kefalas found that 70 percent of fathers were at the hospital when the baby was born, and 40 percent of the couples were living together. By the time the child was old enough to be in daycare, however, 66 percent were separated.[129] Why did the moms send their men packing? In a chapter fittingly called "How does the dream die?" the authors found couples separated for all the reasons one would expect a woman would kick a man out: criminal activity, incarceration, domestic violence, infidelity, drugs, and alcohol abuse.

Conservatives often worry that poor people "don't value marriage." In fact, the interviews revealed that these moms valued it a great deal—too much, in fact, to risk marrying the wrong guy. One woman said frankly, "I'd rather say, 'Yes, I had my kids out of wedlock' than say, 'I married *this* idiot.' It's like a *pride* thing." Indeed, contrary to the notion of an imagined "oppositional culture" that devalues everything the middle class claims to it cherish, many young moms venerated marriage to the point that, like this woman, they wanted to wait until they found the right man. Most poor moms did get married—not when they first had children, but later, by the time they were in their forties.

Why do more poor women have children at a young age, why do middle-class women wait to have kids, and why is everyone so upset about it? Why, as Edin and Kefalas frame it, do middle-class women delay marriage and childbirth, whereas poor women delay marriage but not childbirth? Some provocative data answers why and demonstrates how people who make different decisions are in different situations.

For middle-class girls, the data is clear: as they become adults, their salaries climb, year after year, and continue to climb *until they have babies*, at which point their salaries flatten out.[130] Researchers led by David Ellwood at Harvard University looked at wages and child-bearing for women who had taken a job-skills test in the US military. Among highly qualified women, those who had a baby before age 23 were earning only about $14 an hour by the time they were 38, while women who had waited until they were over 30 earned $22 an hour at 38. The author Ta-Nehisi Coates described having a baby with his partner at 24 and feeling, among college-educated peers, like a teenage parent.[131] Among women with high levels of job skills, the longer someone can put off having a baby, the better off financially she and the baby will be.

But the numbers change for poor women. For women with few marketable job skills, having a baby younger or older has no noticeable effect on how much someone earns. At age 18, the low-skilled women in the study made minimum wage. Twenty years later, they made about $10 an hour—whether they had had children at 21, 31, or anywhere in between. They suffered from real income inequality, earning significantly less than their middle-class counterparts. But when they had a baby didn't affect their financial future.

What about all those other dreams? What about prom? This is perhaps the most dispiriting portion of Edin and Kefalas's book: girls as young as fourteen described a bleak future ahead of them.[132] Even when they tried to express hope for their own children, it was in contrast to hopelessness for themselves. As Anderson concludes in his research, many poor Philadelphia teens "see no future to derail—no hope for a tomorrow much different from today."[133] At a very young age, they had a distinct sense that the promise of their own life had run out, and that what hope there might be had passed to the next generation.

These findings explain only why some of the things that discourage middle-class girls from having babies are not so discouraging to poor girls. The question remains: Why do kids have babies? Some researchers have posited an oppositional culture in which disadvantaged teens had babies (or did poorly in school) to reject middle-class values.[134] This is a classic case of egocentric causality, as a slice of society feels their values are being challenged (an effect); thus, they assume pregnant teens or high-school dropouts must have *wanted* to challenge them (a cause). But the answer is much more human. Low-income teenage girls have babies for the same reason middle-class women have babies: *Babies are really beautiful and special.* At some point, *everybody wants to have babies.* It's fundamental to who we are; the one thing that we share with every one of our direct ancestors is having babies. There is no special explanation needed that takes into account income, race, or deindustrialization. Society has erected strong disincentives against middle-class girls having babies, with everything promised to those who wait—a college degree leading to a promising career, a sufficient salary to build a stable home, a high-status partner who will have an even better salary—but that offer isn't even made to poor girls, and from an early age they're smart and perceptive enough to know it.

What Edin and Kefalas found contradicted the prevailing wisdom and public policy—left and right. President George Bush had suggested that rather than economic support through welfare programs, what poor women needed was a marriage cure, and he began an office that promoted marriage to poor men and women. Although the women in Edin and Kefalas's study already valued marriage, they were fearful of falling into marriage with a man who was not reliable. In communities where so many young men fall prey to incarceration, substance abuse, or are unable to establish long-term employment, it would be extremely difficult to know if a twenty-year-old man was going to be a reliable partner in decades to come. As a result, couples often married in their forties—when potential husbands had made it through the crucible of urban young adulthood.

Democrats understandably dismissed Bush's marriage promotion scheme as Republican moralizing dressed up as public policy. But go-to elements of progressive policy ran up against Edin and Kefalas's findings as well. In particular, people often argue for comprehensive sex education, access to contraceptives, and affordable family planning and abortion services. But the young mothers in Philadelphia had visited Planned Parenthood. They used birth control but stopped, or used it inconsistently, as they and their partners began considering having a baby. Many women had abortions later in life but did not want to terminate their first pregnancy. Education and access were there, but for a mother for whom a child was, in the authors' words, neither planned nor unplanned, simply promoting education failed to grasp the social situation in which women were making decisions.

The conclusion to be drawn about middle-class social worry—at times verging on moral panic—from Edin and Kefalas's study of young, poor mothers is clear. Rather than worrying about young women's morality, controlling their sexuality, or criticizing their choices, if we don't like the choices people make we need to change the difficult social circumstances in which they make those decisions. If you don't like the choices people are making, give them better options.

In the case of low-income single moms, it's clear that teens would be less likely to have babies if they saw promising prospects for themselves that warranted putting off having a baby—as girls with middle-class prospects for college and work do. Likewise, if young men had prospects for stable, satisfying, decent-paying employment, they would be in a position to be more present and supportive husbands and fathers. Street-corner drug dealing, according to several studies with detailed access to drug gangs' financial records, pays about minimum wage. It is likely that a good supply of $20-an-hour jobs would not only make young men into more contributing fathers, but do more to end small-time dealing than the War on Drugs ever did.

What Caused the Drop in Teen Pregnancy?

Those jobs never appeared, but somehow the pregnancy rate dropped. The decline is astonishing news for anyone, like me, who came of age in the years of the "crisis of teen pregnancy." The pregnancy rate peaked in 1990 at 116.9 pregnancies per 1,000 teenage girls. In twenty years, it dropped by more than half to 57.4.[135] Abortion and birth rates dropped in tandem, so it was pregnancy itself that was declining. By 2013, the United States had the lowest teen birthrate since such data was first collected early in the twentieth century.[136] The drop occurred across all racial and age groups. Even though Hispanic and African American teens have higher pregnancy rates, those rates are now below the rate for whites in 1991.[137]

As valuable as it was for Edin and Kefalas to dispel the myths and answer the question, "Why do poor teens have babies?", by the time they did their research, the more timely and difficult question would have been, "Why aren't they having babies anymore?" The answer to this question requires that we step away from the fear that permeated the public debate and look more plainly at sex and the larger story about pregnancy.

As plainly stated by the Guttmacher Institute, a respected repro-ductive health research organization, decreases in pregnancy result from two things: less sex or more birth control. Evidence indicated that girls were having sex somewhat later, but the biggest change was that more teens were using birth control, specifically condoms. (In one study the use of a condom increased from a third to a half of all recent sexual encounters between 1995 and 2010.)[138] However, given that the teen moms Edin and Kefalas interviewed had used birth control but stopped when they were in a relationship with their baby's father, the historic decline only raises the question of why more teens were continuing to use birth control, instead of slacking off as they contemplated having kids.

Halving the teen pregnancy rate in twenty years marks an astonishing change. Why haven't we identified, in order to harness, the causes behind such a dramatic social change? For one thing, we research problems far more than solutions. The peak "epidemic" of teen pregnancy prompted an increase in money to research the causes, measure the problem, and propose reforms.

Some research into the remarkable decline found that fear of AIDS and publicity about sexually transmitted diseases played a role in increasing condom usage. Some believed better sex ed had helped. Others hoped cuts to welfare had disrupted what conservatives argued was a perverse incentive to have children. We can consider all these factors, but they all fall into the same type of causal explanation: intentional social causes, efforts undertaken by people with the goal of changing the teen pregnancy rate. As always, other influences must be considered: broader social changes that had unintended effects on teen pregnancy and nonsocial changes.

To evaluate the drop in teen pregnancy we need to put it in context. The decline started in 1990, and seems to have occurred among all measured racial groups (Asian, Native American, Black, Latino, white) at roughly the same time and at comparable rates, though African

American pregnancy rates started higher and declined more than other groups (falling lower than Latino rates).[139] We don't have statistics on teen pregnancy rates by race before 1990, but the consistency afterward suggests that pregnancy rates rose across racial categories as well.

The decline occurred across all states in the United States, but also in several other Western countries as well. England, for instance, experienced a decline that was nearly as dramatic as the United States, after a decline that started in 1998, eight years later than the US decline: by 2015, England recorded its lowest teenage birth rate in 70 years (19.7 per 1,000 teenage women, compared to 27 for the United States).[140] Second, at the same time fewer teenagers were having kids, fewer young adults were, too. Presumably, women in their early twenties were putting off having kids for some of the same reasons that younger women were. We can consider several of the most popular explanations.

Changes in welfare policy provide one explanation. In *Streetwise*, Anderson suggested that girls who had babies had the incentive, among others, of a welfare check, which might "allow them to establish their own households" (although other researchers showed payments were too miserly to survive on without financial help from the babies' fathers, grandmothers, and others).[141] In 1996, President Bill Clinton signed a sweeping welfare reform bill, the Personal Responsibility and Work Opportunity Reconciliation Act, or PRWORA. The act made it harder to be on welfare. States were given permission to craft their own programs, restrictions, and sanctions. Many followed federal instructions to limit benefits to five years or less, others refused to provide support for children born after an applicant first received benefits. States required recipients to work—as they do in New York, cleaning city parks that city employees used to clean. In the aftermath, half as many people received welfare benefits as once did.

But the decline in teen pregnancy started six years before the federal act, even before some states received permission to undertake restrictive welfare experiments of their own. And although the US declines happened in a conservative, "neoliberal" age of welfare cuts, the comparable reductions in teen pregnancy in Great Britain happened under a politically progressive government. There, officials praised the effects of comprehensive sex ed, counseling, and access to contraception. The US declines began under Republican President George Bush, Sr., continued under Democrat Bill Clinton, and declined at the same rate under President George Bush, Jr. Bush, incidentally, poured millions of dollars into religiously motivated "abstinence only" sex education that experts said didn't work and that subsequent studies found inaccurate and ineffective (unlike sex ed that included information about condoms and other forms of birth control).

A final argument against the idea that generous welfare benefits encourage teen pregnancy while restrictive programs would reduce it comes from a broader comparison: although the United States and Great Britain have reduced their rates, they still remain two to five times higher than in countries like France, the Netherlands, and Denmark, where social welfare benefits are considerably more generous.

But comparing the United States with social democracies is misleading. The relative options a potential young mother has matters more than the size of the government benefits. Perhaps French teens don't take advantage of more generous welfare benefits by getting pregnant because they have even more financially attractive options without getting pregnant—like a secure job at a living wage, a low-cost college education, or social welfare benefits without becoming a mother. In the United States, choking off money to babies and their young, poor mothers with policies like PRWORA might work if they make life with a baby even worse. That leaves open the possibility that miserly social welfare policies can deter teen pregnancy, but only if opponents acknowledge that they are satisfied with making young mothers miserable. Other countries try to provide teens with *better* options than getting pregnant and living on welfare before they finish high school.

Another explanation is sex ed. This story attracts many proponents because well-educated teens are more likely to avoid pregnancy, either by not having sex, or using contraception. Milwaukee, whose teen pregnancy rate was second to Baltimore's, ran a major campaign and developed a broad sex ed campaign. Its pregnancy rate dropped a remarkable 50 percent in seven years.[142]

Texas went in the opposite direction from Milwaukee by offering no meaningful sex ed. Texas schools that did have the class had to spend more time on abstinence than on birth control, even though abstinence curriculums are correlated with higher state pregnancy rates.[143] As recently as 2007, only 3.6 percent of Texas schools taught about condoms or other forms of birth control (a number that rose to 25 percent in 2011).[144] In concert with a program of sex de-education, Texas significantly defunded women's health clinics, cutting its family planning budget by two-thirds, and actually forcing 50 women's health clinics to close. (Politicians claimed they were trying to shutter abortion clinics but, as it happens, none of the closed centers actually provided abortions, making the war on abortion and the war on women's health indistinguishable.)

Texas' teen pregnancy rate fell 43 percent between 1991 and 2012.[145]

How did two diametrically opposed approaches to sex ed generate comparable results? Nationally, the percentage of students who received no sex ed about AIDS or HIV actually increased from 10 to 15 percent from 2007 to 2013—as the birth rate continued to drop.

Granted, a more careful examination shows that states, like California, which pursued more comprehensive and evidence-based sex ed programs than Texas, saw larger drops in teen pregnancy. Proponents can still show, therefore, that education makes a difference. But the fact that Texas's teen pregnancy rate dropped by a substantial amount suggests that education alone does not tell the whole story; something was pushing down teen pregnancy rates that was not connected to the intentional campaign to increase education about sexual health and reduce unintended pregnancies with better use of and access to contraception.

Like education, contraception use matters, but that tells only part of the story. Black teens, for instance, were more likely to have used a condom than whites, but still had teen pregnancy rates that are higher than whites. Teens' use of highly effective "long acting reversible contraceptives," like intrauterine devices, or IUDs, has increased, but is still too rare to be a major cause of the substantial decrease in teen pregnancy.[146]

BEYOND SOCIAL FACTORS: THE NATURE OF LEAD

Teen pregnancy is just one of the social problems that contributed to the collective mythology of the 1990s as a decade of urban chaos that—like crime and crack—has significantly declined and left researchers searching for reasons why. In recent years, they have repeatedly come upon an unexpected factor in the landscape: lead pollution.

A soft, plentiful metal, lead has an unlimited amount of industrial uses, but the most significant lead pollution in our environment came from the addition of lead to products as ubiquitous as gasoline, paint, and pipes for drinking water.[147] Lead exhaust spewed particles into the air that settled in the soil, and peeling paint contaminated both the interiors of homes and buildings and the soil into which peeling house paint fell. Lead was universally added to paint to create an opaque, white color until about 1930 and remained in older houses. Lead was added to gasoline in 1923 to help engines run more smoothly, and air-borne lead levels rose as gasoline usage increased.

Thus, since the start of the twentieth century, US children were exposed to high levels of lead, first from house paint, until that paint was replaced, then from gasoline in the postwar auto boom. Only when lead additives were removed from gasoline in 1975–1991 did childhood lead levels decline by 75 percent.

The harm lead does has been well-known for more than 3,000 years; the Greek physician Nicander wrote about lead poisoning in verse in the second century BC.[148] At high levels, it can cause blind-ness, brain damage, kidney disease, convulsions, and cancer. But at the levels that characterized the twentieth century, children were most at risk, for lower IQ, behavioral problems, increased impulsive behavior and poor anger management, reading and learning disabilities, hyper-activity, and reduced attention span. Exposing children to lead was a behavioral and cognitive nightmare.

In 2000, Rick Nevin published a work that found a correlation between lead levels in blood and both teenage pregnancy and violent crime. Building on research that suggested children with high levels of lead in their bones demonstrated more violent and delinquent behavior, Nevin found that the amount of lead from gasoline and paint correlated to homicide rates *all the way back to 1900*.[149] Preschoolers' lead levels in nine countries correlated to burglary and violent crime. The role of lead paint and lead exhaust point to another way the built environment shapes our health and our social world.

In later research, Nevin continued to find that exposure to lead correlated to crime rates and pregnancy rates. The "lag time" varied: teen pregnancy rose about seventeen years after lead levels rose, but crime rates rose about twenty-one years afterward, consistent with the fact that the criminality peaks in the early twenties. Homicide rates shot up in 1920–1940 when lead paint was ubiquitous, then dropped as it was replaced, only to rise, in the 1960s, as a generation raised in a cloud of leaded gas fumes was coming of age. Lead was removed from gasoline, and suddenly, in 1991, seventeen years later, pregnancy rates began dropping again—the same year that homicide rates in places like New York City began an epic decline.

Other data supports the link between lead and pregnancy. Lead levels declined at different rates in different states. Economist Jessica Wolpaw Reyes looked at groups of teens in different states across different years and found that knowing how much lead there was in the air in a given year in a given state helped predict how likely teenage girls were to become pregnant.

Reyes quantified the effect of lead this way:

"To be specific, we can consider the change in probability associated with a change in blood lead from 15 µg/dl to 5 µg/dl, a change that approximates the population-wide reduction that resulted from the phaseout of lead from gasoline. This calculation yields a predicted 12 percentage point decrease in the likelihood of pregnancy by age 17, and a 24 percentage point decrease in the likelihood of pregnancy by age 19 (from a 40% chance to a 16% chance). This is undoubtedly large: the lead decrease reduces the likelihood of teen pregnancy by more than half."[150]

Lead levels were related to behavior problems and violence as well. In an era where blood levels of 10 µg/dl were common, Reyes writes that "1 µg/dl of blood lead has approximately the same effect on behavior as a decrease of approximately $5,000 of family income."[151] Higher levels had even stronger effects.

How much does lead contribute to violence? It is important not to overstate the impact of a single variable, blinding us to the role of so many other important factors. Education has a measurable effect, as do better life options. But some of the correlations are astonishing. In 2011, the countries that used leaded gas were Afghanistan, Myanmar, and North Korea; those that used a mix of leaded and unleaded gas were Iraq, Algeria, and Yemen. It cannot be that lead alone causes war; the very repressiveness of some of those countries, and US military incursions into several of these are more a cause than an effect of environmental pollution.[152]

UNINTENTIONAL SOCIAL FACTORS: ROE V. WADE

If reduced lead levels is an unexpected cause for the decline in pregnancy, another is potentially more problematic: abortion. I don't mean that birthrates decline because pregnant young women had abortions. In fact, as the frequency of teen pregnancies has declined in the last twenty-five years, so has the rate of abortions: fewer teens are getting pregnant, and fewer of them are having abortions as well.

Around 2001, John Donohue and Steven Levitt found evidence that the legalization of abortion in the United States showed a correlation with a drop in crime: fifteen to twenty-four years after abortion became legal, crime rates began dropping precipitously. The authors argued provocatively that after the Supreme Court's 1973 *Roe v. Wade* decision legalized abortion, significant numbers of women who were least able to raise children terminated their pregnancies. Eighteen years after abortion was legalized, crime rates began a sharp and sustained drop. Although the researchers' claims can and have been widely critiqued, at a minimum the data is strong enough that the contention cannot be dismissed out of hand: states that legalized abortion earlier saw crime drop earlier. States with more abortions saw crime drop more. Crime rates were reduced among young criminals (born during the era of legalized abortion) more than older ones.[153]

The claim raises difficult questions, and puts people on both sides of the abortion debate in an uncomfortable situation. (One of the researchers, Stephen Levitt, is coauthor of the *Freakonomics* book series, which celebrates just the kind of social science findings that upend conventional debates.[154]) If the data is true, law-and-order social conservatives who oppose abortion could be condoning restrictive health policies that will raise the crime rate to the intolerably high levels of the 1990s. Progressives who want abortion to remain legal risk being tagged as eugenicists who condone a brutal form of social control. There are, of course, ways out of these binds: progressives already emphasize that they support women's choices, not abortion per se, and the data puts additional pressure on abortion opponents to make sure that they are as protective of children after they are born as they are of fetuses in the womb, supporting the kinds of educational and social welfare policies that prevent poverty, precarity, and the conditions that lead young people to criminal behavior. But the suggestion of this causal link rightfully makes anyone uneasy.

Donohue and Levitt's later research contends that abortion has played a similar role in the decline of teen pregnancy as it did to the decline of crime. The fact that abortion and crime declined simultaneously has struck some researchers as a coincidence that needed to be explained in and of itself: to Jonathan Gruber, unlike activities like smoking cigarettes and smoking marijuana (which can rise and fall in tandem), for pregnancy and crime, "There is no direct link between these behaviors."[155] The researchers contend that, as with crime, legalized abortion led mothers to have abortions who would otherwise have had trouble raising children at that time in their lives, and that had children been born, they would have been more likely to have gotten pregnant as teens. With more detailed data than was available for their research on crime, the authors specify that they attribute a quarter of the total decline in teen pregnancy—a 6 percent drop by 2008—to abortions performed fifteen to twenty-four years earlier.[156] (Pregnancy rates also dropped for unwed women age twenty-four and under, but the overall fertility rate was unchanged, apparently because women were more likely to have a child when they were twenty-five or older.) Yet another discomfiting implication of this research is that abortion reduces abortion.

THE GLOBAL SHIFT: DECLINING PREGNANCY RATES EVERYWHERE, FOR EVERYONE

In a strange way there is nothing to be explained in declining teen birth rates. Teen birth rates were at a high between 1947 until perhaps 1966—the classic "baby boom" years after World War II. But from its peak in the United States in 1957 (at 96 births per 1,000 teen girls), teen pregnancy began a steady decline that has now been underway, almost uninterrupted, for nearly 60 years. The entirety of the teen pregnancy crisis was a four-year anomaly, from 1988 until 1991, when teen pregnancy rates rose, from 53 to 62 births per 1,000 teens. (Teen birth rates, as opposed to pregnancy rates, were much lower in 1991 than they were in 1957.) From 1991 on, the historic decline continued to the present, when the teen pregnancy rate is about 24.[157]

Birth rates in the urbanized, developed world have been falling for a century, reflecting the "demographic-economic paradox" that in wealthier countries (where there would presumably be the resources to have more children) people have fewer children. People are having fewer children and having them later. Thus, the decline in births to women in their teens and twenties is accompanied by an increase in the percentage of women in their thirties and forties having kids. (Because people become parents later, they typically have fewer kids in their lifetime.) In this global context, it is not the post-1990s decline in teen pregnancy that needs explanation, because it is part of a larger trend affecting teens and adult women in the United States and elsewhere. What would need explaining is the short-term, late-twentieth century increase. Little research on pregnancy rates has framed its research as an effort to explain that brief, four-year anomaly from 1988 to 1991. A look at the data on lead, for instance, suggests the possibility that against the global trend of falling pregnancy rates, auto exhaust lead exposure rose in the United States enough to first stop the decline for a few years—teen pregnancy rates were static from 1976 until 1988—and then raise pregnancy rates in just the last few years before leaded gas was banned. But that is an argument in search of suggestive data, not a decent explanation for the years of the teen pregnancy emergency.

At this scale, both the previous questions—why was there a teen pregnancy problem, and what made it go away?—evaporate in a long-term trend of women getting pregnant less and having children later. Perhaps not helpful for the very real questions of what public health agencies should do about teen pregnancy, it does illustrate the large-scale causal forces that get forgotten in moments of social panic.

Paying Attention to Dynamic Causes

The teen pregnancy riddle is informative about how we can understand social problems. First, we need to consider explanations beyond the normal roster of social causes. As we've seen, social causes cannot be used to explain the drop in teen pregnancy, because the most proximate causes—increased birth control use and, for younger teens, some delay in the first time they have sex—require causal explanations.

Meanwhile, more distant causes, of the sort that would satisfy the "fundamental causes" approach used to understand diabetes (in which fundamental inequalities like poverty, lack of education, and discrimination drive outcomes like teen pregnancy), don't suffice because those fundamental causes didn't improve in the period when teen pregnancy was again on the decline. (The state of the economy seems to influence the decision of adult women to have kids but not teens, yet the rates for both dropped.) Further, the effect of those fundamental causes on pregnancy can vary: in many circumstances poor people are more likely to have children than rich people, but during the Great Recession after 2008, as is often the case, economic hard times and an increase in poverty led to a drop in the birth rate.

Even with only suggestive explanations for the changes in teen pregnancy rates, the totality of the evidence, and the earlier findings of social science researchers, point us in useful directions. First, recall that among poor women, getting pregnant at any age not did not have the financial penalty that it did for middle-class women: their incomes were likely to stay low no matter what. Thus, there is less to celebrate about the striking decline in teen pregnancy when we consider that it has not left poor women better off. Dispiritingly, the drop in teen pregnancy is evidence that society can "solve" a designated "social problem" without doing anything to address the inequality that underlies it.

Over the last several decades, countless people have worked to increase the sexual health of teens: safe sex educators, activists lobbying for sexual education, AIDS activists, health professionals. The work of each of them has undeniably had an effect on the lives and health of individuals. It also seems likely that public policy changes addressing lead exposure and access to abortion unintentionally influenced the teen pregnancy rate, in an era when fertility trends were undergoing historic changes at a global level.

What caused the drop in teen pregnancy? Perhaps the answer is akin to what Tolstoy said about the causes of war: "each single cause . . . appears to us equally valid in itself, and equally false by its insignificance compared to the magnitude of the event."[158]

To illustrate Tolstoy's observations with an everyday mechanical image, think of a bicycle wheel. The causes of an event (war for Tolstoy, teen pregnancy in our investigation) are like the spokes of the bicycle wheel. We know from seeing a bicycle in motion that the spokes must be sufficient to hold up the weight of bike and rider, otherwise the wheels would collapse and everything would fall to the ground. But each spoke in itself seems insignificant, too slender on its own to support the magnitude of the weight of the cyclist. In this way, the causes of a development like the decline in teen pregnancy are each valid in themselves, but, like bicycle spokes, seemingly too slender to contribute meaningfully to support the weight of such substantial social change.

But a further surprise lies in the spoke analogy: although bike spokes are steel, they don't hold up the rider. In fact, the rider hangs from the spokes: those attached to the top of the wheel hold up the hub of the wheel (and the weight of bike and rider resting on the hub), while the spokes at the bottom of the wheel do little to hold the weight. Bicycle spokes don't hold up, they hang on; they do something we rarely even imagine they do. (Emergency repair kits actually allow long distance cyclists to replace a broken spoke with lightweight twine.) Likewise, in a complex social problem like teen pregnancy (or, for instance, the contemporary causes of racial inequality) the myriad causes look like they're being called to do something that they can't possibly do. They seem too weak to push things along, but more incredibly they're pulling and, for that matter, like the spindly spokes of a back wheel, transmitting the torque that is propelling the whole venture forward.

In this case, each potential cause—sex ed, welfare reform, Baltimore's billboards, access to condoms, a culture more comfortable speaking frankly about sex—is a spoke that couldn't support or propel an immense social phenomenon like teen pregnancy on its own. Spokes work because they are not randomly jumbled together but arranged in a particular structure. Similarly, social factors work because they are not isolated but structurally connected. Each factor is being asked not to passively support the weight, difficult enough itself, but to pull it up and push it along. Each spoke on its own is ludicrously weak, thoroughly discreditable, and with no substance at all. Then these factors do what they cannot do. Dozens of filaments with virtually no weight are entwined. Bundled together, unanticipated causes have the pull to shift immense social structures.

The tensile rods pulling along declining teen pregnancy rates exert force on the precipitous drop in crime in the United States as well. Proponents of get-tough policies want to point to intolerant policing strategies, but, in New York for instance, homicide rates were dropping for several years before such policies were implemented. Progressives with an eye toward economic inequality, like myself, could point to an improving economy that accompanied much of the decline, on the assumption that people who can find work don't need to turn to crime. But when the economy got worse in the 2008 recession, the crime rate stayed at historic lows. The possibility of a lag owing to the absence of the ecology of crime—the criminal gangs, pawn shops, syndicates, social norms, and corruption that facilitate widespread criminality—is tempting, but how long does it take for an ecology that sustains criminal activities to develop? We don't know. And, again like teen pregnancy, from a larger perspective there is nothing to be explained: crime rates have been declining in tandem with modernization before anyone even noticed, as social norms, government oversight of society, and increased prosperity put the brakes on the lawless ways of our ancestors, just as it did their birth rates.

In the same way the public put more effort into understanding why teen pregnancy rates were climbing than why they were dropping, other social changes have been front-page news when they were deemed crises, only to be ignored when they declined in ways that could teach us something about changing social conditions. Like teen pregnancy, crime rates, homelessness, and war are among the phenomena that decline—sometimes broadly, sometimes in specific moments—without provoking much public interest in why.

Proximate fear influences those events we try to explain and those we don't. Economist Paul Krugman wrote about "the dramatic decline in crime rates. For those of us who remember the 1970s, New York in 2015 is so safe it's surreal. And the truth is that nobody really knows why that happened."[159] Reasons are things that we construct in particular ways—and which we deem satisfactory when they give us a workable set of instructions about what to do next. To say that no one knows why crime declined is to say that no one has constructed a satisfactory explanation. Without the impetus of fear, we don't invest the time and resources to know why, to develop an explanation that gives us a roadmap to greater safety.

The more fearful we are, the more we want a causal story reassuringly rooted in a moral explanation—that virtue will win out over vice, not that declining lead levels will slowly return us to the century's historically declining teen pregnancy rates. That may be what happened, but even in its success it's a thoroughly dissatisfying answer. It shouldn't be: we control environmental pollutants more than we control the imagined immorality of teenagers. Causal explanations often seem to lie outside of our consideration simply because they are too challenging to our existing structures of power. Anyone can lecture teenagers, it's harder to stop pollution by big industries. Anyone can encourage overweight people to eat less and exercise more, it's more provocative to ask why people in our societies are in such precarious situations that their bodies store up calories in uncertainty about what the future brings for them. In fearful situations we both demand causal stories and restrict the range of causes we're willing to consider.

For events that begin in danger and end in safety, we can posit countless explanations of why they occurred, classic causal explanations that include moral, sequential, and logical sequences. The stories we tell about pregnancy and crime in this country attempt to explain why troubles started, not why they ended or diminished. When there's no crisis, there's no causal thinking.

part three
....

THINK BETTER

9.

what we know,
we know socially

I s drinking and driving a bad idea? Anyone who has driven a car on one occasion, and had three drinks on another ought to figure out that drinking impairs driving.

Yet people have not always thought of this as obvious—not even doctors. In 1957, Ross McFarland and Roland Moore wrote an article for a no-less-respected publication than the *New England Journal of Medicine* about the risks of auto accidents in which they suggested—timidly—that maybe, just maybe, drinking too much might increase the risk of an accident—at least for some people, particularly poor drivers. After considering the influence of inexperience, age, and intemperate personalities, the authors observed that "There have also been a few experiments on the effect of alcohol on driving performance. Wide individual variation in this regard were noted," they offered as a caveat, but "the driving skill of many persons is adversely affected with relatively small amounts of alcohol in the blood."[160] That left a group of other persons who, presumably, could read the article believing that they could hold their liquor and drive.

The tone of McFarland and Moore's article is remarkable. The prevailing wisdom was not that accidents were the result of risk factors—fatigue, alcohol, and weather. The first concern was "the accident prone." We, dear reader—we doctors, we men, we excellent drivers—were not a risk on the road. The accident prone among us cause most accidents and, therefore, need our attention. Leave me alone with my highball or my fourth martini and deal with the accident-prone bad driver.

It's not just drinking and driving. No less reputable a source than the journal *Nature* pooh-poohed the idea that smoking was bad for pregnant women as late as 1973. To the contrary, smoking could help! "Cigarettes often keep both weight and nerves under control," an editorial countered.[161] Experts back then could deny smoking harmed fetuses even though a doctor today can clearly see the effects of smoking: women who smoke have placentas that are brittle and falling apart, peppered with brown clots.

We can be blind to the evidence in front of our eyes, and often are blinded by a framework of thought we learn from society. That is, because we see the world through preconceived notions and inherited stories—a shared framework of thought—we often see the framework itself when we think we're seeing the evidence. This is the same framework that makes us think we can see race on bodies, when what we're really seeing are socially determined racial categories.

In the case of drunk driving, one can think "if accidents are the fault of a small minority of bad drivers, and I'm a good driver (and can handle my liquor besides) then that foggy, blurry feeling I get when drinking is just a sign that I need to pay extra attention on the road." And that's exactly what most drunk drivers believed for decades, until the nationwide organization Mothers Against Drunk Driving undertook a campaign in the 1980s not only to lower the blood alcohol standards for driving under the influence but to change the social framework regarding drinking and driving.

Social frameworks blind us to the facts from an early age. The feminist critic Katha Pollitt once wrote about a toddler who stated while playing dress up, "Women are *nurses*," not doctors. The child said this to her own mother, a doctor. Pollitt attributed kids' views to the gender-stereotyped pop culture characters they watch. "Like medieval philosophers," she wrote, "the text . . . is more authoritative than the evidence of their own eyes."[162]

Our inability to see what's right in front of us shouldn't surprise us. Many factors influence whether someone has an accident, or gives birth to a baby with a health condition. And such situations don't occur often enough for most of us to detect a pattern. There is too much potential data to make sense of it without an explanatory framework, and we can't develop those frameworks by ourselves.

So far, we've focused on causal stories intended to explain what has already happened, and how those stories are often inadequate. Here in the final part of the book, we look forward, using what we've learned about cause and effect to make better decisions about some of the most important issues of our time: climate change, the realignment of US political parties in upcoming elections, and responses to terrorism. These are urgent issues where what we've learned from society molds— and restricts—our expectations about what to do. Sociology doesn't make predictions about the future. (Most fields don't, really.) But it can help us understand why situations are taking shape, and how we should act given those circumstances.

Better causal thinking—an awareness of what our causal stories overlook, and a mistrust of rigid frameworks—that I call dynamic causality extends our vision from the past into the likely future. Understanding a political situation more clearly doesn't mean an end of politics or guarantee a solution on which we can all agree. It means we can have more productive arguments: how to address climate change, not whether to acknowledge it; how to respond to terrorism, not how to feel tough. The decisions still remain to be made. A better grasp of causality gives us the edge in making them.

In this section, we'll look at how dynamic causality can sharpen our understanding of problems in real time, not just improve our stories about what has already happened. We can't afford to fail in our response to life-or-death problems like climate change, racial inequality, and the dangerous space where the two meet. We must break out of the conventional stories we tell. A richer understanding of how we connect social and natural causes will help us recast public debates in a way that moves us forward.

In this chapter, we'll look at one of the most urgent issues facing the planet, climate change. It is a prime example of nonsocial causes, in the sense that drastic changes in the climate (even though they were induced by human activity) are already occurring and will continue to escalate—no matter how quickly we mobilize to respond. But the issue of climate change also shows how there's no way for individuals to respond to natural conditions without thinking about the larger society's response to them.

The causal story we've told about climate change focuses on regulating emissions and modifying consumer preferences. That is an inadequate story in the same way diet and exercise being the cure to the diabetes epidemic is an inadequate story, or the way teen pregnancy being about moral choices is an inadequate story. Those stories each posit one cause and one solution, and suggest that the respective problems result from people's personal behaviors. In fact, we can understand neither the problem nor the options for taking action without understanding the social context of that problem. In the months after Hurricane Sandy struck the East Coast, my own house became a perfect example of why, and of the interplay of natural and social forces.

In 2012, my family and I moved into a brick-fronted Brooklyn row house. It was a catch. Built in 1901, it was wide, deep, with a nice backyard, and, as many Brooklyn homes have, a rental apartment on the first floor for added income. The house needed work, to be sure, but we had been looking forward to renovating a house for years. In the high-priced world of New York real estate, we could barely believe we had finally been able to buy a house where we could settle down and make our permanent home. Our house sagged and leaned a bit, but the rest of the neighborhood was so fancy that I was afraid we'd have trouble relating to the locals. As expensive as our house was, it felt like a secure investment.

We moved in October 19, 2012. Ten days later, on my daughter's birthday, Hurricane Sandy hit. At the height of the storm, the strong winds made it unsafe to go outside. We ate slices of a birthday cake my mother-in-law had delivered the day before as the wind howled through the aging windows. I propped my pillow against the brick wall of an old chimney to read, and when strong gusts blew, I could feel the wall flex and the house shudder.

We stayed dry. The hundred-year-old basement was slightly damp, but our new house had withstood this test. No leaks, no broken windows, no destruction.

We found out only later that the nearby Gowanus Canal had over-flowed. Video posted online by residents showed the Gowanus flood-ing Bond Street, just a block away from our house.

How should we respond to the news that our house was worry-ingly close to a flood-prone waterfront? Climate change meant that this problem would become only more urgent. I started mentally calculat-ing the difference in elevation between Bond Street and our street. How deep were the basements? When our old landlord had announced she was evicting us and we started looking for a house we could buy, I had hoped we'd be able to find somewhere higher up. But every house has advantages and disadvantages, and the higher houses we had looked at all had disqualifying problems. Any choice is a compromise. Our old apartment had been at the same elevation (but on the other side of the canal), and we had looked down a long, gently sloping block toward the canal. The water, it seemed, had a long distance and a reasonable height to climb before it would threaten us. There had been flooding two years earlier when Hurricane Irene hit the city, but not near our neighborhood. We had hoped we'd be safe.

After I told my wife about the video, she said, without much con-viction, "Well, maybe we should fix this place up, sell it, and move to higher ground?" Without even getting into the ethical problems of off-loading our problem onto someone else, I wondered if we could ever bring ourselves to do that. It made a certain sense, but I immediately doubted that would happen.

The reason was not just that the house seemed perfect for us in every other way. It wasn't just that we had started to like the neighbor-hood—it was more diverse than we thought—and wanted to stay. We were likely to stay, as the rest of the residents were, because knowledge is social.

That is, we as human beings rarely know something all by ourselves. My wife and I could connect the dots, rationally, without much trouble: we were at low elevation, the first week we lived in the house a hurricane—which was only Category 1 strength and had actually hit land several hundred miles south of us—had brought flood waters within a block of our home. Climate change insured that there would be more of these storms, not fewer, that they would increase in strength, not weaken, and that sea levels would be higher, not lower. For a decade or more, we had heard warnings that low-lying coastal areas of the world might become uninhabitable, and not being climate deniers, we had no reason not to believe them. Renting an apartment for a few years in a low area had only put our possessions at risk, and we didn't have expensive things. Buying, however, jeopardized not just our possessions but our life investment. Planning to stay there for the rest of our lives considerably increased that risk.

Still, we balked at the idea of leaving. Why? Several biases in the way we, as people, think, made moving less likely.

First, knowledge is social. We could calculate the risk, and deem our house risky. But until more people agreed on that, we were unlikely to act in ways that indicated that we actually believed that was true. If, in several years, banks declare our neighborhood at high risk of flooding and refuse to lend money for people to buy houses, people will stop buying houses here, home values will plummet, and we will know, along with everyone else, that perhaps we made a bad investment. By then, of course, it will be too late. But today, without having gained a neighborhood consensus, that information feels less real, less reliable, and less worthy of acting on.

There are lots of situations in which we act on things that we know only collectively. A graduate student of mine described a waterfront neighborhood where everyone knew Hurricane Sandy was coming. They had been told to evacuate, but all stayed put in their homes.

Then, when one neighbor left, they all got in their cars and left. That we act on something socially doesn't mean we all necessarily have equal influence. Society has structures. After a plane hit the first tower of the World Trade Center, some groups of employees in the second tower (minutes away from being struck by a plane as well, unbeknownst to anyone in the building) left, others stayed (as they were instructed to do by security personnel). Whether a group of employees left or stayed depended on their boss: if the boss left, everybody left. If the boss stayed, everybody stayed.[163] The choice was, in almost every case, between life and death, and made socially and within a hierarchy.

Our hesitance to act without social consensus, however, is not by itself a bad idea. In complex situations, factors that we don't know about could change our response. For instance, what might the city have planned for flooding around the Gowanus Canal? The canal is very narrow, and it's hardly used for navigation anymore. The federal government is spending millions of dollars cleaning up the pollution that industry has dumped in the bottom of the canal over the decades; a fraction of that sum could be used to build a seawall. Or perhaps there is a considerable difference in the likelihood of a storm with a ten-foot storm surge of water and one with a twenty-foot storm surge. Selling a house to avoid a risk is a huge decision, and no one would suggest doing it without collecting outside advice. It's generally a strength not to think alone, but to think socially. Collective assessments of situations are regularly much more well informed, and accurate, than the errors of individual guesses.

Hurricanes are natural, not social, but it's not so easy to decide how much weight to give to natural factors and how much to focus on the social response. What my family should be considering is not the likelihood of a natural phenomenon (a hurricane) but society's response to the natural phenomenon. Will our nation provide global-warming flood insurance? Will we build barriers? Will other people continue to pay to live here? In a presentation about famine, the peripatetic Marxist scholar Mike Davis described how for centuries in India, local rulers stored grain reserves and distributed them when drought struck so the populace wouldn't starve. When the British colonized India, they eliminated that system as outdated, and when famine hit, people starved. Davis's point was that whether it *rains* or not is determined by nature. But whether people *starve* or not is determined by society.

If social interventions can change the risk that our neighborhood will be harmed by flooding—technology, changes in greenhouse gas emissions, flood insurance—then we have the potential to alter some of those critical conditions. Residents could form a group to lobby for a seawall, or push the city to better prepare for a disaster in other ways. We can move from the natural phenomenon to the social response.

In that regard, it makes sense to put more weight on social considerations than natural ones. After all, we would starve every winter if our society didn't have a complex network of highways, trucks, and grocery stores to keep us fed. We shouldn't pay attention to the climate, but to the society.

About half the residents of Lower Manhattan's Battery Park City neighborhood moved out after the Trade Center collapsed just outside their windows. Far fewer moved out of Lower Manhattan after it was flooded by Hurricane Sandy. We respond more to actions that other people cause—in this case terrorists—than to natural events. My research in that neighborhood suggests that, unsurprisingly, the people who left saw the threat of another terrorist attack very differently than the people who stayed.

Although half the residents around the World Trade Center moved out, property values didn't fall. The government moved in immediately with a subsidy program that paid people an extra $500 a month for two years to stay in Battery Park City apartments, with the explicit goal of buoying home values. Ten years later, even in the midst of a worldwide real estate slump, Battery Park City homes had skyrocketed in value.

Three months after Sandy, Governor Andrew Cuomo of New York made a similar intervention. He proposed a $400 million fund to buy out homes in certain low-lying areas. Arguing forcefully that "Mother Nature owns those properties" and that the rising waters would return, Cuomo said it made more sense to leave the areas permanently vacant than to rebuild. The state would pay 10 percent above pre-Sandy market value for the homes (with an additional 10 percent premium for blocks where everyone sold, and a 5 percent bonus for residents who stayed within the same county).[164] It was initially unclear whether his proposal would include my house. But it further complicated my idea of selling before another big storm hit. Strangely, when I heard about the proposal, I *hoped* that our house would be included in the offer. The market is good and our house is worth more than we paid for it, so there's no reason we couldn't sell right now, without the program, if we wanted to. The public acknowledgment of such a program would provide more than the price premium. Knowledge is social, so to move out early and alone would be to abandon the tribe. But if a critical mass of people moved out, to stay behind would be to ignore common sense.

And so, I've reached a stalemate in my thinking. I can *calculate* a significant risk to our investment if we stay in the house we just moved into. However I *want* to stay—to follow through on our plan to make this house our home, to get to know this glittering new neighborhood, to have a base that will keep our family together. Humans aren't good at responding to nature; we respond to each other. We rarely take individual action against natural threats. We look for a social response. It will take longer to convince anyone to build a seawall than it would take to sell our house. But we're more likely to do the former than the latter.

In both causality and action, in both explaining what happened and deciding what to do, we're oriented toward socially sanctioned views. It is not coincidental that the people who take climate change seriously tell a causal story about it being caused by people. Those who don't can't take it seriously.

What Next?

As I wrote in the introduction, the debate over climate change comes from the second, misleading sense of *why*: we don't seek to know the mechanism by which it happens, but the social, often moral, story that could explain it. Scientists have named this period of Earth's history the Anthropocene, because activities by humans (who give the word its "anthro" prefix) have changed the Earth's climate and a network of systems connected to climate.

Many argue that the current epoch should not be called the Anthropocene but the Capitalocene, because global warming is not the fault of all people on the planet, but the fault of capitalism or the industrialized world—particularly through the burning of carbon fuels.[165] Although that makes sense, it is also true that communist economies, to the extent that they have existed in the world, also burned large quantities of fossil fuels and used large quantities of natural resources. It's unclear that other economic systems would have done differently. If mercantilism continued to the present day, would no one have wanted to burn coal? And if people could have formed more egalitarian and humane economic system in the last two hundred years, isn't it likely they would have wanted the warmth, food, easier labor, and creature comforts that burning fossil fuels have provided to us? Certainly no one seems eager to go back to the pre-carbon era.

A period like the Anthropocene is the expected outcome of a planet's species figuring out how to supplement their own muscle power with energy from burning carbon-based fuel at a large scale, and any innovating species would have started burning things that give us energy to heat, eat, and work. A less consumerist or more tradition-bound society might have burned slower, but in geological terms the result would likely have been comparable.

Solutions to climate change generally propose an anticapitalist approach. I support that, because capitalism does a lot of damage beyond climate change. But it is doubtful there is exactly one effective response to climate change. It may be the case that there are *zero* effective responses to climate change.

Sometimes we adopt responses that get at the root causes of problems, more often we adopt responses that don't. Soldiers patrolling the city after a terrorist attack don't get to the root causes of terrorism. Arresting homeless people doesn't get to the root causes of the housing crisis. Sanctimonious billboards don't get to the root causes of teen pregnancy. But a good political process will almost always reveal multiple responses that do promise to be of some value.

Climate change has many possible responses. Perhaps the most obvious is the ongoing effort to get people in powerful positions to greatly reduce our dependency on fossil fuels. There are, undeniably, other responses: a second option is the acceptance of coming climate chaos and the reorganization of society into a defensive posture to deal with the predicted increase in storm damage, drought, crop failures, fishery collapse, and economic disruption. Such reorganization could take a myriad of forms: collective, egalitarian, and anarchistic as one option; or hierarchical, military, and inegalitarian as another. A third response to climate change is analogous to the disruption of social networks: the further sequestering of resources—clean water, high

ground, agricultural produce, emergency resources, and power supplies—by wealthier and more-powerful classes and nations to insulate
themselves against the negative impact of climate change's dramatic
manifestations. A fourth theoretical possibility is for leadership to take
no action at all, determining instead to allow individuals to address
periodic crises on their own or in self-organized groups, a concept
that could be described, depending on one's predilections, as either
"self-organizing anarchist" or "every one for themselves and the devil
take the hindmost."

No doubt different continents, regions, nations, and classes will
adopt different strategies. The shortage so far of collaboration by
smaller groups of nations along lines of locality, region, or class reflects
either a continued hope for a global (and therefore more effective and
economical) solution, or the difficulties of planning and agreeing to
climate change crisis contingency plans at the local as much as at the
global level.

One can only hope that conservative, capitalist interests will artic-
ulate their proposals for responding to climate change. They are likely
to be far worse, more costly, unequal, and effective for fewer people
than current proposals for reduced emissions. (Prove me wrong.) But
at least once new proposals were unveiled, we could get to the political
work of fighting over options rather than debating the reality of climate
change or wading through misinformation regarding its origins—in
other words, looking forward rather than wasting our time arguing
over causality.

Evolutionary psychology has theories for why people are poorly
wired to respond to the risks of climate change that echo some of the
arguments I've made in this book. One claim is that we perceive immediate risks very well, but distant risks very poorly: everyone knows to
back away from a snarling dog, but not to avoid smoking cigarettes,

because the first one might bite you today but the second one will likely kill you in forty years.

But now climate change is the snarling dog. Any country can identify weather changes like more frequent storms or hotter average temperatures. Lives have been lost to climate change. Were we ruled only by our brain as it evolved from primates, we would back away from climate change like we would a snarling dog. But human minds, as they evolved, enwrapped themselves inextricably in social systems we cannot live without, and without which we can make no confident statements about the world or the future. It is time, at the national, regional, continental, and global level, to start a fight. If a few forward-thinking regions were to develop resilient mutual aid agreements for natural disasters and put them into place, it could inspire others to follow. Others might begin building flexible but practical contingency infrastructure (I'm thinking of upland urban planning that made room for resettling lowland populations who were likely to be flooded out). They would no doubt be derided as a climate Maginot Line, and indeed, it is risky to invest too much in preparation for one climate scenario when another can play out instead. But how would the populations in other nearby countries without such infrastructure—say, for rapid resettlement of displaced people—react to their political leaders when plans were needed but lacking?

10.

a black republican president? party realignment

One of the challenges of thinking about our biggest problems is that we tend to imagine that the conceptual categories we use are stable and real, when they are shifting and temporary. Dynamic causality helps us recognize that not only do causes reorganize our world, but those seemingly firm frameworks through which we see our world are shape-shifting at the same time. Land can become ocean. Races change, genders are recategorized. The future threat of climate change can become an inevitable and present reality.

As demonstrated in Part 1, socially constructed notions as seemingly real as racial structures are changing in the United States, possibly to our benefit. The role of our stories, our spaces, and ongoing social changes in what Du Bois called "the color line" help us better understand the frustrating resilience of racial inequality and identify a few of the openings, in desegregation, police reform, and electoral politics that we might take advantage of in the near future. Just as understanding the likely environmental future requires recognizing that the climate is changing, understanding the US political future must take into account that race, demographics, and politics are changing.

Understanding changing racial realities requires accounting for social causes, unseen causes, and historical realities, while having a delicate sense of which of these are changing and which realities remain firmly in place. This chapter examines specifically how US society and politics have oppressed African Americans, and some of the ways those injustices might be corrected.

Segregation Stories

A high level of segregation, of Blacks in Black neighborhoods and whites in white neighborhoods, is an observable phenomenon in the United States. As narrative-making machines we seek to explain it. One explanatory story, frequently told by my students early in the semester, is that people "like to live with their own kind." This simple, effective (in the sense that it is catchy) causal story naturalizes what could otherwise be an ugly manifestation of racism and has the benefit of reflecting the preferences of the students and their many communities: many of them are indeed happy living with their own kind.

Yet the explanation can't account for the peculiar level of racial segregation between Blacks and whites in America. First, only those two groups are so segregated: we can use census data to measure the level of segregation of various racial, ethnic, and immigrant groups (with measurements like the segregation index, an index of isolation, and other calculations), and Asians and Latinos are much more likely to live in diverse neighborhoods than either whites or Blacks. City by city, the highest levels of segregation for immigrant groups are actually lower than the lowest levels found for African Americans, and this has been true for a hundred years. Among other groups, the richer one gets, the less one lives in an enclave concentrated with members of one's own group: as generations of Chinese or Mexican families move up economically, they move out of Chinese or Mexican neighborhoods. In contrast, wealthy African Americans live in neighborhoods that are nearly as Black as the poorest African American neighborhoods: segregation works differently for Black Americans than for other groups.

Social scientists have developed a second story about segregation to better explain this phenomenon that the first story overlooked. Douglas Massey and Nancy Denton contradict the idea that people like to live with their "own kind" in their landmark study of racial segregation, *American Apartheid*: until the 1920s in America, African Americans lived in mixed communities with other groups.[166] Even today, African Americans don't express a preference to be as segregated as they are: in surveys, the largest percentage of African Americans want to live in neighborhoods that are a 50-50 mix of Blacks and whites. But few such neighborhoods exist, and almost none stay mixed for long.

This second explanatory story of segregation suggests that government and business implemented policies that separated Blacks and whites. Laws prohibiting Blacks from living in white neighborhoods were tried out in many cities before being ruled unconstitutional after an early NAACP challenge in 1914. Afterward, the National Association of Realtors maintained a policy instructing members not to sell homes in white neighborhoods to Black buyers. Banks exercised similarly restrictive policies, not lending to Blacks at all or looking at the race of the borrowers and neighborhood before making a loan. An early government homeownership program, the Home Ownership Loan Corporation, drew color-coded maps and explicitly labeled mixed-race neighborhoods as "hazardous." (The Mapping Inequality project at the University of Richmond recently uploaded 1930s redline maps for cities around the country, providing a block-by-block snapshot of the racially and ethnically determined real estate valuation.[167]) Realtors and rental agents may steer Black people looking for a home away from white areas as often as one in every three visits.[168] The response to this story of segregation has been the Fair Housing Act and other laws prohibiting discrimination by landlords, banks, and realtors.

Laws against discrimination serve an important purpose; otherwise, African Americans and other people of color pay more for housing, are given more expensive loans, are restricted to all-Black schools, even pay higher taxes and see their homes stagnate or decline in value. But it's not clear that existing laws have been effective at reducing deeply entrenched discrimination, an additional reason to think story two doesn't help us explain racial discrimination.

There's a third story about segregation that doesn't get told very much, although the facts are in plain sight. What is sometimes called the ghetto, a large, almost entirely African American neighborhood near the center of many US cities, is a creation of violence. As African Americans moved to Northern cities during the Great Migration of the late nineteenth and early twentieth centuries, they were kept out of many areas and squeezed into increasingly crowded, poorly maintained neighborhoods.[169] In city after city in America, in the 1920s, white resentment of the growing Black population boiled over into race riots in which white citizens and police attacked, beat, and killed Black residents, damaged Black businesses and burned Black homes and institutions. In the ignominious (but largely forgotten) race riots of Tulsa, Oklahoma in 1921 over three hundred people were killed in attacks that included police dropping incendiary bombs from aircraft onto areas where Blacks lived.[170] African Americans were forced, as a defensive strategy, to leave the scattered mixed-race settlements that they lived in and retreat into large all-Black neighborhoods that could provide some measure of protection from marauding whites and dangerous forces of law and order.

The danger of straying outside these majority-Black neighborhoods is not in the past. Today, African Americans identify plenty of places they wouldn't want to live. One resident in the suburbs of Baltimore told me proudly that he looked for a house all of five miles past where he lived, a place "most Blacks don't go, because you know, there could be problems there." What they worry about, he said, was the Klan. Anyone who lives in a Black neighborhood can name nearby white neighborhoods with reputations for intolerance, prejudice, and violence where they'd rather not go. Even in less-hostile territory, Black Americans find the prospect of being constantly judged by white neighbors—and having to be on their best behavior to disprove white stereotypes—tiresome. One Washington-area resident said, "I really wasn't interested in moving into an all-white neighborhood and being the only Black pioneer down there. I don't want to come home and always have my guard up. After I work eight hours or more a day, I don't want to come home and work another eight."[171] Well-to-do African American professionals don't want to live in well-to-do white neighborhoods because they'll be harassed by police who are suspicious of any Black person driving through the area. An African American judge once recounted to me the number of times her husband was stopped, and followed home, after coming home from work or evening church meetings.

This third narrative—that Black people mostly live in overwhelmingly Black neighborhoods because white neighborhoods are unsafe for Black people—breaks the mold of stories we prefer to tell. The first makes the segregation seem natural, so that nothing need be done. The second gives people the evidence they needed to propose fair housing legislation, and the sense that they have solved the problem. The third narrative suffers from a diffuse actor: not a bad apple here or there, but a hostile white society that was far more daunting to tackle and difficult to legislate away. Such a story fails to gain traction because it lacks a moral explanation of the sort a white narrator is likely to want to convey.

In fact, this overlooked third narrative goes a long way to explain our recent racial tragedies.

As recent shootings by police—of Michael Brown in Ferguson, Missouri; Trayvon Martin in Sanford, Florida; Philando Castile in Falcon Heights, Minnesota; John Crawford in an Ohio Walmart—show, something has changed. Today, stories of violence against African Americans come not just from the inner city, but the suburbs.

In the hundred largest metropolitan areas in the United States, half of African Americans live in the suburbs, not the cities. Suburbs were never as lily-white as their reputation, but today they're even more diverse. Black families have transcended the color line. But some police and white residents haven't.

In the 1990s, police brutality headlines came from cities: Amadou Diallo was shot to death by the NYPD in the Bronx; Rodney King was beaten by the Los Angeles Police. Today, the stories come from areas in transition, according to research by sociologist Richard Moye and his colleagues.[172] They're not all Black or all white. They're closer to an even mix. Ferguson is 67 percent Black. Sanford, Florida is 30 percent Black.

These dangerous encounters happen at borders where Black and white neighborhoods mix. Former college football player Jonathan

Ferrell got in a car accident, knocked on a door for help, was mistaken by the resident for a robber, and shot by police. It happened in a Charlotte, North Carolina suburb that's 40 percent Black, where a Black community ends and a white rural area begins.

In a white Dayton suburb next to a mixed Black-and-white neighborhood, John Crawford was strolling through a Walmart chatting on the phone with his girlfriend. He picked up a pellet gun from the toy section. Shoppers called police because they thought he looked like a threat. Police shot him with little warning while the end of the gun was leaning against the floor. The problem is, some residents and police haven't updated their image of their new neighbors from the scare stories they told each other when the neighborhood was all white.

Eric Garner's death in Staten Island shows police violence against Black people still happens in cities, but even that happened in a comparatively mixed part of the borough (27% Black).

The nineteenth-century Black experience was rural. The twentieth-century Black experience was urban. The twenty-first-century Black experience will likely be suburban. We need to make those new neighborhoods safer for new Black residents. That begins with changing outdated white stories.

Researchers David Jacobs and Robert M. O'Brien found that police shootings were more likely to happen in areas where African Americans made up a growing percentage of the population, but were less likely in areas with a Black mayor.[173] In other words, police shootings peak in the middle: beginning with an all-white area, they rise as the Black population begins to get bigger but is not large enough to be politically dominant. When the Black community is large enough to have significant political influence, fewer shootings occur. To Black families living in Black neighborhoods, the view beyond the Black community looks dangerous.

Just as the "realtor discrimination" explanation provided narrative justification for legislation against housing discrimination, a narrative of the dangers lurking in mixed neighborhoods supports growing actions against police violence by groups like Black Lives Matter. The movement is not just an effort to punish police abuses, just as the Fair Housing Act was not just legislation to catch discriminatory real estate brokers. Making it difficult for the police to violently control or harass African Americans in public space takes away a process that has contributed significantly to the ongoing residential segregation of African Americans, and the negative consequences that spring from it.

In the meantime, if Black families are hesitant to move into mostly white neighborhoods, policy makers should think twice before pushing them into those areas. The federal Moving to Opportunity program gives low-income households incentives to move out of large housing projects and into more economically mixed neighborhoods, on the theory that poor families will do better if they lived in mixed areas where schools are likely to have more resources, where crime may be lower, where neighbors are likely to have jobs with better-paying employers who may have job openings. Indeed, some initial studies showed that Moving to Opportunity was working: participants were earning a few hundred dollars more per year. Later studies that charted the long-term effects determined that wages weren't improved for parents who moved, and outcomes may even have been worse for teenagers who moved. Kids under thirteen, however, grew up to make $3,000 more a year—a big chunk compared to the $11,000 they were likely to make otherwise.[174]

The policy, of course, targeted low-income people not Black people, but in many cities it was seen as a way to deconcentrate poverty and disperse mostly Black housing projects. (In cities, Black poverty is concentrated, white poverty is dispersed. There are actually more poor white people in New York than poor Black people, but census maps show they're spread across the whole city, except in Black neighborhoods.) I want our neighborhoods to be integrated, and I appreciate that the government is doing something, for a change, to desegregate them. But we should pause: because poor people have so few options, they often have to make difficult tradeoffs to receive public benefits in exchange for certain behaviors. For example, when welfare payments were made only to families with no father in the house (and case workers arrived without warning to look for evidence a man was living in the home), families had to choose between an intact family with two parents, and a father who lived elsewhere in exchange for a little of the money the family so desperately needed.

In the case of efforts like Moving to Opportunity, we should at least ask how hard we should push poor families into new neighborhoods: a few hundred dollars is nothing compared to the worry that you, your spouse, or your kid will be harassed by the police, or the concern that your child will be singled out as trouble in school. Who wouldn't give up income for greater safety? Perhaps if the mission of the police were radically redefined—from harassing people of color in ways that made it clear to them that they were neither welcome nor safe in non-Black neighborhoods, to protecting Black citizens so that they were safe in all neighborhoods, then people would consider moving to white neighborhoods without the push from Moving to Opportunity.

Today, many working-class Black neighborhoods are characterized by long periods of calm and moments of acute crisis: everything goes smoothly until the foreclosure crisis, a hurricane, job loss, or a recession throws things into uncertainty. If government does less to protect African American residents than others, during a crisis are African American families more vulnerable in a largely white neighborhood, or in a largely Black neighborhood? Distinctly high rates of residential segregation testify to Black Americans' collective conclusion that, no matter how considerable the differences and diversity among them, they are better off together. The same has been true politically. The danger Blacks find in white neighborhoods comes both from neighbors and from the government, in the form of police who harass, schools that label children as problems, public services that seem to diminish as the proportion of white residents declines. Politicians foster other racial problems too: the racialization of welfare recipients as Black and their simultaneous vilification, the promotion of a racialized crime hysteria, voter disenfranchisement, and the scapegoating of people of color at every turn. The racial hazards that people experience at the neighborhood level, then, are relentlessly renewed through our racially polarized politics. Although US politics have been organized around racial issues for as long as any of us can remember, political parties' orientations toward important racial questions has changed more frequently than we acknowledge. Those reorientations can pose valuable, if risk-fraught, openings for progress.

New Politics

We think Democrats are Democrats and Republicans are Republicans. Even if we know the history of party realignments, we tend to think that process has stalled out. It hasn't.

Republicans were the anti-slavery party of Lincoln, until the 1870 Tilden-Hayes election where they sold Southern Blacks' civil rights to white Democratic segregationists in exchange for a Republican presidency. Many observers date the next realignment to FDR, when Blacks, who for sixty years had been terrorized and disenfranchised by Democrats, started voting for Democrats on the strength of FDR's social programs, and Eleanor Roosevelt's symbolic gestures like inviting African Americans to the White House. But the transition was not yet complete. In Baltimore, a Southern border city, Black people continued to vote for Republicans (rather than candidates of the segregationist white Democratic machine) into the 1960s. Black Republicanism expired when the Republicans ran Barry Goldwater for president (the era's Donald Trump), and Goldwater's racist, anti–civil rights, dog-whistle politics were too shrill for Black voters to abide.

For readers who have always voted for the same party, imagine how disorienting the 1870s, 1930s, or 1960s must have been, as voters who had vowed never to vote for the other party experienced a perverse attraction to candidates in the party that was their sworn enemy. As those shifts happened, the coalitions that had adhered to the old party's structure delaminated, like plywood left in the rain until its layers, each thin and brittle by itself, separate one from the other, and the seemingly solid plank revealed itself to be a glued-together mishmash of different layers of fibers, each pointed in different directions. That delamination is happening right now in the United States.

To understand party delamination requires a moment to identify the components of the current coalitions. Democrats can quickly recognize the contradictory parts of the Republican Party that have been glued together since Goldwater ushered in the Southern Strategy that united an anti-tax, anti-regulation, capitalist business class in an unholy alliance with evangelical Christians, and incited white working-class voters to take racist bait and vote with the white Republicans. The contradictions are elementary in this configuration: the working class doesn't share the same economic interests as the capitalists, and evangelical Christians prior to this electoral realignment were fundamentally suspicious of wealth as a corrupting influence and (though they might not recognize it) shared more theology with Black

Christians than secular, cosmopolitan capitalists who cared little about abortion, prayer in school, or integrationist busing to public schools their children never attended.

Perhaps less contradictory on the surface, the layers of the recent Democratic coalition could likewise be read as the testimony to the work required to forge unlikely political alliances. Today, the Democratic Party includes African American voters as one of its most consistent voting blocs, side by side with immigrant voters, despite the fact that historically the first thing immigrants have done is prove their worthiness as Americans by disparaging African Americans. The Democrats have lots of working-class and low-income voters in their coalition, along with a specific part of the upper-middle class: the Republicans get campaign contributions from industries like coal and oil, which need little investment in education or human capital for their employees but benefit from a foreign policy that opens up other country's resources to US extraction. But the Democrats get more money from another type of capitalist, the Silicon Valley computer magnates who benefit from government investment in educating their future employees, and Hollywood entertainers who value investments in culture.

On an issue like free trade agreements, both parties endorse a position at odds with a significant segment of their supporters. For both Democrats and Republicans, the US political system forces parties to find a way to glue together a portion of the business class with the money and a section of the working class with the votes.

The current party alignments are so well established that they seem natural. Imagine, in contrast, the difficulty of being a progressive, educated urbanite circa 1920, at the height of both immigration and the reform era. Urban Democrats clearly represented the immigrant working class. But as the reformer Republicans pointed out, the

Democratic machine was criminally corrupt, systematically handing out favors and taking in bribes, and allied to Southern Democrats who were unvarnished terrorists. Those reserved, waspy Republicans promised a more modern, scientific, open way of running a city government, but that promise of efficiency came from people who believed they were qualified because of religious and eugenic superiority to the darker and poorer Catholic and Jewish immigrant classes. Would you vote for the corrupt party that sold out the people, or the reformers steeped in eugenic racism? Time travel to that era would leave today's progressive voter with a tough election-day choice, assuming they were of the race and gender that was allowed to vote at all.

Examples of party realignment can be startling because they upend things that we take for granted. Consider, as just one example, the electoral preferences of gay voters. We're not surprised that gay and lesbian voters lean strongly to the left, because right-wing parties tend to be socially conservative, ally with religions, emphasize an imagined set of "traditional values" that are not inclusive of gay people, and are often explicitly homophobic in their policies. Imagine the surprise, then, of Laurie Essig when she was conducting research for her book, *Queer in Russia*, in the 1990s. In an interview, the sister of a gay Russian was surprised that Essig, who is lesbian, did not vote right wing. Her brother, after all, was "part of a neofascist punk band, and of course they're all gay," she said. "I thought that homosexuals were always connected with fascism."[175] The anecdote caught Essig's audience by surprise, but her explanation made sense: in the Soviet Union, the party that repressed "sexual minorities" was the *only* party in the USSR, the Communist Party. People therefore allied with the opposition if they were not sexually conventional, leading many gays and lesbians to ally with the nationalist party whose leader, at the time, "consistently defended" the rights of gays and lesbians and was seen

surrounded by attractive young men who could be read as a represen-
tations of the nation's virility or a kind of gay friendly propaganda.[176]

Moving across Europe, a survey found that while support for the
far-right nationalist party, the Front National, had grown to 28 percent
nationwide in the first round of voting in France, a full 32.45 percent
of same-sex couples had voted for the neo-fascists (compared to 34 percent who voted for the Socialist Party, the ruling party on the left).[177]

Leaders of gay organizations attributed the right-wing party's
rising popularity among gay voters to a speech the FN president,
Marine Le Pen, gave in 2010, where she intoned that "I hear more and
more testimony to the fact that, in some places, it's not good to be a
woman, homosexual, Jewish, or even French or white."[178] What was
Le Pen saying? The Front National was built by her father, Jean-Marie
Le Pen, from French resentment of the victory of the Algerians in their
War of Independence, and the core of the party has been a xenophobic
anti-immigrant position (which in France translates into particular
hostility against "Arabs," foremost Algerians). Jean-Marie was also
anti-Semitic and made offensive comments about the Holocaust, and
showed his intolerance of homosexuals and a range of other people.
His daughter Marine has won more supporters by trimming the FN's
message of intolerance, and stokes a populist sense that if immigrants
are invading France, then French culture must be at risk, and French
people must be an endangered species in their own land. Thus, her
comment simultaneously articulates that resentment (French people
and white people are somehow oppressed), bolsters that group's sense
that it's aggrieved by comparing it to oppressed groups like women
and Jews, and (perhaps unintentionally) tips her hat in recognition of
the oppression of other groups like homosexuals.

Far-right gestures toward gay voters are not inevitable; right-wing
parties (particularly in Europe) opposed gay marriage on the grounds

that the next step was legalizing polygamy, particularly egregious because it's practiced by some Muslims, demonstrating that gays, like other groups, can be opportunistically placed on either side of the scapegoat pale. But in many countries, a realignment of gay voters is already underway.

The candidacy and presidency of Donald Trump, even more so than the ascendance of the socialist candidate Bernie Sanders, signals another major party realignment in this country. The Republicans' Tea Party schism foretold this unraveling; it marked the outcome of decades of the Southern Strategy, where the moneyed elite of the party attracted working-class white voters with demagoguery about Blacks, immigrants, abortion, and prayer in school, and then did nothing to make life better for that white working-class base. As the resentful white demographic that was central to the Southern Strategy got old and died off, the Republican Party tried changing the message and was abandoned by a base that had drunk the Kool-Aid it was served. But the Tea Party couldn't win. Nor could the Romney elite win without enough resentful white voters. (Romney won the white vote by 20 percent, but still lost, with not enough white resentment left in the electorate to propel him to victory.) As much as Trump seems to break from the Republican establishment, his new brand of resentment hints at one solution to the Republicans' problem: working-class faux-populism and elites could have realigned behind a new scapegoat: the imagined enemy of Muslims and immigrants. Alternately, Republican elites may leave the party; during the 2016 presidential campaign, Charles Koch, who has spent a fortune supporting Republican candidates, snubbed Donald Trump, and even suggested that he might support Democrat Hillary Clinton.

Bernie Sanders, like a Tea Party of a different flavor, gave loyal progressive Democrats the take-no-prisoners populist economic politics they wanted. He did so at the expense of the wealthy wing of the party (with whom they'd have had to break if they were truly going to institute socialist-style, income-equalizing taxes) and also at the expense of African Americans and immigrants of color whose issues are never, contrary to progressive imaginations, reducible to a set of economic policies. To the contrary, Sanders was slow to use his civil rights experiences to put forward racial justice proposals that would attract voters of color. He illustrated the possibility of a Democratic realignment: a party more politically progressive than its predecessors, but less engaged in racial justice. It could attract more disenfranchised whites than it had in the past, but leave Blacks and other voters of color with no obvious reason to be Democrats rather than Republicans.

If Trump's fake populism and Sanders's social democratic promises sounded too close to the old formulations of Republican and Democrat to be a revolution, look at the implications. A Republican party that truly relocated its scapegoat from Black Americans to Muslim foreigners would be a party that has abandoned the Southern Strategy— as it must for demographic reasons. In such a party, African American and arch-Republican Ben Carson would not be a walking contradiction; conservative Blacks could vote for such a party for the first time in two generations.

Likewise, if Sanders's position were a model for the new normal, capitalists in technology and the "creative class" (an odious expression if ever there was one) could join with members of the white working class to lower college tuition. But Sanders's program for accessible college educations did not restore affirmative action admissions to universities that were stripped of them by the activist Supreme Court of the Scalia era, and Hillary Clinton has shown no more enthusiasm for putting Black civil rights programs in the center of her political showcase. To the contrary, Clinton, and even, implicitly, Sanders, accept Ronald Reagan's assumption that if the Democrats talk about equality for Black people, white people will not join in unity but desert in droves. As a Senator, Sanders got a 100 percent rating from the NAACP, but most of the bills they rated Senators on were about economic justice, not racial justice (because the Senate takes so little initiative today regarding civil rights issues).

If Republicans refocused their fifty-year scapegoating away from Blacks, African American voters might, for the first time in US voting history, have two parties to choose from (particularly if the Democrats embraced an economic populism that left out civil rights). Such a development could signify abandonment of African American issues by both parties, or the final arrival of an American political landscape not determined, first and foremost, by race. Democratic abandonment of even their present, inadequate discussion of racial justice could be dangerous. At the same time, if American politics, for the first time, were not oriented around race and the scapegoating of African Americans, the very threats to African Americans (by race-baiting politicians and the in-the-neighborhood white terrorists who those politicians agitate) would be less acute. Our politics has long produced and incited racist violence. To the extent that anti-Black racist violence has been carried out to congeal a white political identity, the possibility that American electoral politics might be oriented around something other than racism (and conceivably give Black voters choices between two major parties) could certainly count as progress.

The exact contours of the new alliances are not firmly established, and now is a valuable opportunity for progressives to secure as much space as possible in the new parties. Nationally, Latino voters have leaned Democratic, but each generation after immigration votes less reliably along ethnic lines than its predecessor, and at least some portion of upwardly mobile Latinos, despite the astonishing inability of Rubio, Cruz, or Bush to create widespread Latino interest, could back a conservative or capitalist party if it didn't scapegoat them personally.

Other groups are less uncertain. Whither voters in agricultural, rural, and Western areas, with their disproportionately large share of electoral votes? Will they rally behind the antigovernment, libertarian ethos represented by Apple's refusal to grant government agents access to electronic communication? If so, they may join the Silicon Valley libertarians among the Democrats. Or will they support a Republican Party that actually follows through on threats to shut out the immigrants that do the heavy lifting in the agricultural sector, hoping a wall would raise wages for US-born workers? If either party opposed free trade orthodoxy, they would attract voters from the other party.

In foreign policy, will one party be more isolationist, or will both be aggressively interventionist, Republicans under the guise of military might, or Democrats believing in their own civilizing influence as peacekeepers?

And what, precisely, will be the position of each of these new parties regarding climate change? Given that climate change is already happening, politics must face the social, environmental, economic, and dietary challenges that come with it. As such, Trump's hysterical, virulent, deadly anti-immigrantism is a climate change policy of the siege mentality. Sanders's strategy of investment in human capital and potential is either a nostalgia for the days when science, growth, and industry could fix everything, or a last ditch effort to improve human scientific and technical understanding to the level that we can address the changes of a warming planet without catastrophic loss of life through drought, flood, and food chain disruption. In the current moment, when the business page's main concern is that oil is cheap, none of the candidates have built their campaign around any energy alternative. What will the new parties' proposals be in this critical realm of climate change reaction? Cast against type, the Republicans could endorse subsidies for their supporters among oil and energy companies to develop other profitable energy sources.

Questions of climate change bring to the fore the urgency of a party realignment. As African American neighborhoods demonstrate, the manifestation of inequality for African Americans today can often be one of punctuated equilibrium: periods of relative stasis punctuated by moments of absolute crisis.[179] Predominantly Black communities persist because African Americans still require safety in numbers from the economic predation, brutal policing, and neglect by white America. Climate change is on schedule to cause displacement on a large scale, and most analysis suggests that low-lying areas, although they include beach resorts and waterfront luxury as well, are disproportionately home to people of color and poor people. How serious is the post-displacement risk that African Americans will face in the age of global warming? As long as the Republican Party keeps African Americans in the crosshairs of a scapegoat strategy, climate displacement makes African Americans doubly vulnerable. They are at disproportionate risk from storms and flooding in the first place, and as a result of displacement could be exposed to the kinds of abuse that African American communities provide some modest protection against today.

The difference in the federal response to African American victims of Hurricane Katrina and to the largely white and affluent residents around the World Trade Center, noted by my colleagues Miriam Greenberg and Kevin Fox Gotham, suggests poor people displaced by natural or man-made disasters are less likely to be helped than neglected or taken advantage of.[180] In addition to evacuation plans that take social networks into account, realignment of the Republican Party away from the Southern Strategy could reduce the political impetus to demonize African Americans after they have been displaced by disasters.

The old party system—in many ways a holdover from the Cold War era, which in the United States forced the right to prove they were not as evil as the communists claimed, and the left to prove that they did not support communist programs—has become outmoded. The period of party reorientation is upon us, and the better we prepare for it, the more we can gain from it.

We have a short time, no longer than Trump's presidency, to outline the positions of the new parties. Two pieces of advice from right-wing economists are apt here: first, never let a crisis go to waste; second, in a crisis, the actions that are taken depend on the plans that are just lying around.[181] Perhaps, in the crisis of climate displacement, plans lying around for better relocation of displaced people could provide the opportunity to either ensure racial groups' collective security, desegregate long-segregated areas, or create different, more inclusive, valuable kinds of social solidarity among people who have shared the experience of such a disaster.

One can only hope that political activists working in the midst of the coming party realignment will secure, conceivably even in both parties, politics that are economically progressive and explicitly ethnically inclusive. Perhaps we can forge a politics that can avoid the pitfalls of earlier US progressive movements by making racial justice and immigrant ethnic inclusion an explicit centerpiece of its platform for social justice. The coming political realignment could even bring the political priorities of working-class people, poor people, and people of color back onto center stage. To do so would require recognizing some of the ways nonelites draw complex causal stories with valuable predictive power, as the next chapter describes.

II.

social class and conspiracy theories that work

Because we understand our world by constructing causal narratives, we obsess over them and can be swayed by them. A good story built on bad facts will travel halfway around the world, while facts without a narrative fall off the radar. In this chapter we look at social class, a category more common in the social sciences than public debates, to see how groups that have less power may lack access to specialized information but can still formulate accurate predictions and make insightful choices. Class shapes everything from what movies we watch to what we expect from our government. Surprisingly, sometimes we can get farther by worrying less about causal mechanisms—those features we try to figure out through our stories—and paying more attention to the patterned outcomes we see over and over again. Dynamic causality can generate practical predictions even when we can't create a causal story that neatly connects every observation to a cause and an outcome.

Scientists, celebrated for their impartiality, never conduct research blindly. In practice, researchers begin with a hypothesis and typically seek to confirm that hypothesis: a belief that a particular lifestyle change *will* reduce diabetes mortality, or that a vaccination program *will* reduce childhood illness. This bias of motivation is good if we want to discover anything. As the great Stephen Jay Gould pointed out, Charles Darwin didn't go to the Galapagos Islands and observe evolution. (It evolves too slowly for him to have seen it.) He embarked with a theory of evolution, in search of a rich array of natural observations that he could use to test, or support, his theory. He found it.

The two primary theorists of capitalism, Adam Smith and Karl Marx, began with two different theories, but only one, Marx, did the research, grinding away long hours in the British Library, to support his theory with substantial evidence. The difference is noteworthy. In works like the first volume of *Capital* (1867) and the more accessible *Communist Manifesto* (1848), Marx concluded, consistent with his original hypothesis, that capitalism creates two fundamentally different classes of people: those who own *capital*, which is money they invest to make more money through the labor of (under)paid employees, and everyone else, who is an (under)paid employee. We can certainly elaborate on this simple schematic, but the fact that the determining feature of the system we call capitalism is *capital* ends up seeming so self-evident that it would likely be universally recognized were it not for the explosive political implications Marx also proposed from this insight.[182]

Marx and Smith marveled over the apparently unprecedented material surplus of the ages in which they lived, and which capitalism had produced. Both concluded that the division of labor, in which work became more specialized and each worker performed only one part of a much larger project, was central to this surplus. How the surplus was organized, and who had legitimate claim to it, were among Smith and Marx's disagreements. Marx concluded that the surplus rightfully belonged to the workers who produced it, while Smith had no objection to capitalists taking a heaping share of that surplus for themselves.

Smith defended the system as beneficial to the workers themselves. Workers were far wealthier, Smith hypothesized, under capitalism, than almost anyone under noncapitalist systems. "Yet it may be true, perhaps, that the accommodation of an European prince does not always so much exceed that of an industrious and frugal peasant, as the accommodation of the latter exceeds that of many an African king, the absolute master of the lives and liberties of ten thousand naked savages."[183] Despite the weasel words ("yet it *may* be true *perhaps*?") and the convoluted four-way comparison, his central point was provocative: If an industrial and frugal peasant might be better off than many an African king, capitalism must have much to recommend it.

But were laborers under early British capitalism really better off? Smith did not do the research. In fact, it's not clear that life in England during Smith's day was better. Life expectancy had been falling, not improving, from the mid-1500s to about the time that Smith was writing.[184] It's unlikely that the peasant's life was better or longer than the African king's, or than that of the non-nobility in Africa. For some time, industrialization created such crowding, malnutrition, and disease that many historians argue conditions got worse.[185]

The meaning of class has always rested on the evidence. As a social construct—class exists because we create it in our societies—class is a slippery feature. Like race, it is socially constructed but real, but unlike the body in race, we have not isolated a single place to look to imagine that we "see" class. We don't even have substantial agreement in the United States that class exists, and social scientists don't share a standard definition for each social class. Yet class, like race, shapes our day from the moment we wake up in the morning until the moment we look to see if we have a place to go to sleep at night.

Researchers use a range of definitions for class. In quantitative research, class is sometimes reduced to income. More elaborate versions of this measurement look at a number of features, like income, education, occupational status, and wealth (the amount of money one has, versus what one earns—a critical distinction). But the best definitions see beyond the often-misleading question of income. Class is a power relation. It typically stems from one's work, and what class one belongs to depends on how much power one has politically and socially, how much autonomy one has at work, and how someone relates to what Marx called the *means of production*. In other words, do you work for the company or does the company work for you?[186]

Even these quantitative measures of class don't grasp the full meaning of class: there are unionized construction workers who make more than plenty of teachers, poets, even small business owners, yet the former fit into the working class, the latter, less so. (A public high school teacher once called his profession the most well-educated of the working class.) Class is not only about money, not only about the means of production, but about culture, preferences, and a way of seeing the world and making predictions about the world. Class is about causality.

People avoid talking about class in the United States. A founding myth of the United States is that class *shouldn't* matter, everyone can be successful. After all, what is the American Dream? It's become such a buzzword that no one remembers anymore what the American Dream *is* exactly. To James Truslow Adams, who coined the term in 1931, the dream wasn't about how grand one's success could be, but that one's success wouldn't be determined by their inherited class: "It is not a dream of motor cars and high wages merely, but a dream of social order in which each man and each woman shall be able to attain to the fullest stature of which they are innately capable, and be recognized by others for what they are, regardless of the fortuitous circumstances of birth or position."[187] The American Dream hopes to dispel privileges or stigma conveyed by family or class and, instead, to celebrate hard work and performance.

We can try to dream away class, but it remains real, visible, and so pressing in our everyday lives that its effects need some illumination.

The American Dream is wedded to an equally foggy notion: the middle class. Politicians love the expression "middle class" so much they rarely name any other class, certainly not the working class. Recently more than one elected official has talked about the "middle class and those struggling to enter the middle class."

Who counts as middle class? Well, the 2015 median household income in the United States—the point where half of all households make more, and half make less—was $56,516 (and had risen for the first year since the 2008 recession).[188] The median for Blacks is a third less, at $37,000, 20 percent less for Latinos, 10 percent higher for whites, and a third higher for Asians.

But the middle class is not the median. A family on the median income could not afford the average house in the United States. When politicians say "middle class," they hope to conjure images of a family with a house, a car, vacation, and prospects of college for the kids; a family on $56,000 would have trouble living that kind of life; in many places, they'd have trouble paying the rent. In New York, a family with that income can still apply (and wait) for public housing.

The key: *the middle class is not in the middle.* The middle class was initially the people between the masses and the nobility. Today, researcher Michael Zweig suggests reasonably that the "middle class" sits between the working class and the upper class. The bottom two-thirds are working class, then comes the middle, then at the top are the 10 percent. Considering lifestyle, power, and income, we can say that the middle class typically makes between $85,000 and $165,000, comprising not more than a third of the country.

As important as economic measures of class are, class shapes much more than our income. The sociologist Herbert Gans directed his perpetually provocative attention to the effects social class has on our tastes in movies, TV shows, music, and other cultural products. Gans argued that different classes enjoy different types of entertainment—and that there's nothing better or worse about high art or mass media, they just play to their audiences. Gans divided viewers into upper class, upper-middle, lower-middle, and low. Most Americans belong to the lower middle. Gans found that audiences from the lower-middle class don't mind if the heroes in their action movies live in a world where even the good guys are corrupt. (Think of the good cop in the city where the mayor is on the take and his boss is inept and hamstrung by bureaucracy.) Those lower on the class ladder like their movies made of pure good and evil: martial arts master against the bad guys, no questions asked. Upper-middle class audiences like plenty of movies where not much happens at all, and high culture connoisseurs are off at museums and concert halls where the art can't be understood without reading up on it first.

Today, big data lets us study these cultural preferences in particular detail. Netflix can rank which movies are most popular by zip code. A few years ago, the *New York Times* took this geographic data about movie preferences and mapped out which neighborhoods were watching which movies throughout the country.[189] The results support Gans's findings: class and income do correlate to movie tastes. But the Netflix data also shows class interwoven with race.

The maps of Netflix movies expose a country organized by class and race, showing three different types of divisions. There are upper-class and working-class movies. Within those classes there are conservative versus liberal subgroups, and mixed in with class there are Black and white movies. Consider the map of New York and its suburbs as an example.

New York's upper-middle class sought movies about artistic and contemplative topics, and it's not a surprise that *Man on Wire*, the documentary about the performance artist who tightrope-walked across the World Trade Center in 1974, was watched not only in Lower Manhattan, but by all of cultural-capital-rich Manhattan. Self-portraits of the white-collar class also do well, explaining *Mad Men*'s early popularity in neighborhoods with Manhattan professionals. Working-class Brooklyn and New Jersey favored action-adventure movies like *Valkyrie* or Ridley Scott's *Body of Lies*.

Within those economic classes, two subgroups emerged: Manhattanites liked "serious" movies with artistic, political, or social themes. Critics liked those films too, so films with high rankings by critics, like *Milk*, the biography of pioneering gay politician Harvey Milk, were often watched by upper-income New Yorkers—sometimes almost exclusively by people in areas with high quantities of financial and cultural capital. Equally wealthy suburban New Jersey and Connecticut viewers preferred films with broader audiences, or a film about the suburbs themselves like *Revolutionary Road*. Gans argued that within each economic group, there was a more liberal, tolerant cosmopolitan side, and a more conservative, restrictive, traditional one. Thus, rich and poor New York united in watching the stoner movie *Pineapple Express*, while the more provincial and upstanding suburbs flocked to the saccharine *Last Chance Harvey*, which no one in New York watched.

But among the class and culture divides, clear, and overlapping, racial divides appeared. Working-class neighborhoods in New York City were often neighborhoods of color. Some viewing habits demarcated Black neighborhoods as reliably as a census map could. Movies with Black stars were certainly in this category, though one has to wonder if the Tyler Perry franchise is so popular why white neighborhoods refuse to check them out. (White working-class areas that year were busy watching action heroes defying the Nazis, in *Valkyrie* or *Defiance*, which critics dismissed as "slick, facile entertainment" or comedies about getting married, like *Mamma Mia!* or *The Proposal*.) A map of an area's favorite movies charts the terrain of economic class, but it can't be separated from race. Around New York, the areas with shared tastes in films created a patchwork of several distinct areas: working-class neighborhoods of color, working-class white neighborhoods, upper-income cosmopolitan areas inside the city, and more conservative upper-income areas out in the suburbs. Class was real, but it never existed alone.

One of the most useful aspects of the extensive Netflix movie map is that it can rank movies by how much critics like them using "metascores," which aggregated many professional reviews. Gans wrote that the upper-middle class was more likely to choose their movies based on the opinions of critics, while the working class referred to the opinions of friends. Sure enough, movies that had high metascores tested best in the upper-class, high-culture neighborhoods (sometimes critics' favorites were *only* popular in those areas; on some occasions, critics loved a movie and absolutely everybody saw it, as in the case of *Slumdog Millionaire*).

We can't argue that one strategy is superior to the other: critics are experts who watch hundreds of movies a year, but friends are people who share your tastes, whose biases you know well. Official sources don't necessarily provide better information than word of mouth, particularly when two social classes need different types of information (because they apparently like different types of movies).

The conclusion one is tempted to draw is that working-class movie-goers find official sources of information—newspapers, critics, online reviews—less useful or accurate. Instead, they use informal networks to gather the information they need. Certainly college professors hear about movies from friends, and transit workers read movie reviews in the newspaper, but the difference remains visible on the maps of what people watch.

This subtle divergence in where people get information about the world—from official sources or social networks—has enormous implications. The fact that we all get information from people we trust, but that while the working class has only trusted friends, the upper class has allies in mass media too, may have something to do with the divergent ways the two sides define fake news. Word-of-mouth is not vetted to weed out rumors, but the news-ingesting upper classes are more likely to swallow government-sourced justifications of wars, police misconduct, or corruption that the working class are more quickly skeptical of. In some areas, like movie choices, both sources have their strengths. But move far enough away from the official account of an event, and one enters the realm of conspiracy theories, an effort to get "the real story" that official sources must be concealing or unable to reveal.

One of my earliest memories of a real conspiracy theory is of a high school friend's older brother, who had compiled massive knowledge about the "real story" of President John F. Kennedy's assassination. I remember him sitting down with a book on the subject, and showing me all the graphics I came to recognize as classics on the topic: the drawing of the bullet's trajectory showing it was impossible for Lee Harvey Oswald to have fired all the shots as official sources said, the frame-by-frame images of the Zapruder film, shown to demonstrate that the president had been hit not from a lone gunman high in the Dallas Book Depository, but from furtive operators on the infamous grassy knoll. To any good conspiracy theorist, the "real story" provided evidence of a cover-up, and a cover-up was demonstration of deception, dishonesty, greed, and malfeasance at the highest levels of government—a suspicion of government that, I should note, comported not only with his own at the time but with mine today.

If word-of-mouth movie recommendations fill in for filmgoers who find that movie reviews lack the information they need, conspiracy theories serve a different function. Conspiracy theories do not merely appear where verifiable information is in short supply (they often develop regarding events with the *most* intense investigation). Instead, the contemporary genre of political conspiracy theory inverts causality—switching the roles of perpetrator and victim—so that the "real" perpetrator aligns with the experiences, ideology, and political understanding of the believer. Thus, Kennedy's assassination became an incident where the government was not the shot at, but the shooter. A group of conspiracy theorists believe that, on September 11, the United States was not attacked but the attacker. To people who believe the Sandy Hook school shooting massacre was perpetrated by a gun-control advocate, gun control is inverted from the unavoidable response to the ghastly perpetrator. Because of the moral nature of causal explanations, the claim that climate change is one vast and endless conspiracy theory tries to rehabilitate global capitalism from epochal perpetrator to innocent victim.

Conspiracy theories put ideology and experience ahead of data, and often do so by assembling a not-credible causal story of "how" an event supposedly actually occurred. As we've seen, our causal stories can be artificial and illogical. Thus the fact that conspiracy theories assemble casual stories that make no sense (the moon landing was faked in a movie studio, or the people who died in the hijacked planes on September 11 were flown to Ohio) is not what discredits them. Narratives become conspiracy theories not when they're wrong or outrageous, but when we decide that the causal story for a specific event *must* illustrate a specific moral point. Often that means that a conspiracy theory's narrative follows contorted, complex, or otherwise inexplicable narrative paths to travel from the event to the morally freighted cause.

Contrary to our assumptions about the usefulness of conspiracy theories, some examples that have a strong moral line but hew closely to the observed data can have strong predictive power even when it lacks a believable causal story. If the JFK-style conspiracy theory is a conclusion in search of data, a different sort of conspiracy theory reflects the working-class alienation from movie reviews. It is an effort to make sense of data from repeated observations, close to the action but far enough from the powerful that powerful people's actions are less comprehensible but more damaging. We don't know how elites do it, but they've done it to us again and again so now we expect it.

During my research on recovery in Lower Manhattan after September 11, I heard plenty of conspiracy theories. For years I went to the annual commemorations of the attacks on the Twin Towers. The first year it was an emotionally raw event, with victims' families in labeled t-shirts comforting each other, at times literally supporting each other from collapsing. But as the years went by, the annual memorial took on the feel of a carnival fairway. Amid the hooded religious orders selling CDs, the motorcycles and pickup trucks painted in elaborate patriotic motifs, and boxing promoter Don King promoting the war in Iraq, were groups of people who offered materials arguing September 11 had been an inside job. I was offered—and watched—more than one copy of the "Loose Change" video, which promised proof that the attacks could not have happened as the official account said they had, that it had been, to the contrary, a staged event intended to justify a US war against Iraq. The videos were tedious in the extreme, shamelessly slanting the evidence, and conflating metaphor and reality. Any discrepancy was taken as *prima facie* evidence that the mainstream account could not be true— and that the conspiracy theory must therefore be correct.[190]

The lack of acceptance of ambiguity, contradiction, and fallibility showed a failure to recognize how we construct accounts of anything. Any mildly complicated legal case presents contradictory evidence that cannot be reconciled: in the infamous O.J. Simpson murder trial, for instance, if he was guilty how do we explain that the bloody glove didn't fit his hand? If he was innocent, then how do we explain the bloody print left by a shoe he owned that was so expensive only a few dozen existed in the world? In any reconstructed story eyewitnesses contradict, timelines overlap, cell phone records fail to correlate with time-stamped videotape. Such is the contingent and imperfect nature of our ability to develop causal accounts (or collect perfect evidence). As Richard Hofstadter said in his essay "The Paranoid Style in American Politics," the mentality of the conspiracy theorist "is far more coherent than the real world, since it leaves no room for mistakes, failures, or ambiguities."[191]

The themes in this book give us another way to consider conspiracy theories. Causal explanations spring from particular times and places in history, and we've already seen how as time passes those historically specific explanations start to show signs of wear. Just as the motivations of characters in a movie written in 1967 make less sense to us today because we don't share the screenwriter's assumption about what behaviors make sense, a conspiracy theory proposed in 1963, if inaccurate, should look less plausible over time. Indeed, when Kennedy was shot it was the first time in over half a century that a president had been assassinated, and the event seemed so incredible as to demand a more satisfactory explanation.

But the rest of the twentieth century started to reveal just how common such acts of violence were. Robert Kennedy. Malcolm X. Martin Luther King, Jr. Twelve years after John Kennedy, President Gerald Ford faced assassination attempts not once but twice. Six years after that, John Hinckley, Jr. shot President Ronald Reagan. Attempted assassinations, like that of Congresswoman Gabrielle Giffords in 2011, have made such attacks seem even more common. Although some attackers had connections to organizations, or articulated political motivations, most showed signs of mental illness—a maelstrom of political issues and personal slights—that metastasized into the compulsion to kill a public figure to make a statement of uniquely personal importance. One of Ford's attempted assassins, for instance, wanted to kill him because she believed auto pollution would make redwood trees fall down. Hinckley famously sought to kill Reagan in the belief that doing so would impress actress Jodie Foster.

Often the assassins had a vast reservoir of anger that they targeted at particular individuals, but which made no sense to the rest of us. The assassins' biographies show a history of run-ins with people in power, and an outsized anger directed at an idiosyncratic grouping of political figures. Such people gravitated toward symbols on the political extremes, but mixed and matched them indiscriminately in ways healthy people—even with politically extreme views—do not. For instance, Jared Lee Loughner, who killed six people and injured thirteen, expressed intense hatred toward Democratic Representative Gabrielle Giffords, telling friends women should not have positions of power, but those close to him also said Loughner's anger would "well up" at the sight of President George W. Bush. John Hinckley, Jr., tried to kill the conservative Republican Ronald Reagan, but told a psychiatrist that he had also considered shooting liberal Democrat Senator Edward Kennedy.[192] Likewise, Lee Harvey Oswald's life was a confused whirl of contacts with both the pro-American and pro-Soviet poles of Cold War America: he joined the Marines but studied Russian while he was there. He defected to the Soviet Union, but returned disillusioned to Dallas and socialized with anti-Soviet emigres rather than left-wing radicals. Finally, while he assassinated Kennedy, a symbol of liberal Democratic politics, later police investigations tied him to the attempted assassination of the outspoken right-wing former US general Edwin Walker. Each of these young men shared an anger and a focus on poles of power, simultaneously dabbling in political extremes and angry at those who they believed were unacceptably politically extreme.

Although it was incredible at the time of the Kennedy assassination that one angry individual could bring down a president, it has since become nearly commonplace: young people, almost always men, almost always twenty-two to twenty-six years old (the ages of Loughner, Oswald, Hinckley, Booth, Sirhan, and Fromme), angered and unstable, take aim at public figures. With the benefit of hindsight we can see a pattern in contemporary manifestations of mental illness amid abundant handguns, and no conspiracy theory is necessary to provide a satisfactory causal account of how such shootings happen.[193] Conspiracy theories actually obstruct our understanding, because they ascribe too much rational calculation and strategic maneuvering to the shooter, rather than seeing the act as a disturbance.

Applying that lens to earlier assassinations is revealing. We interpret the assassination of Lincoln as a cold statement of Southern anger at the president. But what about John Wilkes Booth? A twenty-six-year old with "wild tirades, which were the very fever of his distracted brain and tortured heart," according to his sister. He was a man of troubled anger. The fall of Richmond, Virginia, she concluded, had "breathed air afresh upon the fire which consumed him" and led him to assassinate Lincoln.[194] We accord Lincoln's assassination considerable politi-

Those who commit torture can become wrapped up in it, but those who have not are often no less consumed by it. Many of the most prominent members of the White House administration that implemented and defended the US torture program after September 11, 2001, did not have military experience. Much of the posturing of that period has a strong odor of the dysfunctional model of masculinity, of men who still believed, naively, that masculinity is tied up with physical toughness, but who neither experienced violence nor engaged in violence in a way that would allow them to recognize its destructive danger.

Fear stokes this kind of reactionary decision making, just as it did in policies about teen pregnancy or the war on drugs. Fear is a less than ideal, but sometimes unavoidable context in which to make decisions. But here as in so many situations, fear is not merely a passive reality but an actively created situation; fear both drives our political leaders and is promoted by them as a justification for their decisions.

We have an odd obsession with the confession. In the Jeffrey Mac-Donald case, had he said nothing the case would have seemed like an open-and-shut domestic murder. The only thing that has made it an unresolved story in our national news cycle mythology is MacDonald's insistence on an alternative narrative. We want more than just the evidence that he did it—that's available. We crave an admission—a story that matches what we already believe to be true. This type of thinking has driven some of history's greatest atrocities: the Spanish Inquisition sought, and tortured for, confessions; show trials during eras like China's Cultural Revolution required confessions, forced, apparently, through torture, when without confession the victims could have just as easily been condemned. Yuri Nosenko was tortured in the hopes he would give his interrogators the confession they wanted—that he was not a defector but still a Soviet spy. (Three years of torture failed to resolve the question, and his handlers disagree to this day about what he was.)

cal meaning, but Booth's motivation looks very similar to the disturbed and senseless drive behind John Hinckley, Jr.[195]

Our readings of these assassinations demonstrate our tendency to spin meaningful causal stories out of nothingness. We create the meaning ourselves. Looking at the patterns among assassins and the instability of their mental health calls into serious doubt the political meaning we have ascribed to those acts. These assassinations could retain political meaning if we think of an individual's actions as the outcome of knowledge they share with a larger group, and that extremists operate in a worldview sustained by the narratives of a larger movement. But mainstream political movements justifiably bridle when outsiders blame them for fringe violence committed in their name.

Our drive to create meaning is deep and broad. In one experiment, people were more likely to conclude that a page of random dots appeared to have a pattern than be random; researchers concluded that human minds are biased toward seeing patterns and presuming causal relationships. Since then, researchers have posited an evolutionary advantage to erring on the side of causality rather than randomness: if an early human heard a rustle in the leaves nearby and assumed it was a predator even when it was not, no harm was done by being startled, grabbing a stick, and striking a defensive position (or running away). The person with the overactive tendency to see causality (that the rustling leaves were caused by a predator) lived to pass on their high-strung heritage. But other early humans less inclined to presume causality were too likely to presume rustling leaves meant nothing even when they signaled a predator's approach, and their genetic predisposition toward carefreeness was lost to humanity. Perhaps that tendency to see causality or meaning even when none exists, results in twin phenomena: the disturbed assassin's belief that a politician had to be killed, and the public's belief that that killing must mean something.

Early agriculturalists seeking to understand why the Earth was dry (and what to do about it), lighted on a range of causal explanations that sought to find meaning in the absence of meaning: sinful behavior by other villagers, lack of animal sacrifice to the rain spirits, the anger of a god (which inevitably just kicked the causal can down the road, begging an explanation of why the god was angry or capricious). Perhaps from drought sprung religion, or at least many religious rituals.

The effects of a drought—crop failure and perhaps famine—are completely different from the cause of the drought, which are meteorological. Likewise, the effects of an assassination—the loss of a historically significant head of state like Lincoln or Kennedy, the end of an era like the Civil War or Camelot—are completely different from the causes of the assassination—the particular convergence of mental health chemistry, anger, and armaments in a twenty-six-year-old man. True to egocentric causality, we want the effect of the assassinations to be the cause. Most often, these assassinations have been as devoid of meaning as a weather pattern.[196]

The good news for the conspiracy minded is that some theories hold up quite well. For instance, "The Plan"—a belief among residents in Washington, DC that there has been a plot to displace Black residents with white residents—has lingered since the 1970s. The Plan sounds like a classic conspiracy theory, except the ideas behind this conspiracy theory have had surprisingly strong predictive success: in 1970, 71 percent of Washington, DC residents were Black. Today, 49 percent are. Consistent with The Plan, affordable housing has made way for luxury condos, largely inhabited by whites, and central neighborhoods in DC have become predominantly white.

A similar theory spread on the South Side of Chicago, that the city government would evict Blacks from public housing projects along the coastline of Lake Michigan and cede the property to whites. Officials denied such allegations, even as they evicted residents from complexes of public housing towers. The demolitions were part of the federal HOPE VI program discussed in Chapter 6. Eventually, some affordable housing was rebuilt, but the "mixed income" plan meant that more whites lived in the area than had previously.

Working-class whites harbor their own theories. A colleague researching the industrial New York neighborhood of Red Hook twenty years ago heard many of the neighborhood's white residents speak about a similar plan: the city had moved Blacks into housing projects in Red Hook to scare away working-class whites, which was, they insisted, a strategy to deliver the neighborhood to rich white people. The conspiracy theory didn't make any sense—how would introducing poor Blacks make a place more attractive to rich whites? Yet a glance at any of the half-dozen redevelopment plans for Red Hook today, or the gourmet supermarket, the IKEA, and the outcroppings of trendy bars, restaurants, and waterfront parks lends the claims a strange amount of predictive power.

Gentrification can have an air of inevitability to it today, and some commentators have suggested that growing white populations in cities from Washington to New York to Chicago are no more remarkable than the inevitability of demographic change.[197] What is forgotten is how unimaginable it was, in the 1970s and '80s, and even, to the general public, well into the 1990s, that affluent whites would want to move into cities, which at the time seemed to be nests of intractable problems of crime, poor-quality schools, people of color turned into pariahs, drugs, and crumbling infrastructure. To foresee that urban America would once again be a crystal city was a feat of visionary imagination few people could muster.

Even those with a strong interest in forecasting such things had a difficult time anticipating gentrification: corporations moved their headquarters from New York City to places like suburban Connecticut in large numbers and at significant expense, department stores closed central city locations and relocated to the suburbs where the action seemed to be. The Plan was ignored—until it came to pass.

What are the key differences between the retrospective and predictive types of conspiracy theories, and how do we explain the differences in accuracy between the two? The first type tries to tie an event that has already occurred to a predetermined causal explanation, selectively using evidence to claim cause and effect are connected. The second uses repeated outcomes to make predictions about future outcomes, using a history of effects to make predictions even when there is poor information about the causes.

The first type, like JFK conspiracy theories, begins with an idea about the malevolent way government and powerful people work, chooses an event (an assassination or terrorist attack), and then tries to work backward to demonstrate how the event originates in a particular party whose presumed moral culpability is the real evidence of their causal responsibility. Beyond the obvious, one problem, as I've found in my research, is that any effort to reverse engineer a process based on observing the outcome fails. There are too many variables, too many actors, at work. Sure, there were elements in the federal government that were hostile to Kennedy, but no theory can take into account every politically engaged but mentally unstable Lee Harvey Oswald. Likewise, in the case of September 11 conspiracies, although there were prominent members of the Bush administration who, even before entering the White House, wanted to take military action against Iraq, no theory of Republican scheming or Western petroleum imperialism can take into account actions by mujahideen-trained terrorists.

While the JFK-variety of conspiracy theory starts with the moral component of a causal narrative, chooses an event that has already occurred, and seeks to go back and explain the event to get to the moral, conspiracy theories like The Plan start with a theory of how the world works, largely skip over the question of mechanisms, and predict the outcome. Conspiracy theories that follow whatever contorted causal path leads to the predetermined moral of the story typically fail to uncover the truth. But conspiracy theories that do not try to describe *specific causality*, but instead move from an informed theory of how powerful actors work to the kinds of outcomes those actors are likely to achieve, has a track record worth paying attention to. Indeed, the JFK conspiracy theory industry has been a failure. But The Plan correctly predicted an urban reinvestment few could have imagined at the height of urban flight. We need to sit up, take notice of the type of conspiracy theories that have strong predictive power, and understand why.

One reason for the accurate outcomes is that people disadvantaged by class and race have perforce done their research, like Karl Marx (but not Adam Smith). Conspiracy theories in the Black urban community have been so right because the theorists cannot afford to be wrong. African Americans' lives have long hung on people's ability to accurately predict the white man's behaviors. When are they most likely to be violent? Where will they be, and how can they be avoided? What angers them? What tricks can be played on them without them noticing? How can one get around, get by, or get over a white man who is most dangerous when he is unpredictable? One could argue then that African Americans have observed this situation closely and over a long time, and come to recognize many fine spokes of causal connection between motive and action.

The intermediate "why" of causality is functionally less important: whether white malfeasance is the result of being a white devil, a fool, or a bad person is less important than having some accurate prediction of the outcome. In this situation, causality does not matter: it is an unknown algorithm, but the algorithm generates outcomes with meaningful predictive power.

For that reason we ignore such predictions at our peril. In a New York City version of The Plan, many believe that the city seeks to evict people from public housing (many of them Black) to make room for gentrifying whites. This is, unequivocally, not the policy of the New York City Housing Authority. Although other cities have taken millions of dollars of federal money under the HOPE VI program to tear down public housing high rises, New York has not. To date, they have taken HOPE VI money to renovate exactly one of their 345 public housing developments. The current mayor of New York, Bill de Blasio, strongly supports affordable housing.

And yet green space and parking lots around New York housing projects are already being sold to developers. In the Bronx, the city's housing authority gave a private developer a stake in publicly run apartments that could be renovated and re-rented. The New York City Housing Authority, unlike housing authorities in other cities, still has a very strong commitment to maintaining affordable, city-owned public housing projects. But what will the federal government's increasingly tight financial constraints on public housing drive the agency to do? What will the next mayor do? Despite visible public policy to the contrary, the risks of that conspiracy theory—privatization hand in hand with gentrification—cannot be ignored.

The case of conspiracy theories that can skip over causality to get to accurate outcomes brings Occam's razor—the adage that the simplest explanation is normally the best—to causality in a useful way. Take the case of class: politicians regularly pay homage to the American Dream by denying that class matters, arguing instead that anyone can overcome disadvantage through hard work. The American Dream tells a good story but ignores inconvenient facts. The fact that the circumstances of one's birth and upbringing increasingly determine a person's wealth, occupation, and education speaks to the reality of class. Here, our human preference for causal stories prevents us from narrowing the wealth gap, or even fully understanding the problem of inequality. Paying more attention to the patterns of inputs and outputs, and less attention to trying to connect them with a moral narrative, would provide us better predictive power about the role of privilege than an American Dream that remains a dream.

Attention to outcomes without a causal explanation occurs, oddly enough, even in drug research, where chemical compounds are approved for prescription use on the basis of measures of outcomes, even when researchers say that the causal mechanism is only hypothesized, that is, unproven. It is more important to measure that a drug works than to understand how. It may seem surprising that a book about causality would highlight explanations that work without causality. But the point throughout the book is that causality is a human construction: we invented the word *why*, and we invented its answer. All sorts of things happen without us formulating a causal story about them, and we can even study and understand things without imposing a conventional casual story on them. We may not know exactly *why* there are class-based movie preferences, educational outcomes, or voting patterns. But the outcomes of class are real.

Dynamic causality encourages us to account for many factors we've ignored until now. So the paring down done by Occam's razor is welcome. The accuracy of the second class of conspiracy theories suggests not only that less-powerful people are better positioned to expect misuses of power and their end results, but that, more broadly, we can afford to miss some of the details if we look more closely at related outcomes. Particularly in observing society, no situation repeats itself precisely, so the common counterargument that "things are different this time" doesn't discredit the use of previous patterns to understand contemporary events.

With the tools of dynamic causality, we can grasp a situation better, understand what has worked in the past and gain a real, usable sense of what might go right or go wrong this time around. But how might we become better at confronting stories intended to mislead, or disrupt, a clear understanding of what's going on? Our final chapter shows how stories can gain authority, no matter how shoddy they are, precisely because they justify the actions of a society steeped in egocentric causality, victor-victim duality, muddled social categories, and crisis-driven decision making. As the next chapter shows, in cases where the inaccuracy of the story is the point, the blunt but learned skepticism of The Plan would serve us well.

12.

ticking time bomb

Would you torture someone to prevent a terrorist attack?

After the attacks of September 11, 2001, that destroyed the World Trade Center and damaged the Pentagon, advisers in President George W. Bush's White House insisted that national defense required a more aggressive strategy. At a press conference, Secretary of Defense Donald Rumsfeld claimed "substantial monetary rewards will incentivize—through the great principle of University of Chicago economics—incentivize a large number of people to begin crawling through those tunnels and caves, looking for the bad folks."[198] Rumsfeld was referring to the Chicago school organized around economist Milton Friedman, who had been an architect of deregulated capitalism around the world. His model presumed that people are essentially rational actors who respond reliably to economic incentives. In this case Friedman was correct, if the predictable outcome was that local authorities captured and exchanged any foreigner they could find and turned them in for the government's $5,000 bounty, without regard for whether they were actually connected to terrorism. The United States paid for 440 out of the 517 men held at the US base in Guantanamo by 2006, and the Defense Department concluded soon afterward that at least 92 percent were not al Qaeda fighters.[199] Two million dollars in bounty for nothing.

In keeping with a desire to be more aggressive, the United States established torture centers for those who the US army collected both with this bounty and "on the battlefield" of Afghanistan and later Iraq. The most visible was the US center at Guantanamo Bay, Cuba (where the United States still had a military base left over from the days when Cuba was run by a compliant, pro-US dictator). The irony was rich: the primary American torture center would exist not on US soil, but isolated from investigation by the American public and media by an embargo that kept most Americans out of Cuba. Any nation that was a US ally might well have objected to a torture center on their territory, but Cuba was already anything but an ally, so their opinion mattered little, diplomatically, to the United States. Torture also occurred at so-called "black sites," which were essentially torture centers run by other nations, particularly US allies with dim human rights records. The United States flew prisoners to black sites in hopes they could later disavow the torture as US policy.

Torture springs from our worst impulses as narrative-making machines. It seeks to force a nonconforming narrative into aligning with the dominant narrative: the fate of the doomed dissident, heretic, or traitor is sealed, but first the authorities extract a confession that suits the party line. Because torture complicates our dual identity as predator and prey, we simultaneously embrace contradictory narratives that justify and deny torture. Information agencies deploy denial narratives that, no matter how transparent, tangle up the human rights opposition, testifying to the trouble we have acting on knowledge that is socially contested. If we can use dynamic causality to understand situations better, we should understand that false narratives about torture do not take place in a political vacuum, and that sometimes stories are *designed* to impede our understanding. For a society that professes a bedrock opposition to torture, it is striking how readily a flimsy official narrative can sway opinions about the practice.

After September 11, one of the few skeptical voices about the US war on terror came from France, which announced it would not participate in the US-led invasion of Iraq. The Bush administration and its supporters, like the Fox News network, responded by denigrating all things French, to the point of excising the word "French" from the English language. In the congressional cafeteria, French fries became Freedom Fries. Bush's defense secretary maligned nations like France that failed to support the United States, saying they were part of "Old Europe." Among the ironies was that the United States had learned its torture techniques from France.

The Ignominious Origins of the US Torture State: France

The conventional origin story of the US torture program, included in a Senate report on CIA torture, is that the United States had first trained soldiers to resist torture techniques they imagined communists might use, then "reverse engineered" these techniques to use them against suspected terrorists. This story, the government may have hoped, gives human rights watchers no reason to think that techniques plucked from a torture-resistance training, based on what the United States imagined might happen in a hypothetical prisoner of war camp, would be an effective offensive tool.

But this is not where the United States got its torture techniques. France supplied the United States not only with torture techniques but also with the modern justification for torture. For them, torture was a means of keeping colonies under imperial control. France had lost significant colonies in the eighteenth and nineteenth centuries: the British took Canada, the United States bought the region called Louisiana, and Haiti gained its independence in the most successful slave revolt in human history. Then, relatively late in the European empire-building game, French politicians declared that their nation needed colonies once more. In fact, they declared that the colonies needed the colonizers, too. Socialist leader, Marxist historian, and politician Jean Jaurès— whose left-wing bona fides include not only his prominent support of Alfred Dreyfus, but a resolute antimilitarism for which he was assassinated at the start of World War I—spoke so affectionately of colonization that it sounded as if it were unfair to deny people the opportunity to be occupied by France. "When we take possession of a country," Jaurès said seductively, "we must bring with us the glory of France, and be sure that we make it welcomed, so that it is as pure as it is large . . . We can say to these people, in honesty, that never have we intentionally harmed our brothers, that we were first who gave men of color the liberty of whites, and abolished slavery . . . that where France has established itself, it was loved, that where it has only passed by, it was missed . . . that where it no longer shines, it has left behind only a long, sweet twilight where sentiments and hearts remain attached."[200] No less than Victor Hugo could call colonialism the march of civilization against barbarism[201] (providing the language of *civilization contre la barbarie* that would be repeated after the 2015 terrorist attacks in France on the political left and right).[202] Across the political spectrum, French politicians endorsed the idea of empire and France quickly set its sights across the Mediterranean on nearby Algeria, which France invaded in 1830.[203]

The roots of Algerian resistance to French occupation grew almost immediately. Not until more than a century later did the Algerian FLN, the National Liberation Front, effectively challenge French control. The FLN used terror attacks to frighten the colonists into leaving Algeria and ceding it independence. The French responded by torturing and interrogating suspected members of the FLN and others.

Paul Aussaresses was an officer who directed the French program of torture and assassination in Algeria. He claims to have personally tortured and killed at least twenty-four people.

Aussaresses came to Algeria in 1955 with the French special forces after serving in Indochina. He was put in charge of intelligence in the town of Phillippeville (today Skikda). Aussaresses claimed that while he was with the military in Vietnam he observed torture only rarely and that it was "exceptional," but he quickly made it widespread and gruesome in Algeria. He learned his torture techniques from the local colonial French police, using wires from generators to shock prisoners' ears or testicles. The tactic was later used by the CIA in Vietnam. After he tortured prisoners, he executed them.[204]

Aussaresses coined the term "death squad" (*escadron de la mort*) to describe his troops rounding up and executing prisoners. In 2000 he claimed to have participated in the 1957 executions of two leaders of the FLN that the French government had until then alleged were suicides.

The publication of Aussaresses's memoir was so outrageous in France that he and his publishers were charged and convicted of justifying torture (French law does not provide as broad protection for freedom of expression as the US Constitution does) and fined a small sum.[205] Significantly, Aussaresses was never tried for the torture itself, perhaps because he claimed that knowledge of it extended all the way to former President François Mitterrand, who had been minister of the interior at the time.

History has shown that Aussaresses's death squad campaign failed: France ceded independence to Algeria in 1962. Aussaresses claimed torture was necessary because the government had insisted to him that the FLN be defeated *quickly*. Other tactics might have worked, he implied, but expedience mandated torture.

Paradoxically, while the Algerian victory traumatized many French people, the failure of the campaign in Algeria did not tarnish Aussaresses's image, or that of torture more generally. Afterward, he took his methods abroad and trained military officers for the United States and Latin America in French torture techniques.

In the 1960s, the US military knew nothing about waging war against insurgents—that is, against groups fighting for their own independence from colonizers, according to Vietnam counterinsurgency veteran General John Johns in a 2013 documentary interview. His counterpart, Colonel Carl Bernard, explained that Paul Aussaresses had given US officers copies of fellow Algiers veteran Roger Trinquier's book *Modern War* (*La Guerre moderne*) in draft form, before it was published. "We went over it in detail, and unfortunately, I'm one of the ones who studied it," said Bernard, who then developed the US torture program in the 1960s.[206] The notorious American torture program in Vietnam, Operation Phoenix, was developed directly from what Aussaresses had taught the Americans. Bernard, who later lobbied against the use of torture, concluded that a minimum of 20,000 civilians were killed in Operation Phoenix. Aussaresses, he said, "exported torture."[207]

But Aussaresses did not end his torture training with the United States; he moved on to train the death squads of Chilean dictator

Augusto Pinochet. In the military coup of Argentina in 1976, torture was again a key tool of repression. All of the generals in the Argentinean junta had received French training.[208] Argentinian General Reynaldo Bignone, accused of raping and murdering women and children who were disappeared, was asked in an interview what the difference was between the Argentinian model and the torture in Algeria. "I would say it was a copy; there was no difference."[209]

The Ticking Time Bomb

Governments' most common justification for the transgression of torture—the "ticking time bomb" scenario, a simplified version of Aussaresses's "expedience"—is also a French creation from the Algerian War. In his 1960 novel *The Centurions* (*Les Centurions*), Jean Lartéguy imagines a scenario in which an Algerian terrorist has planted fifteen bombs around the city, set to go off the next morning. In what is now a well-known scenario, the colonel tortures the prisoner to determine the location of the bombs.

To defenders of torture, what has become known in its many versions as the "ticking time bomb scenario" became the most important justification for torture.

Significantly, this thought experiment about a tough choice between morality and humanity replaced the previous justification for torture that was fundamentally racist: that the enemy—often a colonial enemy—was so inherently simpleminded that they only understood brute force.[210]

For a book that is today largely unknown, out of print, and was long virtually impossible to obtain in English, the influence of *The Centurions* is hard to understate. It has been credited for saving the novel in

France, where it sold half a million copies. Known as a favorite read of US generals, it was much sought after by those who served under them, and sold for as much as $1,700 on Amazon.[211] General David Petraeus, who oversaw part of the US war in Iraq, successfully pushed for a small press to bring the book back into print; some readers see the book reflected in the US Army counterinsurgency manual Petraeus revised. General Stanley McChrystal, who directed forces in Afghanistan, claimed that he and his troops "had a level of unit cohesion just like in *The Centurions*."[212]

The book is a pulp fiction page-turner, and it's not hard to understand its attraction in 1960s France, or the US military today. A macho story of wartime fraternity with a hard-boiled moral code that allows for sex and violence, the book glorifies keeping one's head high and one's hands dirty to deliver the thrill of the dangerous and forbidden without the discomfort of moral uncertainty.

Jean Lartéguy's account was fiction, and there's no evidence there was ever a ticking time bomb scenario in French-controlled Algeria or Indochina. But the novel remains a founding myth for the contemporary justification of torture. If the ticking time bomb was a cleaner justification than the old, racist justification of torture, it wasn't exactly enlightened: as the plot builds to the final showdown in Algiers between the FLN and the French paratroopers, one officer rapes a woman brought in to be interrogated in a classic Orientalist scene of the white man who is obsessed with, and must protect and destroy, the feminine Orient. ("I love you and I hate you," she cries, in both a victor/victim duality and an Orientalist fantasy that legitimates domination, politically and sexually. "You raped me and I gave myself to you. You are my master and I will kill you. You hurt me so badly and I want you to do it again."[213]) In another room, a member of the liberation movement is interrogated, killed, and dismissed as a suicide (all of which Aussaresses reported he did).

When the ticking time bomb scene finally arrives, it is carefully set up, and discreetly carried out. The captain receives a call in the night informing him that a dentist named Arouche knows the location of time bombs set to explode at 9:30 the next morning in stores frequented by French colonists. The captain must find out where the bombs are. The novel rules out any possibility of misidentification of the suspect when an officer conveniently telephones at the start of the interrogation to give an exacting description of the would-be bomber: his scars, his injuries, his age, the shape of his face. Even better, Arouche—driven to hate the French, we are told, by a man who hurled a racist insult because he tried to approach a European woman at a club—proudly gives his captor the information that ensures a nice, neat ticking time bomb situation, a perfect construction of egocentric causality, reassuring the captain that "I am the only one who knows . . . Your bomb squads can search the stores of Algiers all night, they won't find anything. You can kill me, torture me, I'll die of joy in your grasp because tomorrow . . ."[214] Arouche stares at the clock, taunting the interrogator with the knowledge that each passing minute brings the vindictive terrorist closer to bloody success. Even so, Captain Esclavier tries to convince the dentist to talk. But, two factors overwhelm his civilized instincts: his own memories of being tortured when he was captured by the Nazis, and another well-timed phone call, this time from his mistress, who tells him the rebels have killed her grandfather and his three servants. Unlike in the objective, philosophical thought experiment of the ticking time bomb, in Lartéguy's original scenario torture is driven by the torturer's own traumatic torture and his fury at the violence of his opponents. (Is Captain Esclavier a slave—an *esclave*—to his past, to the passion for revenge, to Algeria, or to his country? Or is this supposed liberator really an enslaver—a *négrier*—of Algerians?)

In the novel, the French never consider simply warning stores to stay closed in the morning to keep customers and shopkeepers out of harm's way. Much as the Americans learned their torture from the French, the scene implies that Esclavier used the methods imparted on him by his Nazi torturers. The torture by the French captain, however, is merely implied modestly in a single sentence: "When, in the early morning, the dentist was carried out on a stretcher, he had said it all; none of the fifteen bombs exploded."[215]

Since *The Centurions*, the ticking time bomb has taken on a life of its own, from the philosopher Henry Shue's often-cited formulation (in which there is a nuclear bomb under Paris, perhaps a tribute to Lartéguy) to the plot of the popular television show *24*, which confronts its protagonist with a series of ticking time bombs he must disarm over a single day.[216]

The ticking time bomb has since been the primary rhetorical justification for torture. American politicians, jurists, and commentators have all borrowed from the French novelist to ask people who are opposed to torture whether they wouldn't justify extreme measures in such a scenario. It's an image that is as widespread and pernicious as it is wrong and dangerous.

Both the power and the dangerous deception of the ticking time bomb lie in its apparent simplicity. Although first articulated by Lartéguy, the question is often credited to Shue, who put it this way: "Suppose a fanatic, perfectly willing to die rather than collaborate in the thwarting of his own scheme, has set a hidden nuclear device to explode in the heart of Paris. There is no time to evacuate the innocent people or even the movable art treasures—the only hope of preventing tragedy is to torture the perpetrator, find the device, and deactivate it."[217]

Human rights organizations have published considerable breakdowns of the time bomb scenario. In particular, the Geneva-based

Association for the Prevention of Torture published a concise and compelling critique of this rationale in 2007.[218]

First, the Association points out, the scenario too readily assumes that we know things for certain: that there *will be* an attack, that a person is in custody who *has* critical information to prevent the attack, and, critically, that engaging in torture *will* get information from the person in custody, and that it is the *best* means of gaining such information. An interrogator wouldn't know all of those things.

The scenario oversimplifies typical real-world experience in other ways. For instance, one must assume that the attack is imminent enough to foreclose the possibility of obtaining the information from other sources, but not so imminent that the interrogators couldn't use the information to disarm the bomb or stop the planned attack.

The ticking time bomb may be the least sound causal story ever. As such, it serves as a reminder that understanding causality is not an academic exercise of cleaning up innocent mistakes, but a political undertaking to challenge the deployment of manipulative causal stories like the ticking time bomb. The fact that people who oppose torture are fighting against a *made-up story* gives a sense of just how much influence narratives have over people.

The ticking time bomb is not real life. But this fictional case has real-world implications. Senator Dianne Feinstein, who headed the committee that wrote the Senate report, explained that "The Committee never found an example of this hypothetical ticking time bomb scenario."[219] But, more tellingly, the administration disagreed. They argued that there had been a ticking time bomb scenario because, as former CIA director George Tenet and five other CIA administrators wrote, they believed that terrorists had met with Pakistani nuclear experts and were smuggling weapons into the United States. "It felt like the classic 'ticking time bomb' scenario—every single day," they wrote. Those reports turned out to be not true, they conceded. This is, in fact, critical: to the director of the CIA, the ticking time bomb scenario justified torture not when there was a terrorist attack, but when he thought, erroneously, that there might be. Such a scenario is not the classic justification—"Wouldn't you torture someone if you *knew* this were true?"—but the opposite, presented by opponents of torture: "Should we torture someone if there is no plot?" At best, it is muddied into "Should the public endorse torture by government agencies as long as those agencies can collect uncertain evidence that tends to support their foregone conclusion that there might be some threat?"

Buying in to the time bomb scenario makes torture routine, not exceptional: if it were justifiable to torture one person to stop the bombing of a school bus of twenty-five children, then at the rate of one torture victim per twenty-five lives saved, it would be ethical to torture two people, if one of the two were known to know the locations of two such bombs. Following the math, we could justify torturing three people (each with a 33 percent chance of being the bomber) to prevent 75 victims, 4 people with a 25 percent chance of knowing how to save 100, until the possibility of a mushroom cloud over New York's 8 million person metropolis justifies torturing 320,000 people if any one of them might be able to head off a nuclear attack. These figures better represent that statistical reality of the American torture program than the ticking time bomb. The ticking time bomb scenario smuggles in a fundamental deception: that we can know anything for certain. In the real world, answering yes to the scenario inherently endorses torturing innocent people who cannot provide the information demanded—the very reality that the ticking time bomb's certainty seeks to exclude from our consideration. The scenario's powerful narrative dissolves completely and reverts to the formation, "Should government employees torture suspects as routine policy?"

From Fiction to Reality: Torture Doesn't Work

The use of torture by the CIA for years after the attacks of September 11, 2001, has been exhaustively studied—and vigorously defended. In 2012, the US Senate's bipartisan Select Committee on Intelligence issued a 525-page report studying the outcomes of torture. They found, unequivocally, that torture did not work and was even counterproductive. First, torture did not generate useful intelligence. Sometimes detainees provided valuable information *without* torture, but stopped providing information when they were tortured.

It is worth noting here that the CIA, not inconsistent with its nature as a bureaucratic institution officially charged with duplicity, has for years given two contradictory narratives about torture: what it says and what it does. The CIA has long been on record opposing torture for humanitarian and practical reasons. Beginning in 1964, the CIA tortured Soviet KGB officer Yuri Nosenko for *three years* with techniques including solitary confinement and forced standing. (Nosenko had defected but the CIA didn't believe he was a real defector, so they tortured him. With friends like that who needed enemies?) Then came the horrors of Operation Phoenix in Vietnam from 1965 to 1972.

Asked to review the treatment of Nosenko, a CIA officer in 1978 testified that after thirty-one years with the CIA, "To me it is an abomination, and I am happy to say that . . . it is not in my memory typical of what my colleagues and I did in the agency during the time I was connected with it." Five years after that, the torture techniques used against Nosenko were nonetheless incorporated into interrogation training and used to train torturers in Latin America in the 1980s. By 1988 CIA officials were again in front of Congress taking a strong stand against torture: "physical abuse or other degrading treatment was rejected not only because it is wrong, but because it has historically proven to be ineffective." This was followed up by a performance a year later in which the CIA avowed to Congress that "inhumane physical or psychological techniques are counterproductive because they do not produce intelligence and will probably result in false answers."[220] At the same time, an unnamed CIA officer was torturing people during interrogations in Latin America. This individual was admonished for that behavior, but, apparently after September 11, was put in charge of the CIA's kidnap and torture group.[221]

After September 11, the CIA claimed to the White House, Congress, and the public that torture had extracted information and "thwarted" specific terrorist plots. The Senate committee reviewed the twenty cases most frequently cited by the CIA and found that the CIA was lying. Either no information had been gained through torture, the information had already been extracted through other sources, or the information was obtained from prisoners during interrogations that did not involve torture. (The committee says of the CIA claims of terrorist plots foiled by torture that "The examples provided by the CIA included numerous factual inaccuracies."[222]) CIA torture systematically used solitary confinement, as well as slamming detainees into walls, nearly drowning them with waterboarding, threatening to kill them, sleep deprivation of more than a week, assaults on bound detainees by groups of five CIA personnel, threats to kill their families and rape the mother of one detainee, ice water baths, and assurances that the detainees would be killed because the world would not be permitted to learn of the torture visited upon the detainees. At least one detainee died from exposure to the cold. Further, the CIA lied to oversight agencies like Congress and the Justice Department (the torture was far more severe than they admitted) and impeded investigations into the torture program. Simultaneously, the CIA fought a public relations war against the

American people, releasing (inaccurate) classified information to the press that suggested that the torture program was working.

The White House administration had promoted just such a "muscular" response. Maybe that's why the CIA ignored their own previous finding that the torture they were conducting wasn't going to help them do their job.

One obvious takeaway from the CIA's history of torturing and denying it tortures is that the public and the press should systematically ignore any public statements made by the CIA and other government agencies tasked with deception. Trafficking in false narratives may have taught intelligence agencies that people's causal explanations do so little to link A to B that lies and philosophical justifications don't even have to make that much sense. Powerful actors benefit from our compulsion to resolve contradictory narratives—as we squabble, and become paralyzed waiting for social consensus—even when those stories are patently unreliable.

Revealingly, the CIA itself never conducted a review of the effectiveness of the torture program. To the contrary, several abortive efforts to evaluate whether the torture program was working stopped before they began, concluding that it was impossible (or, in one Orwellian turn, unethical) to evaluate the effectiveness of the torture program.[223]

The result is a contradictory record. The CIA insists repeatedly that torture doesn't work, yet their practice over the decades, in a range of countries and contexts, has been to engage in torture as if it did. The final record is unambiguous: the CIA's ventures into torture do not work.

General Paul Aussaresses, that proud veteran of the Algerian War and exporter of human suffering, would disagree. He insisted that he used torture because it worked, and because the expedience demanded of his political superiors required it. But his own real record, like the

CIA's, tells a different story. A *Soldier of Fortune* magazine article claimed to have interviewed Aussaresses in a Paris hotel once used as a meeting place by the Nazi Party. In fact, the article was a wholesale plagiarism of his memoir *Services Spéciaux*. (The article was later quoted in Aussaresses's *New York Times* obituary.[224]) In that excerpt, he describes the first time he tortured: it was June 18, 1955, but the victim, who had attacked a civilian with an axe, died without providing any information. Aussaresses's greatest success of that period stands in stark contrast to the justification of torture: he obtained early warning that rebels were gathering outside the city of Philippeville thus providing him adequate time to prepare and save the lives of his troops. The information came not from torture, but from relationships with locals developed over time: one grocer reported that he was now selling two tons of flour at a time to a buyer who paid cash. A pharmacy noted individuals were buying bandages in bulk. Informants told him the date and time of the attack. Torturers claim the practice works, but their own memoirs and reports establish it does not.

The ticking time bomb scenario presents itself as a rational calculation: doesn't sacrificing one culpable individual to save many innocent lives have an irrefutable, almost mathematical morality? The question goes against human nature, insisting we should be more violent. But there is already no shortage of human violence, nor of torture, and we know it doesn't work. A situation like the ticking time bomb would be frightening, angering, frustrating, and desperate. One can easily imagine becoming violent in the face of a recalcitrant terrorist. The anger and desire to harm such a person is palpable. In such a situation, a more challenging question is, if you were interrogating someone who could stop a deadly attack, knowing torture doesn't work, could you resist the urge to hurt them? If the time bomb were ticking, could you *not* torture?

The reality of torture is that for fifty years, the CIA has *both* tortured *and* stated publicly that it does not. The CIA tortured *and* produced evidence it did not work. The CIA is victor and victim, compelled to be the aggressor and unable to admit that they are. This duality expresses itself at every opportunity: the Bush administration stated that it would engage in conduct that previous administrations had prohibited, and argued that such action was justified after September 11. Yet they denied the actions were torture, renaming them "enhanced interrogation techniques." Terms like secret prisons, black sites, and secret police all obscure practices that we collectively know are torture. Just as torturers fight against the cognitive dissonance of knowing something is true (you're a terrorist!) and hearing it denied (no I'm not!), people in power profit from the public's response to cognitive dissonance in which powerful people say contradictory things (We must torture. We don't torture.) both justifying and denying unacceptable behavior.

While these contradictions play out on the public stage, the backstage contradicts itself as well. Sociologists often identify the *normalization of deviance*, in which a specific group of people redefine what counts as "acceptable" behavior, even though the general public agrees it is not acceptable. Chefs stick their fingers in the soup, police beat prisoners, engineers build space shuttles that they know put astronauts at risk, all because they believe they must break rules to expedite the completion of their tasks.[225] In this respect it's not exceptional that the CIA would endorse prohibitions against torture publicly if they engaged in it privately, but our mistake has been to confront each of these contradictions one at a time. Instead, we must interrogate the entirety of the situation: While torture is happening, the appropriate question is not whether an institution like the CIA is torturing, but why it simultaneously tortures, denies it tortures, and defends torture, all while knowing torture doesn't work.

The precise answers may vary, but they mark the intersection of how people think and how social structures push people to certain behaviors: how, for instance, an image of masculine toughness, an institution tasked with violating social norms to achieve its ends, a mandate to gain intelligence it does not have, and a bureaucracy with minimal legal constraints drive its employees to engage in hopeless and self-defeating violence.

Causality and Torture

These contradictions make clear that, contrary to the simple rationality implied in the ticking time bomb question, torture is not rational. It is part of the victim/victor dialectic discussed in Chapter 4. We are thrilled and repulsed by war, thrilled and repulsed by a fantasy of righteous torture. As human rights organizations point out, torture is not a just-this-once event. Torture creates a bureaucracy that must be fed, like the specially built torture prisons of the CIA in Iraq. (One was called Cobalt, or the Dark Prison, among other names, where prisoners died.) People must turn into torturers. Paul Aussaresses said that he committed torture himself, to spare younger, enlisted men, but the CIA seemed to assign the responsibility to employees who did not even have training, much less experience, in interrogation.[226] Just as Barbara Ehrenreich asked about the effect of killing in war, what psychological damage is done to people who commit such horrible acts? All accounts indicate that torture soon becomes a practice not of last resort, but of routine. It also creeps from aiming to save lives, to a tool for torturers to exact revenge, dole out punishment, and express anger (these torturers, it is no less frightening to consider, must, one day, have returned to the civilian world).

We must recognize that we as people want confessions, demand confessions, *need* confessions, *torture* for confessions. Confession is a form of submission, it is about power, and no power is as obvious as physical violence. The need for confessions is a product of our social and psychological makeup: what we know we know socially, and if a centrally important person in a narrative disagrees with our account of events, we work to gain consensus, even potentially inducing pain to get consensus. We not only want a conviction for Jeffrey MacDonald, we want a confession; we not only want to prevent the terrorists from attacking, we want them to share our egocentric view of their place in the world.

Dynamic causality can teach us to be properly skeptical of causal stories and avoid foreseeable but frequently overlooked pitfalls. We're seduced by stories, but we need to be able to dismiss those that contain no substance or evidence. At other times, we need to recognize when our compulsion for satisfying stories impairs understanding a situation and, as in the case of torture, even drives us to violence.

Much like the opposition to solitary confinement that opened the first chapter, opposition to torture ebbs and flows in waves of revelation, revulsion, prohibition, complacency, and complicity. We need to maintain our collective memory of the unacceptable horrors of torture, resist the siren song of would-be torturers who imagine, wrongly, that it is a shortcut to enormous and poorly defined goals like defeating terrorism or ensuring national security. We are not perfect, but we can construct a more robust opposition to one of the most repulsive behaviors that human societies can bring into being. We are better at opposing torture before it happens than we are at stopping it once it has become normalized.

conclusion: dynamic causality

As the species that invented the question *why*, it's a shame we haven't advanced very far toward answering it. As we've examined in the chapters of this book, in creating our causal explanations we face constraints on how we think borne of biology, social prejudice, and our own tendency to create certain types of narratives. And we ignore important causal factors—natural, physical, and spatial. Finally, we exist in a social world in which we rarely have confidence that we know something until it's collectively agreed upon, where we work hardest to determine cause and effect under the worst conditions of fear and stress, and where if we're lucky enough to eradicate a problem, we don't have much interest in retroactively figuring out how we did it. It's no wonder that some of our best predictions come from ignoring the question of *how* things happen, and instead preparing for what is likely to happen.

Putting It Together: Dynamic Causality

Think back to the discussion of solitary confinement in the first chapter. A question many people, parents in particular, ask is whether social media and our addiction to our phones is creating a more isolated world. When I ask parents this question they often say yes, noting that even when their teenaged children are sitting with friends, each of them are often on their own phone, not conversing or interacting with the people right around them. When I ask college students the same question, they often say it makes them more social, not less, because three people sitting around the table at a fast-food restaurant may actually be having conversations with a dozen friends, near and far.

We know from Chapter 1 that when isolated, even for small amounts of time, people can rapidly exhibit the agitated behaviors observed in proper solitary confinement. These symptoms also express themselves when people don't have their phones. David Denby wrote about a class of high school students who participated in their teacher's experiment to go phone-free for two weeks. Like naïve prisoners, they thought they could handle the isolation. "I started off thinking I could get through it," wrote one student. By the second day, familiar symptoms arose: They were bored. They couldn't focus. They were lonely. They needed more stimulation, like music, to be satisfied. Unwittingly mimicking the behavior of prisoners in solitary confinement, one student reported, "I was so restless. I had to do push-ups and running in place."[227]

Researchers have been divided on the role of cell phones. Some note approvingly that smart phones "strengthen bonds among family members," facilitate "maintenance of symbolic proximity" and "continue to facilitate relationship maintenance."[228] A different group of researchers worried that "overuse" of "wireless mobile devices" (which they gave the same abbreviation as "weapons of mass destruction") caused anxiety as soon as the device was removed from a heavy user of WMDs.[229]

The disagreement centers on the idea that human needs and behaviors are static instead of dynamic and changing. Allostasis tells us that the "baseline" level for a range of basic physiological needs—like blood pressure, blood sugar, and fat—can change. Evidently, a world that puts social media constantly at our fingertips raises our baseline for social interaction. The amount of social connectivity someone needed before smart phones was less than it is once someone is accustomed to them. Increasingly, people use text messages and social media to mediate such intense conversations, and even emotionally sustaining romantic relationships, suggesting that the meaning of physical isolation could be changing once again, as it did with television and radio. Research has yet to address that question. Whatever the effect, there is no going back to life without cell phones (since even for research purposes the authors were only able to pry cell phones out of people's hands for a short series of tests, not a longer time); the question is therefore not what social media does to sociability as we understood it *before* smart phones, but social media's role in socializing as it exists today. Irrespective of how childhoods *were*, we can decide what kind of social world we want children, and adults, to have now.

Dynamic causality more nimbly considers the past and the social structures that in our everyday experience seem so intransigent, but are constantly evolving. It recognizes the ways that our particular breed of storytelling privileges certain factors and overlooks others, how we put ourselves in the center of the narrative and assume that others are acting not with their own objectives but with the intent to affect us personally. Broadening our analysis beyond the fear-laden reasoning often disseminated by politicians and the press, adopting perspectives from a wider range of disciplines, integrating causal factors outside of the human intentions we gravitate to, dynamic causality allows us to better make sense both of what we see and what we miss.

Dynamic causality is not just a better way to understand, but an insistence that understanding can bring about social change. Social scientists often borrow from physics and use the Heisenberg Uncertainty Principle to say that observing something changes it. In the sciences that means that, to look at a subatomic particle, researchers have to shoot high-energy particles at it to find out where it is; however, those high-energy particles immediately send it off in some other direction at a new velocity. Social scientists worry by analogy that watching kids in a classroom to see if a new teaching technique works alters the kids' behavior because they *know they're being watched*.[230] But to develop the analogy further, the principle in physics says that someone can know a particle's location or velocity—but not both. The more precisely someone knows one the less they know the other. Situations in the social world have location and velocity too. Social scientists' data is skewed toward letting us understand where things stand at this moment in time, not the rate and direction at which they are changing. In contrast, politicians and other decision-makers, I would argue, focus on velocity: they may not have as detailed a snapshot of where things are at this moment, but they want to be leaders in where they will go. The aim of dynamic causality is to help us know both. To think dynamically, we must embrace a few concepts:

THE PULL AND PUSH OF SPOKES

Taken individually the spokes of a bike wheel seem too flimsy to hold us, yet in the proper arrangement they can pull from the top of the wheel to keep us from falling, and push from the gears outward to propel us forward: surprising outcomes can come from a welter of tiny little spindles. While conventional explanations focus on a small number of proximate causes, many others are interlinked and play unrecognized roles. We overlook these other causes at our peril when discussing a contentious issue: African Americans are worse off than whites in a range of concrete and substantial ways: median income, poverty rates, life expectancy, home value appreciation. Yet skeptical conservatives can dismiss each of the individual proposed causes: microaggression (they're micro, some argue), lending discrimination (Are default rates lower for Blacks? If not, some argue, there's no evidence of discrimination.), police profiling (just obey the officers), and so on. If we fail to think holistically, opponents can dismiss each of those causes individually, arguing that no single cause seems sufficient to explain the totality of Black disadvantage in America. And so that disadvantage remains.

DON'T REASON FROM FEAR

Easier said than done, because moments of fear present the most urgent need to find explanations and counterstrategies. But undertaking serious post-incident assessments, with an eye toward future application is a start: What ended the teen pregnancy epidemic in the United States? What ended the rash of terrorist attacks in the 1980s? What led to the end of ozone-depleting chemicals?[231] Although fear may be useful for fight or flight responses or grabbing headlines, sometimes pulling the fire alarm isn't the smartest way to exit the building.

Fear can be mitigated by cautious use of comparisons. For a given social problem (like teen pregnancy, terrorism, or diabetes), what is the situation in Europe compared to the United States? The developed world versus the developing world? Today versus a decade ago, fifty years ago, a hundred years ago? Not all comparisons are relevant, but they can often provide the perspective that is lost in a moment of fear: How many people die of terrorism? What were the causes and outcomes of terrorism fifty years ago? In moments of fear, we are often unable to understand mechanisms, but data about previous outcomes is easier to grasp and allows us to see that not every crisis is unprecedented. From that starting point, we are less likely to become paralyzed and complacent, and more likely to act effectively.

UNDERSTANDING IS NOT PREDICTING

Physics is a science with astounding predictive powers: Einstein's theory of general relativity first predicted the existence of black holes in 1916, but evidence for them (though they are, by definition, impossible to see) was not found until the 1990s. In contrast, sociology is not a predictive science.[232] No matter how accurately scientists can model the different possible outcomes for global warming depending on our future consumption of carbon fuels, no one has tried to model or predict the totality of human responses. How and when will governments respond? At what scale will people reach out to help, and against whom will they pull up the drawbridge?

Our inability to predict human responses to climate change moves us from the realm of science to the realm of politics. We have adequate scientific knowledge about global warming. We will need the very best decision making possible. We show no signs of cutting off all fossil fuel use. This sets up a direct relationship between the rate at which we will burn fuel and the cost of preparing for damage or cleaning up the mess. In coming centuries we will be repeatedly and inescapably faced with the question of how much to defend and how much to retreat, how much to spend protecting, and how much to focus on rebuilding. To respond smartly, we will need good structures and decision-making processes on personal and global scales.

Though understanding is not predicting, we are not defenseless. As the various flavors of conspiracy theories demonstrate, we don't always need to understand mechanisms to predict likely outcomes and fashion strategic responses. It's just as well that we don't need to understand the causal narratives, because we increasingly act without them. Machine-based learning, for instance, is a process in which computers examine massive quantities of data to make predictions. After sifting through thousands of scans of patients' bodies, for instance, computers can more accurately identify breast cancer or predict the onset of an epileptic seizure than doctors can. Because the computers identify patterns and rules from the massive number of cases they examine, researchers don't always know *how* a computer predicts, from a scan, that a patient will develop a condition, only that the prediction is probably correct. If "big data" increasingly draws conclusions that humans can't on their own, we may increasingly accept a perspective that stops demanding neat causal explanations and favors the persuasiveness of consistent results. Each time we follow GPS driving directions informed by traffic data, we are doing just that: taking a different route because a computer's algorithm has determined, in ways it does not inform us, that a different route is better. Thinking of conspiracy theories, what will determine whether big data validates elite official sources or popular local wisdom?

We are not about to abdicate our decision-making prerogative. But with dynamic causality, social science's insights help us see problems in their larger context, shifting our focus from stories to results, and allowing us to move forward.

Our Greatest Problems, Seen Through Dynamic Causality

TERRORISM

The fact that decisions made in fear tend to be poor decisions is exacerbated after terrorist attacks, where one strategic intent is to provoke leaders to overreact in fear and make bad decisions. Those bad decisions—overreaction, collective punishment, torture, and terrorism in response—galvanize the potential allies of the terrorist actor.

That the United States has responded forcefully to terrorism is well known: the United States has spent over $300 billion dollars fighting this threat since 2001.[233] In addition, it has passed significant legislation and deployed increasingly sophisticated spying operations that have collected trillions of communication records of Americans and civilians from around the world. During this period, attacks have increased substantially, then decreased meaningfully though more modestly. Terrorism is still a major concern, and despite a global decline in attacks, the number of deaths from terrorist attacks inside the United States has increased moderately but consistently since 2011.[234]

What has worked in the past? By at least one accounting, terrorism was most prevalent in the United States in the 1960s, Western Europe in the 1970s, Latin America in the 1980s, and in the Middle East today.[235] Far from being a constant threat, terrorism clearly rises and falls in different regions in different times. Interestingly, the available (imperfect) databases indicate that the overall number of terrorist attacks has been decreasing worldwide. Government militaries cause most of the terror in the world and most civilian deaths, but the convention is to consider nonstate terrorism separately from military bombs, mines, and violence.[236] The number of suicide attacks worldwide peaked sharply in 2007 and has dropped considerably since then.[237] (Most terrorist attacks happen in Iraq, where they occurred only after the US invasion and occupation; Iraq had the most terrorist attacks in the world in 2015.[238]) Inside the United States, thirty-six Americans died in attacks between 2004 and 2013.

As with teen pregnancy, "What works?" is a critical question we rarely ask. The rise in terrorist attacks could have be an anomaly, or a crisis that is passing while our alarm remains as high as ever. Certainly some of the actions taken to combat it, like invading Iraq, have increased terrorism, not reduced it. The key question that receives too little attention is what has reduced waves of terrorism in the past.

The first thing we should note is what often does not work against terrorism. Counterproductive strategies are often borne of terrorists' intent to provoke a disproportionate response. When President Bush said, "On September the 11th, enemies of freedom committed an act of war against our country," he made no distinction between an attack by a small terror cell and a war that can be waged by an actual national army.[239] Going to "war" is often less of an antiterrorism strategy than it is the terrorists' desired outcome of their attacks. Going to war is the mistake terrorists want their more powerful targets to make.

We need to differentiate between war and terrorism, organizations and disturbed individuals, because the causes and solutions are different for each, and because equating a lone individual with a large organization with a national army symbolically conveys enlarged importance to anyone who engages in terrorism.

It is true that military responses sometimes prove effective: observers claim Latin American nations' attacks against Maoist rebel groups— who used terror attacks as a strategy—reduced terror. Sri Lanka brags of being the only country to have eradicated terrorism in its country with the defeat of the Tamil Tiger rebels, which was largely accomplished through a military campaign. But these cases, in which a government has defeated a single (paramilitary) organization inside its own borders, differ from most situations involving terrorism. And, despite their success, the military responses still carried very high costs in casualties and human rights abuses. Military responses have not succeeded in most situations.

One answer to what works is hidden by the bluster that accompanies our uneasy identification with both victor and victim. As every president insists, we do *not* negotiate with terrorists. In fact, we *do* negotiate with terrorists. First, governments try to wipe out terror cells through violence. Such a tactic is unlikely to succeed with a geographically and organizationally diverse terror movement. Then countries negotiate with terrorists. Israel negotiates with Hezbollah. Great Britain negotiated with the Irish Republican Army. President Reagan negotiated with Iran. Even Sri Lanka negotiated with the Tamil Tigers.

Dynamic causality demands an understanding of why terrorism develops, and research in this area is useful, if too often overlooked. The causes break down into three levels. At the most basic level there are "fundamental causes" like modernization, urbanization, the legitimation of violence, and an avant-garde (often middle-class) group of aggrieved actors. These causes point to important inequalities in societies.

At the intermediate level, longtime terrorism researcher Martha Crenshaw pointed to "the lack of opportunity for political participation. Regimes that deny access to power and persecute dissenters create dissatisfaction."[240] Twenty years before September 11, Crenshaw was thinking of terrorists in 1870s czarist Russia, but the Saudis who hijacked planes on September 11 to express their objection to US-Saudi policy in their country could not make those claims politically in Saudi Arabia either. Crenshaw went on to point out, intriguingly, that "terrorism is essentially the result of elite disaffection; it represents the strategy of . . . Combining the intermediate causes of a lack of political participation and elite dissatisfaction . . . Perhaps terrorism is most likely to occur precisely where mass passivity and elite dissatisfaction coincide. Discontent is not generalized or severe enough to provoke the majority of the populace to action against the regime, yet a small minority, without access to the bases of power that would permit over-throw of the government through coup d'état or subversion, seeks radical change."[241]

At the third level, dynamic causality would consider the immediate trigger that drives a small, dissatisfied group to terrorist acts. For a hundred years, governments have overreacted, pushing dissidents toward terrorism. An "unexpected and unusual force in response to protest or reform attempts often compels terrorist retaliation," noted Crenshaw. "There are numerous historical examples of a campaign of terrorism precipitated by a government's reliance on excessive force to quell protest or squash dissent." She cited crackdowns by the czar, the British execution of Irish leaders, and the nineteenth-century French government's repression of anarchists as precipitating terrorist responses.

Since September 11, our fear of terrorism has particularly focused on suicide bombings. Recently, Robert Pape studied every suicide bombing he could find for twenty years and concluded that occupying a territory is the leading cause of suicide bombing.[242] Pape found that an astonishing "95 percent of the suicide attacks were in response to a military occupation."[243] Whether the French colonization of Algeria that triggered FLN terrorism in the 1950s, or Israeli and US troops in Lebanon that bin Laden cited as motivation for September 11, a foreign power occupying a community proves particularly incendiary.

Pape also found that such terrorism works: for people with few other ways to fight occupation, suicide bombings killed large numbers of people, and often extracted costs big enough that the occupying army withdrew, like the US Marines who left Lebanon after 241 were killed by a 1983 suicide mission.

Military escalation is counterproductive, states negotiate, individual attacks are legitimated by being compared to war, and terrorism recedes when troops leave. Do less. Deescalate. Negotiate. Move on.

From my observations of Battery Park City after September 11 and after Hurricane Sandy, terrorism and climate change look like different sides of the same coin, both in terms of the neighborhood displacement they triggered in New York City, and the patterns in causal explanations. The insightful observations by Crenshaw and Pape nevertheless fall into the trap of explaining social facts (terrorism) with recourse only to other social facts (repressive political regimes, occupying armies). The nonsocial factors that we overlook tell us something useful about terrorism we otherwise miss. As usual, a crucial factor we ignore is the spatial component.

As Eyal Weizman has pointed out, the Middle East is bordered by the so-called aridity line, the edge beyond which the environment is too dry to farm conventionally.[244] Along that line, to give one example, Syria recorded its worst drought on record, which displaced farmers and 1.5 million people within Syria, contributing to the conditions that led to civil war and the terrorism of the Islamic State. More strikingly, Weizman found that Western drone strikes followed the line of aridity from Western Africa, across Northern Africa, through the Arabian Peninsula, and across central and South Asia. From this angle, we can see that there is a natural and spatial component to social violence. Terrorism looks very different as a symptom of an environmental problem the world already needs to address, rather than as an ideological war we've vowed to fight.

CLIMATE CHANGE

Climate change presents us with a challenge beyond just responding to the intimidating, global danger: we need to convince other people of the need to take action. Once again, the natural problem recedes to the background, and we spend more time thinking about the social problem. And so, it's worth asking if we'd even want to convert deniers into participants in climate change response. Why not, instead, shift our focus to actually developing responses, and minimizing the political friction that could arise?

Climate change is not hard to grasp, and it's not new. It was as early as 1824 that Joseph Fourier first theorized that burning fossil fuels would increase global temperatures; by 1896 Swedish chemist Svante Arrhenius's calculations of the effect of doubling the amount of carbon dioxide in the air were within the range of predictions from the most advanced models today.[245] Nor is the evidence for climate change obscure or distant; to the contrary it appears unambiguous to any casual examination: For those of a quantitative bent, the level of carbon in the air has increased 43 percent, from 280 parts per million to 400 parts per million, a level the Earth has not experienced in 3 million years.[246] For those struck by superlatives, every month for the last thirty years has been hotter than that month's historical average.[247] For those who are more visually oriented, there are photos of glaciers that have shrunk dramatically in recent years. Against those who hope that this is just a periodic fluctuation in the Earth's temperature and not an upward trend, imagine how many brutal winters, or how many summers blotted out by a major volcanic eruption (and thus how many failed crops) would be needed to restock the ice and snow in global glaciers. No matter what you believe the Earth is doing, the only thing it can't do is go back to the way it was a few years ago. The climate is changing, and those changes will permanently alter the weather and sea level, and adversely affect current agriculture.

Climate change clearly poses a natural problem as well as a social problem. Dynamic causality can help us understand the problem on both of these seemingly separate levels. Our response to the natural force of climate change, after all, will require a collective and social response.

It is not impossible for us to address climate change—millions of people already are. Climate deniers are not simply evolutionarily and cognitively obstructed in trying to grasp the problem. Climate deniers are also socially, politically, economically, and dispositionally inclined to reject the problem. We make choices about how we frame the story of climate change, and the story we choose has consequences for both how we try to respond, and who our allies are.

As we've seen, for a causal story to be meaningful to people, the cause needs a moral component. The issue of climate change demonstrates the stakes in identifying the moral component. Although people who recognize the reality of climate change believe it is the Right who has mixed politics and morality into climate change, this is not entirely evident.

George Marshall, who studies climate change debates, looked at the connection between the stories we tell and the actions we want taken on climate change.[248] Marshall found that a compelling story has four elements: cause, effect, perpetrator, and motive. For climate deniers, those elements can coalesce in statements like: Governments (perpetrators) pass environmental rules (cause) that control our lives (effect) because they think they know better than us (motive).[249] It's no coincidence that those among us who are most likely to accept the reality of climate change are more likely to have a world view that agrees with the perpetrator, cause, effect, and motive found in accounts of climate change such as: Corporations (perpetrators) spew chemicals out of their smokestacks (cause) even though they disrupt the climate (effect) because all they care about is making money (motive). If you believe corporations do harmful things, that statement is consistent with your beliefs. If, in your view, corporations are good guys, bringing us great products, making life better, and making money doing it, then that statement is hard to swallow, or even square with what you know about businesses. Given the world's predominate causal story of climate change, godless communists are at an ideological advantage to accept climate change. If the scientific consensus was that climate change was caused by the Devil, Christian capitalists would be the ones with a story they could believe.

Even people who recognize the real dangers of climate change identify their favorite "enemies" as culprits: people who campaign against oil companies blame oil companies, people who oppose American consumerism blame excessive consumption, farm activists blame Big Agriculture. It's not that they're wrong, but it's also true that climate-minded people emphasize reducing the use of things they already don't like. So we *can* blame capitalism for climate change, but we don't have to. We could frame it differently, as, for instance, the inevitable result of smart primates finding out that they can get great things out of burning the coal and oil that's in the Earth.

As long as we blame capitalism, people who defend capitalism will take a defensive position. Thus, one way beyond the current climate debates is to change the causal story. Rising temperatures can be the fault of human nature (we're innovators and energy burners), or a growing population, or more people wanting to live like the West lives. Hell, if people's goal is just to get others to admit the temperatures are rising dangerously, all this heat can be the result of the Devil directing fire at a hubristic and sinful world.

The more important question is what to do. Facing climate change, we are often faced with two types of responses, to be mixed and matched in some proportion: mitigation and adaptation. Mitigation aims to reduce the amount of warming (by decreasing the amount of fossil fuels burned, for instance). Adaptation seeks to adjust to rising temperatures, and the related fallout.

How we frame a problem typically influences the response we take to it—whether we try to stop fossil fuel burning, rain forest leveling, cattle ranching, or sinful behavior. Adaptation is inevitable. Millions of people have already been displaced by climate change. While there is talk about mitigation, there is immediate need for adaptation—and there will be no matter what mitigation measures the world might put into effect.

The Intergovernmental Panel on Climate Change has presented four different mitigation scenarios, from severe greenhouse gas reduction to continued high emissions.[250] Because carbon stays in the atmosphere, all four involve roughly similar temperature rises in the short term. Temperatures will remain "at elevated levels for many centuries" even if there were to be "a complete cessation" of carbon usage. Even the most stringent scenario can't halt a sea-level rise of a foot and a half by the end of the century. There's no turning back.

The dominant framing—that climate change is human caused, the very perspectives that make conservatives into climate deniers—leads to recommendations that seem beside the point. Individual-level solutions make good stories, and make some people feel good. But for a problem of global scale, individual steps for people to take at home are often insignificant. A piece in *Scientific American* titled "10 Solutions for Climate Change" starts off talking about reducing fossil fuels.[251] Fair enough. Its third suggestion is "Move Closer to Work," on the assumption that such moves can reduce commutes. But if a thoughtful environmentalist sells their cabin in the woods two hours from the city and moves to an apartment on a bus line, won't the person who buys that cabin move into it and have a long commute? By suggestion number four, *Scientific American* is telling readers to stop climate change—the three-foot rise of the ocean, the possible collapse of the Greenland ice sheets, drought, and species extinction—by "employing a reusable grocery sack." This, unfortunately, validates the individual consumer gestures that a minuscule fraction of the Earth's population—the fraction that consumes the most resources and produces the most greenhouse gases, not coincidentally—makes to feel like they're part of the solution when the problem rages unchecked, irrespective of their shopping choices. Even suggestions for big-ticket items—"if you are in the market for a new car, buy one that will last the longest and have the least impact on the environment" don't seem scaled to IPCC reports, in which the only scenario to actually stop global warming would almost inevitably require all cars on Earth to burn no gasoline in just thirty-four years.

This critique is not to argue that mitigation is futile; the speed with which glaciers deteriorate, or ocean levels rise, depends on how much mitigation we can enact. My point is that conditions have already changed, and will continue to change, for centuries at least. Mitigation can be a goal, but adaptation is unavoidable. I happen to be skeptical that the planet will soon reduce, much less eliminate, carbon emissions. When presidential candidate Hillary Clinton called for "half a billion new solar panels,"[252] it seemed obvious to me that without other restrictions, the US economy would just add that electricity to the energy it already produces with fossil fuels: an additional source of electricity could produce more products, light more highways, power longer vacations in electric cars, illuminate new, brighter signs and billboards. Or oil companies in Canada, or the United States for that matter, could sell the petroleum and natural gas that Americans didn't buy to the Europeans and Chinese. Solar power can be a real part of a real mitigation scenario, but not if it's a feel-good proposal unconnected to policies that actually reduce fossil fuel extraction.

Mitigation could be enormously effective and save millions of lives. There are no simple responses, but meaningful responses are not inconceivable. As a very rough example, most sources calculate that total US energy appetite today could be met with the equivalent of a block of solar panels 132 miles square.[253] (On a map of the United States that was 12 inches by 20 inches, the solar panels, if in one place, would take up the space of a postage stamp.) This is not a solution. (It would generate no power at night, require massive quantities of raw materials, cost perhaps the whole federal budget to install, and still leave oil pumping.) But Clinton's ambition was not impossible, only missing the key elements that would actually leave carbon in the ground. A dramatic mitigation strategy suggests that even the seemingly idealistic IPCC scenario of zero fossil fuel burning is in the range of consideration.

But note what solar panels would not do: they would not require the dismantling of modern capitalism. People could still carry groceries in disposable plastic bags, drive home in big (electric-powered) SUVs, and eat dinner sold in plastic wrap. The moral critique inherent in the causal story of climate change is not inevitably part of the response to planetary warming.

This is contrary to conventional wisdom about climate change. Scientists often exclaim that "adaptation is agnostic!" meaning that it makes sense to move to higher ground whether or not one acknowledges the rising seas are caused by human activity or imagines (as deniers do) that it is a natural process.[254] I would suggest the opposite: *mitigation* is agnostic and can be pursued without a critique of capitalism. In contrast, it is a humane pursuit of adaptation that requires a noncapitalist mindset.

Any adaptation strategy needs to find as humane a way as possible to help millions of existing and future climate refugees (from flooding, drought, rising seas, agricultural disruption, and civil war) redistribute food globally to address food shortages from local climate change and address social conflicts that may result from these crises. Every region will have consequences, but poorer people, internationally and locally, are more likely to suffer more severe consequences, and they have fewer resources to address those emergencies.

Adaptation is a huge undertaking, and we needed it a decade ago. The numbers in need are growing. With more of a focus on adaptation and less on the social conflict of the debate over climate change itself, the response to climate change looks different. As George Marshall argues, there is no solution to climate change. There are only responses. Such responses would require organizations or pacts of mutual aid. Food would need to be available during famine. Refugees would need the right to escape disasters and wars. To develop such agreements, we would need people's participation (and commitment) over sustained, difficult periods. For it to work, nations would need to commit significant resources to the needs of other countries, either in the belief that they themselves might need help later, or because they were obligated to do so and could not get out of it. Incidentally, such support systems would work equally well whether disasters were caused by climate change or not, and so much the better.

Adequate adaptation requires that people embrace the morality of the causal explanation. In the past, the wealthy in the global North made insufficient efforts to improve the lives of the disadvantaged. Victims of famine in the nineteenth-century colonies were dismissed as having brought the catastrophe on themselves, the troubles of the poor were blamed on them not working hard enough, and when any of those excuses failed, there was always recourse to racism or religious doctrine that suggested that the suffering group were either inherently inferior or meant to suffer by divine design.

The wealthy cannot in good faith "blame the victim" in a climate-changing world. The narrative makes clear that it was the rich whose excessive consumption, extraction, and incineration drove climate change. The only decent thing to do is to establish networks at local, regional, national, and international levels to be ready to aid the poor and victimized who already are, and will continue to be, harmed and imperiled by climate change.

The conservative alternative to embracing this moral could be called Build a Wall. (Donald Trump's most famous campaign promise to build a wall against Mexico was in fact his climate change policy.) That policy could mean attacking other countries to seize and hoard resources, then barricading the powerful countries (or the powerful people within them) to keep out others as they drown. It's not that the only response to climate change is a left wing, social democratic sharing-of-the-burden response, it's that the right's traditional response to scarcity is socially unacceptable, and so indefensible it cannot be proposed. It's inhuman and morally repugnant. That's why I would argue that it's better that conservatives keep denying climate change: so they don't get involved in preparing for it. Right-wing strategies are a disaster: the right's response to terrorism was a disaster of counterproductive torture and military occupation. The right's response to civil rights was a Southern Strategy of rearguard race-baiting. The right's response to social progress was neoliberal insecurity that soaked into our blood in the form of an obesity epidemic. We'll be better off developing a climate change response against their simple denial and obstructionism than in the face of their more dangerous, literal barricading.

Dynamic causality therefore proposes a new kind of narrative for climate change, even for progressives. This new story thinks beyond egocentric causality—for many of the responses to climate change, it is better if we *do not* focus on the role of people in the center of the narrative as causal actors. People caused these changes, but we can't wind back the clock. Nor is it most effective to attack climate change with a victor/victim strategy that expects solutions or victories, or allows us to proclaim our innocence (as victims) while naming others as enemies (and us as victors). Instead, climate change is a massively complex process on a global scale, over which we have very little control. Because the waters are rising, we have no choice but to adapt. As with the most reliable forms of conspiracy theories, even if we don't fully understand or agree on the mechanisms of climate change, we can still foresee the general outcomes and act on those expectations.

RACE

Racism often compounds the damage from climate change and makes the war on terror that much more severe. It is a disaster multiplier that dehumanizes people, makes them more vulnerable, and leads those in power to make bad decisions, at the exact moments that minority communities need the most help.

Progress toward racial equality can be categorized into three general types. First is the strategy of changing hearts and minds—of convincing white people, for instance, to not be racist. This is a terrific idea, but to the degree that racial attitudes improve, they often follow, rather than precede, other changes.

Next are strategies of political power: protests that force government to improve conditions. The Fair Housing Act or the federal affirmative action programs for government contractors did not come as a result of changing hearts and minds; Nixon implemented affirmative actions after all, a substantial majority of whites opposed both, and judging from recent electoral referendums, a majority oppose affirmative action to this day. Such programs were implemented because civil rights leaders demanded that government officials and business leaders change practices.

The third category includes unintentional change, like the shifting racial identity of powerful adversaries in wartime. Changes in the political landscape can give activists new leverage in their campaigns. Occasionally, policies not intended to help racial minorities may still do so, but in such situations, such as the expansion of Social Security and wage regulations, from which industries with large numbers of Black workers were initially excluded, those policies did not change themselves.

Clearly, all three types of challenges can be useful. Politics in the United States has always been more about race than class, as evinced by the framing of the Constitution, Westward Expansion, the Civil War, Dixiecrats, Civil Rights, the Southern Strategy, and the Reagan Revolution. Antiracist politics have used political power to strip segregationists of tools like restrictive covenants or legally segregated schools, changes that have benefitted African Americans and immigrants in the decades since. Many people have also changed their attitudes about race, as polls show slowly increasing support for such basic concepts as the ban on housing discrimination and support for interracial marriage (up to a still-paltry 87 percent from a minority 48 percent as recently as 1995).[255] Other actions have unintentionally changed the racial landscape, as segregation rates have declined because of immigration and gentrification.

The themes in this book outline some of the ways activists are challenging racial inequality. Understanding races as categories of denied citizenship points to the need to demand full citizenship at every turn. Police cannot control and patrol communities of color as if they are occupied places. In this respect current movements against police brutality are central to securing the right to the city—the right of anyone to move to any neighborhood—which can be won only when the police protect rather than threaten people of color. Only when most African Americans feel safe entering into majority white areas will segregation rates decline significantly.

The right to the city can be achieved under the present political configuration, because it involves getting police to do only what they are legally supposed to do already. Critical work toward economic and educational equality requires more active involvement by the state, which determines the rules by which we live our economic lives.

The era of the Southern Strategy slowed social progress. But will the Republican strategy of anti-Black race-baiting hold? If it does not, more progress could be made toward racial and economic equality. Consider the possible outcomes of two issues we have discussed. First, while the country is slated to become majority nonwhite by 2043, the definition of who is "white" and who is "nonwhite" changes over time, with the possibility that descendants of immigrants today could vote with whites or with people of color. Second, the Republicans' strategy of winning white voters through a politics of resentment will become more difficult because sympathetic white voters make up a smaller and smaller percentage of the electorate.

The question then becomes whether Latino, Asian, and other voters of color will ally themselves electorally in 2043 with other people of color, or along other lines. Although the Democratic Party has long been the party of immigrants (even before it was the party of Black voters), Republicans nabbed more and more of those votes as immigrant generations assimilated. White ethnics started Democratic and became increasingly Republican as they moved out of ethnic enclaves and into suburbs. Will the same thing happen again?

Evidence suggests that people of color tend to resist this trend: Asian voters, particularly young voters, are becoming *more* Democratic. Only 31 percent of Asian Americans voted for Bill Clinton in 1992, 43 percent in 1996. Democratic polling among Asian voters continued to climb, so that, in 2016, Hillary Clinton polled 65 percent among Asians. The election was exceptional, featuring especially hostile anti-immigrant rhetoric, but Asian American voting trends continued their long arc.[256] Latino voting patterns have changed less; already being predominantly Democratic they have remained so and also came in at 65 percent for Clinton.[257]

Political parties can be stymied by their own ideology, unable to adjust messages to gain new voters when they are central to the origins of the old guard. Whether Republicans make serious efforts to attract new voters will shape the electoral map and may reshape our larger racial categories as well.

There is nothing inevitable about 2043, but if Americans took it as an opportunity to redefine their national identity—perhaps as a New World racial hybrid, one whose history of immigration, slavery, and genocide created not a country whose ideology looked to Europe (or ancient Rome and Greece) for inspiration, but saw itself as part of the Americas, a millennium-long experiment in modern global population movement—it could contribute the momentum needed to lead the government to protect, rather than disregard, people of color in times of economic crisis like the foreclosure debacle. Reparations, particularly for slavery but for other racial crimes as well, is like an electric fence that no mainstream political candidate will touch. But if reparations means doing whatever is needed to create racial equality in a land built on inequality, then reparations is just equality, and no more or less realistic than that.

There is little time to achieve this equality, and all three strategies will be necessary: political pressure, hearts and minds, and unintended consequences. Especially in light of an impending crisis like climate change, we must make everyone a more secure member of the social community, because it is in crises that people are suddenly most vulnerable. Like the debate over torture, we will encounter baldly misleading narratives that can divide and derail such a unitary effort. In addition to the necessary campaigns of increasing incomes and education, ensuring the right to the city through police reform and desegregation, we need to make sure that displaced communities (increasing in number with climate change and disproportionately, although by no means only, poor and people of color) obtain the respect and generosity they deserve. Likewise, the counterproductive responses to terrorism are driven by narratives that rely on simplistic, often racialized tropes of good and bad. The way that race shapes what we see and don't see, the stories we believe, and the structures we don't realize we can alter means that dynamic causality requires rethinking racial categories in a way that will lead to their disassembly.

Forward Motion

Life is a race, an unnervingly brief one, and we have to draw the map on the fly. The great benefit of dynamic causality is that it functions as conditions evolve, looking deep for answers but recognizing that our most solid assumptions, from racial categories to political affiliations to where dry land ends and ocean begins, are not as fixed as we imagine.

We will always reason like people, magnifying some explanations and diminishing others. But we can check ourselves when falling into old storytelling ruts: Are we reasoning from hypothetical stories like the ticking time bomb? Are our stories too consistent with our society's pre-existing fears and anxieties (about sex, race, terrorists)? Are we assuming that another actor must be behaving in a way that is meant to affect us? Are we acting out of fear and anger emanating from our own dual sense of being prey and predator? Dynamic causality appreciates these reflexes of our primate mind and our social reasoning, but does not leave us hapless prisoners to those tendencies.

Replacing my old ways of seeing the world with new ones is a singu-lar thrill in my life and something that this book has been built around. When I conduct fieldwork, assumptions I start out with are inevitably knocked off their foundations. Seeking better models to explain the world I encounter in research is what led me to concepts like allostasis, egocentric causality, Barbara Ehrenreich's blood rites, the role of space in social conflicts, and dynamic causality. I embrace them not for their novelty, but because they fulfill an urgent need to understand the world better than conventional models do.

We don't have to be perfect at determining cause and effect—we'll never be armed with all of the necessary data in real time—but we can certainly do better. We can step back, for just a moment, and assess what has worked before in a broad sample of comparable situations. We can integrate observations from a wider range of scientific and social scien-tific fields than we often do now. We can determine the nonsocial factors at play in a given situation, and tailor our social responses to interact with them.

With this deepened, dynamic view of causality in mind, we can embrace the fact that knowledge is social, and engage larger groups of people, allies and opponents, in the process of problem solving. We will always have a unique and abiding love of our own humanness. Understanding how uniquely human our thoughts really are will help us preserve and enhance what we love.

acknowledgments

This book was inspired by the stories of participants in my field research and by the insights of students in the classroom. I owe a great debt to everyone involved in those projects. The big secret of teaching is how much you learn when you're supposedly the teacher, and any claim to expertise in a field of research comes from working with people who see far more in the field than the researcher ever can.

This book was intimidating to undertake, because it took me out of the comfort of academic writing. Mark Krotov encouraged me to even propose it out loud. Liza Featherstone offered valuable guidance early on. Along the way, I received unanticipated encouragement, and careful readings, from people who spent time on early drafts and gently nudged me when I needed it. A writing group of my friends and colleagues read some of the earliest drafts; my profound thanks to John Krinsky and Rich Ocejo. James D'Angelo reminded me of the importance of telling a story, especially in a book about stories. Judah Grunstein couldn't be a better friend, and read the whole manuscript and sent transatlantic handwritten notes about each chapter. Colleagues at EHESS (the School of Advanced Study in the Social Sciences) in Paris went out of their way to accommodate me while I spent a year researching and writing at the Institut Marcel Mauss there. I turned to people with specialized knowledge to comb through particular chapters and got invaluable insight and advice from Jennifer Reich, Philip Kasinitz, Alan Takeall, Susan Clampet-Lundquist, Joseph Entin, and Alexandra Murphy, though they bear no responsibility for the elaborations I make beyond their unimpeachable expertise. Jay Schulkin sat down in Georgetown and talked about allostasis when he had never met me. At Melville House, my editor Ryan Harrington gave me the most thorough edits I've ever been lucky enough to receive. My colleagues across Brooklyn College and the larger republic of the City University of New York provided the intellectual environment a book like this needed. A special thanks to my family, especially my kids, Una and Eamon, who were so close to the project that they're the first to call out egocentric causality when they see it. I love you so much. This is for you.

endnotes

[1] Kevin Sack, "A TB Patient Turns to His Inner Lawyer," *The New York Times*, June 8, 2007.

[2] Ross A. McFarland and Ronald C. Moore, "Human Factors in Highway Safety," *New England Journal of Medicine* (April 25, 1957), p. 797.

[3] John McCain and Mark Salter, *Faith of My Fathers: A Family Memoir* (New York: Random House, 1999), p. 206.

[4] McCain has taken positions against physical torture but said little about solitary confinement. He said about waterboarding, which the US inflicted on prisoners during the so-called war on terror, "It's torture. It's in violation of the Geneva Conventions, of the international agreement on torture, treaty on torture signed during the Reagan administration. It goes all the way back to the Spanish inquisition. It is not a new technique and it is certainly torture." McCain on "On the Record," Fox News, May 21, 2009. Transcript: http://www.foxnews.com/story/2009/05/22/sen-john-mccain-on-record-on-torture-pelosi-and-more. Video: https://www.youtube.com/watch?v=fvjn5cKQHQg. He had criticized waterboarding during the 2008 presidential campaign when other Republican candidates did not label the practice torture. But although he introduced a bill to

limit Army interrogation to procedures in the Army Field Manual, he has not spoken out when the US has held POWs or US citizens in solitary confinement.

[5]Testimony of Michael B. Mushlin, "Briefing On Solitary Confinement: Connecticut Advisory Committee To The U.S. Commission On Civil Rights," Hartford, Connecticut, February 7, 2017, p. 4, referencing dismissals of suits brought under the Prison Litigation Reform Act. Solitary is defined as mental torture by Michael Mushlin, a member of the Correctional Association of New York. See "Breeding Psychotics," *The New York Times,* March 27, 2005. http://query.nytimes.com/gst/fullpage.html?res =9802E6DE173FF934A15750C0A9639C8B63.

[6]Atul Gawande, "Hellhole: The United States Holds Tens Of Thousands Of Inmates In Long-Term Solitary Confinement. Is This Torture?" *New Yorker,* March 30, 2009.

[7]Brandon Keim, "The Horrible Psychology of Solitary Confinement," *Wired,* July 10, 2013. http://www.wired.com/wiredscience/2013/07/solitary-confinement-2.

[8]Stuart Grassian, "Psychiatric Effects of Solitary Confinement," *Journal of Law and Policy* 22 (2006), pp. 325–383, p. 331. http://openscholarship.wustl.edu/law_journal _law_policy/vol22/iss1.

[9]Josh Fattal, Sarah Shourd, and Shane Bauer, *A Sliver of Light: Three Americans Imprisoned in Iran* (New York: Houghton Mifflin Harcourt, 2014).

[10]Ramin Skibba, "Solitary Confinement Screws up The Brains of Prisoners," *Newsweek,* April 18, 2017. http://www.newsweek.com/2017/04/28/solitary-confinement-prisoners-behave-badly-screws-brains-585541.html.

[11]Grassian, 2006.

[12]P. Herbert Liederman, "Man Alone: Sensory Deprivation and Behavioral Change," *Correctional Psychiatry & J. Soc. Therapy* 64, 66 (vol. 8, 1962), cited in Grassian, p. 341.

[13]Grassian, 2006, p. 342.

[14]134 US 160 (1890) cited in Grassian, p. 329.

[15]Daniel Defoe, *The Life and Adventures of Robinson Crusoe* (London: Seeley, Service & Co, 1919 [1719]).

[16]Ulla Grapard and Gillian Hewitson, eds., *Robinson Crusoe's Economic Man: A Construction and Deconstruction* (London: Routledge, 2011).

[17]Grassian, 2006, p. 361.

[18]Woodes Rogers, *A Cruising Voyage Round the World: First to the South-Seas, thence to the East Indies, and Homewards by the Cape of Good Hope* (London: A. Bell, 1712), p. 126.

[19]Tim Severin, *Seeking Robinson Crusoe* (New York: Macmillan, 2002).

[20]Henry Pitman, "A Relation of the Great Sufferings and Strange Adventures of Henry Pitman, 1689," in *An English Garner: Stuart Tracts 1603–1693*, ed. Thomas Seccombe (New York: E.P. Dutton and Co., 1903), pp. 431–476.

[21] Grassian, 2006, pp. 363–364.

[22] Cited in Grassian, 2006, p. 358.

[23] Kurt H. Wolff, *The Sociology of Georg Simmel*, (New York: Free Press, 1950), p. 122.

[24] Brent Schlender, "Larry Ellison 'The Internet changes everything,' and the CEO of Oracle is living proof," *Fortune* via *CNN Money*, May 24, 1999. http://money.cnn.com /magazines/fortune/fortune_archive/1999/05/24/260276.

[25] Bill Gates, *Business @ The Speed Of Thought: Succeeding in the Digital Economy* (New York: Warner Books, 1999).

[26] Bill Bryson, *Made in America: An Informal History of the English Language in the United States* (London: Black Swan, 1998), p. 184.

[27] Data is from the United Nations Population Division. Accessed from http://en.wiki-pedia.org/wiki/List_of_countries_by_infant_mortality_rate, January 10, 2014.

[28] Elijah Wald, *How the Beatles Killed Rock and Roll: An Alternative History of American Popular Music* (New York: Oxford University Press, 2011).

[29] Kenneth T. Jackson, *Crabgrass Frontier: The Suburbanization of the United States* (New York: Oxford University Press, 1985, p. 280).

[30] Betty Friedan, *The Feminine Mystique* (New York: Norton, 1963).

[31] Claudia Goldin, Lawrence F. Katz, and Ilyana Kuziemko, "The Homecoming of American College Women: The Reversal of the College Gender Gap," *Journal of Economic Perspectives* 20, No. 4 (Fall 2006), pp. 133–156.

[32] Herbert Gans, *The Levittowners: Ways of Life and Politics in a New Suburban Community* (New York: Pantheon Books, 1967). (For my younger readers, yes, there was a time when calling someone more than about an hour from where you lived cost money by the minute, and people carefully rationed those calls.)

[33] Gans, 1967, p. 272.

[34] William H. Whyte, *City: Rediscovering the Center* (New York: Doubleday, 1988), p. 8.

[35] Richard J. Whalen, *A City Destroying Itself: An Angry View of New York (*New York: William Morrow, 1965). Eric M. Javits, *SOS New York: A City in Distress* (New York: Dial Press, 1961), p. 124.

[36] My reactionary Republican father always confessed with frustration of Jane Fonda, "I *hated* her politics! But I always loved her movies." (Fonda had outraged some when she visited Hanoi during the Vietnam War in opposition to the war and accused US pilots of war crimes.) He wanted to hate her films, but he didn't. I don't know that it would comfort him that I don't have any problem with her politics, but don't like *Barefoot in the Park* all that much.

[37] Douglas Martin, "Charles Tilly, Writer and a Social Scientist, is Dead," *The New York Times*, May 2, 2008.

[38]Charles Tilly, *Why: What Happens When People Give Reasons . . . and Why* (Princeton, NJ: Princeton University Press, 2006).

[39]Tilly, 2006, p. 17.

[40]Tilly, 2006, p. 17. Influences that storytellers ignore (but researchers can measure) include indirect effects, incremental effects, simultaneous effects, feedback effects, and environmental effects.

[41]Trump said, "Hey, I watched when the World Trade Center came tumbling down. And I watched in Jersey City, New Jersey, where thousands and thousands of people were cheering as that building was coming down. Thousands of people were cheering." Glenn Kessler, "Trump's Outrageous Claim That 'Thousands' Of New Jersey Muslims Celebrated The 9/11 Attacks," *Washington Post,* November 22, 2015. https://www.washingtonpost.com/news/fact-checker/wp/2015/11/22/donald -trumps-outrageous-claim-that-thousands-of-new-jersey-muslims-celebrated-the -911-attacks/?tid=a_inl&utm_term=.7e4ca1cf103a.

[42]"Were Israelis Detained on September 11 Spies?" ABC News, June 21, 2002. http: //web.archive.org/web/20020802194310/http://abcnews.go.com/sections/2020 /DailyNews/2020_whitevan_020621.html. Sources sympathetic to Trump, such as Breitbart, have cited a *Washington Post* story, among others, as evidence Trump was not wrong. The *Post* article reported on September 18 that "law enforcement authorities detained and questioned a number of people who were allegedly seen celebrating the attacks and holding tailgate-style parties on rooftops while they watched the devastation on the other side of the river." The account matches that of the Israeli movers, but pro-Trump articles stop at that quote rather than providing details about the actual story, which would disqualify the quote as evidence that Muslims, by the thousands, were celebrating. Serge F. Kovaleski and Fredrick Kunkle, "Northern New Jersey Draws Probers' Eyes," *Washington Post*, September 18, 2001. https://www.washingtonpost.com/archive/politics/2001/09/18/northern -new-jersey-draws-probers-eyes/40f82ea4-e015-4d6e-a87e-93aa433fafdc/?utm _term=.f266602ddc20.

[43]Al Guard, "Trio Who Cheered Attack Face Boot As Illegal Aliens," *New York Post*, September 13, 2001. http://nypost.com/2001/09/13/trio-who-cheered-attack-face-boot- as-illegal-aliens.

[44]Marc Perelman, "Spy Rumors Fly on Gusts of Truth," *Forward*, March 15, 2002. http://forward.com/news/national/325698/spy-rumors-fly-on-gusts-of-truth.

[45]"Were Israelis Detained on Sept. 11 Spies?," ABC News. The source cites the anonymously sourced *Forward* article and adds commentary by a retired investigator not involved in the investigation.

[46]Tamar Lewin and Alison Leigh Cowan, "Dozens of Israeli Jews Are Being Kept in Federal Detention" *The New York Times*, November 21, 2001. http://www.nytimes.com/2001/11/21/us/nation-challenged-detainees-dozens-israeli-jews-are-being-kept-federal-detention.html. Yossi Melman, "5 Israelis Detained for Puzzling Behavior After WTC Tragedy," *Haaretz*, September 17, 2001. http://www.haaretz.com/5-israelis-detained-for-puzzling-behavior-after-wtc-tragedy-1.70005.

[47]Joe McGinniss, *Fatal Vision* (New York: Signet, 1983). Errol Morris, *Wilderness of Error* (New York: Penguin Press, 2012). Janet Malcolm, *The Journalist and the Murderer* (New York: Knopf, 1990).

[48]Michael Omi, Howard Winant, *Racial Formation in the United States: From the 1960s to the 1990s*, 2nd ed. (New York: Routledge, 1994), p. 55.

[49]Charles Tilly, *Durable Inequalities* (Berkeley: University of California Press, 1999).

[50]Vijay Prashad, *Karma of Brown Folk* (Minneapolis: University of Minnesota Press, 2001), p. 72.

[51]The Luce–Celler Act of 1946 allowed 100 Filipinos and 100 Indians to immigrate with the possibility of becoming naturalized citizens, creating an exception to the whiteness requirement adjudicated in 1923. In 1952 the Immigration and Nationality Act was passed eliminating other racial restrictions, but still limited the number of "Asian" immigrants by race, no matter what their nationality in the world.

[52]Kevin M. Kruse, *White Flight: Atlanta and the Making of Modern Conservatism* (Princeton: Princeton University Press, 2007).

[53]Craig Wilder, *A Covenant with Color: Race and Social Power in Brooklyn* (New York: Columbia University Press, 2000), p. 15.

[54]On how people like Ralph Waldo Emerson imagined the mysterious Oriental other to be different from the rational Westerner, see Prashad, *Karma of Brown Folk*.

[55]Note that these three categories are less complete in areas with different histories of racialization, such as Hawaii; the American Southwest, which was Mexican before it was American; and US territories such as Puerto Rico, which developed categories in a different historical experience than the eastern United States.

[56]I use the term after Nell Irvin Painter's use of it in *The History of White People* (New York, Norton, 2010), pp. 37–38.

[57]Risjord argues that "a cursory glance at the statistics . . . will show that the War of 1812 was the most uneconomic war the United States has every fought." Norman K. Risjord, "1812: Conservatives, War Hawks, and the Nation's Honor," *William And Mary Quarterly* (1961) 18(2): 196–210.

[58]H. W. Brands, *Andrew Jackson: His Life and Times* (Random House Digital, 2006), p. 163.

[59] More and less powerful groups outside the United States get conflated in the way we conflate predator and prey, as seen in the next chapter.

[60] Painter, 2010, p. 360.

[61] "Every white male citizen of the United States, and every white male citizen of Mexico . . ." Constitution of the State of California, 1849. Cal. Const. art. I, §4, cl.2.

[62] Painter, 2010, p. 360.

[63] Margaret Montoya, "A Brief History of Chicana/o School Segregation: One Rationale for Affirmative Action," *Berkeley La Raza Law Journal* 12, no. 2 (2001), p. 166.

[64] Roy E. Horton, III, "Out Of (South) Africa: Pretoria's Nuclear Weapons Experience," INSS Occasional Paper 27, Counterproliferation Series (United States Air Force Institute for National Security Studies, United States Air Force Academy, Colorado), August 1999. http://permanent.access.gpo.gov/lps4417/www.usafa.af.mil/inss/OCP/ocp27.pdf.

[65] Zondi Masiza, "A Chronology of South Africa's Nuclear Program," *Nonproliferation Review*, Fall 1993, pp. 35–55, p. 44.

[66] Masiza, 1993.

[67] Horton, 1999, p. 31.

[68] David Albright and Mark Hibbs, "South Africa: The ANC and the Atom Bomb," *Bulletin of the Atomic Scientists*, April 1, 1993. http://docs7.chomikuj.pl/2097156904,PL,0,0,The-ANC-and-the-Atom-Bomb.doc.

[69] Quoted in Mawuna Remarque Koutonin, "The Dark Truth About Why South Africa Destroyed Its Nuclear Weapons in 1990," SiliconAfrica.com, June 17, 2013. http://www.siliconafrica.com/the-dark-truth-about-why-south-africa-destroyed-its-nuclear-weapons-in-1990.

[70] Koutonin, 2013. Apartheid South Africa had also been slowly dismantling their chemical and biological weapons program, which had been aimed (and used) against troops in countries like Mozambique, but also to assassinate specific members of the ANC-led antiapartheid movements. See Stephen Burgess and Helen Purkitt, "The Rollback Of South Africa's Biological Warfare Program," INSS Occasional Paper 37, Counterproliferation Series (United States Air Force Institute for National Security Studies, United States Air Force Academy, Colorado), August 1999. http://permanent.access.gpo.gov/lps4417/www.usafa.af.mil/inss/OCP/ocp37.pdf.

[71] "What, then, shall I say of those . . . who carry their handkerchiefs about in their mouths?" Norbert Elias, *The Civilizing Process: The Development of Manners. Changes in the Code of Conduct and Feeling in Early Modern Times* (New York: Urizen Books, 1978), pp. 143–145.

[72] Painter, 2010.

[73]"More Than 4.5 Million African Americans Now Hold a Four-Year College Degree," *Journal of Blacks in Higher Education,* April 9, 2011. http://www.jbhe.com/news _views/64_degrees.html.

[74]"How Does Race Affect the Gender Wage Gap?" American Association of University Women. April 3, 2014. http://www.aauw.org/2014/04/03/race-and-the-gender-wage-gap.

[75]Barbara Ehrenreich, *Blood Rites: Origins and History of the Passions of War* (New York: Metropolitan Books, 1997).

[76]In French the game is called "cat," making explicit, albeit in domesticated form, that the game is predator-prey play.

[77]Ehrenreich 1997, pp. 10–11. Citing Grossman, p. 28. Grossman also quotes Brigadier General S.L.A Marshall, a World War I veteran who interviewed World War II soldiers. Marshall recalled from his war experiences that "the average and healthy individual . . . has such an inner and usually unrealized resistance towards killing a fellow man that he will not of his own volition take life if it is possible to turn away from that responsibility . . . At the vital point" the soldier "becomes a conscientious objector." A detailed study in World War II found that 85 percent of soldiers did not shoot, even when under fire, and subsequent studies of other wars (and of police officers) found similar percentages. After the Civil War Battle of Gettysburg, 12,000 rifles recovered on the battlefield showed signs that their owners had purposely avoided firing them—such as dutifully loading the weapon multiple times, but never pulling the trigger. Lieutenant Colonel Dave Grossman, *On Killing: The Psychological Cost of Learning to Kill in War and Society* (New York, Little Brown, 1995).

[78]Guillaume Descours, « Une vingtaine de mosquées fermées depuis décembre, annonce Cazeneuve, » *Le Figaro,* January 8, 2016. http://www.lefigaro.fr/actualite-france/2016 /08/01/01016-20160801ARTFIG00129-une-vingtaine-de-mosquees-fermees-depuis-decembre-annonce-cazeneuve.php.

[79]Julia Pascual, « L'état d'urgence repart pour trois mois, malgré un bilan contesté et mitigé, » *Le Monde,* February 25, 2016. http://www.lemonde.fr/recherche/#5A56AmE-2001dQ1bs.99.

[80]According to survivors of the Bataclan attack, the terrorists said, « Ce qui vous arrive, c'est de votre faute. On vient venger nos frères de Syrie. » and « Vous avez tué nos frères en Syrie, nous sommes là maintenant », See the account by Sébastien, and « "Regarde-moi": quand les otages du Bataclan ont été pris à partie par les terroristes, » *Le Nouvel Obs,* November 17, 2016. http://tempsreel.nouvelobs.com/attentats-terroristes-a-paris/20151117.OBS9660/regarde-moi-quand-les-otages-du-bataclan-ont-ete-pris-a-partie-par-les-terroristes.html. « Attaques de Paris : Ceux qui sortaient leurs portables étaient exécutés au Bataclan » *Le Figaro* November 14, 2016. http://www.le-

figaro.fr/culture/2015/11/14/03004-20151114ARTFIG00095-attaques-de-paris-on-a-
bien-vu-les-assaillants-du-bataclan.php.

[81] McKenzie Wark, *The Beach Beneath the Street* (New York: Verso, 2011).

[82] Lest Americans be unjustly proud of their nation's commitment to gender equality, my thanks to McKenzie Wark for pointing out that New York, for instance, had a law on the books at the time allowing the state to make a woman under twenty-one a ward of the court, part of why the artist Samuel Delaney married so young.

[83] Delphine Bancaud, « Rapport de la CNCDH: Pourquoi les clichés antisémites ont pres-péré en 2014, » *20 Minutes*, April 9, 2015. Cited in Thomas Guénolé, *Les jeunes de ban-lieue mangent-ils les enfants?* (Lormont, France: Editions Le Bord de L'Eau, 2015), p. 116.

[84] Richard Hofstadter, *The Paranoid Style in American Politics and Other Essays* (New York: Knopf, Borzoi Books, 1965), p. 32.

[85] Related to the earlier discussion of races becoming invisible, apparently "Johnnie Mae" was a recognizably African American name to white Chicagoans in the 1960s. Norris Vitchek (pseudonym) as told to Alfred Balk, "Confessions of a Block-Buster," *Saturday Evening Post*, July 14–21, 1962.

[86] For instance, see Andrew Wiese's pathbreaking and important history of the suburbs, *Places of Their Own: African American Suburbanization in the Twentieth Century* (Chicago: University of Chicago Press, 2004). Wiese cites Vitchek's article via a master's thesis by Roberta Raymond, who repeats the story as true, though noting that "although there is, from time to time, rumor of panic-peddling in southeast Oak Park, no documentation has yet been provided." Roberta Raymond, "The Challenge to Oak Park: a Suburban Community Faces Racial Change." (Master's Thesis, Roosevelt University, 1972), p. 80. Vitchek is also cited in, among other sources, Talcott Parsons, Kenneth Bancroft Clark, *The Negro American* (Beacon Press, 1969) and in Arnold Hirsch, *Making the Second Ghetto: Race and Housing in Chicago, 1940–1960* (Chicago: University Of Chicago Press, 1998).

[87] For a more detailed examination of "Confessions of a Blockbuster," its origins and meaning, see Gregory Smithsimon, *Liberty Road*, (New York: New York University Press, forthcoming).

[88] Cited in Wiese 2004, 245 who found it in Baxandall and Ewen, *Picture Windows*, 2000, p. 80, who found it in Lawrence Harmon, Hillel Levine, *The Death of an American Jewish Community: A Tragedy of good Intentions* (New York: Free Press, 1992), 195–96, who cite Anonymous, "Confessions of a Blockbuster," *Metropolitan Real Estate Journal*, May 1987, p. 14. That Levine and Harmon no longer have a copy comes from a personal correspondence with Hillel Levine (after checking with Lawrence Harmon), Saturday, October 5, 2013. According to Roger Draper, the second "Confes-

sions" was an anonymous letter to the editor, not an actual article. Roger Draper, "The Death of an American Jewish Community: A Tragedy of Good Intentions" *The New Leader*, December 30, 1991.

[89]Deborah Acosta, "An Improbable Survival," *New York Times*. Video. November 19, 2015. http://www.nytimes.com/video/world/europe/100000004046518/heroes-of-the-bataclan.html.

[90]Text of President George W. Bush's address to joint session of Congress, September 20, 2001. http://www.washingtonpost.com/wp-srv/nation/specials/attacked/transcripts/bushaddress_092001.html.

[91]Although there had been some models of the solar system organized around the sun as early as 150 BC, Copernicus's work wasn't published until 1543. That's late enough to mean, quite stunningly, that in addition to the ignominy that Christopher Columbus did not discover America, that he insisted wrongly his whole life that he had sailed to India, and that he didn't prove Earth was round, he died not knowing that Earth revolved around the sun.

[92]The University of Chicago has long considered itself the birthplace of American sociology, but that history is now contested by those who point to the pioneering work of W.E.B. Du Bois. See Mary Pattillo's review of *The Scholar Denied: W.E.B. Du Bois and the Birth Of Modern Sociology* by Aldon Morris in *City and Community* 15: 2 (2016), pp. 184–186.

[93]Hakim Bey, a problematic author to say the least, is the author of *The Temporary Autonomous Zone, Ontological Anarchy, Poetic Terrorism* (New York: Autonomedia, 1985).

[94]"XII Aniversario de la masacre del 11 M en la Puerta del Sol de Madrid," *Nvarra Informaciones*, March 11, 2016. http://www.navarrainformacion.es/2016/03/11/xii-aniversario-la-masacre-del-11-m-la-puerta-del-sol-madrid. "Un monumento de cristal recuerda en Atocha a las víctimas del 11-M tres años después," *El Mundo*, March 11, 2007. http://www.elmundo.es/elmundo/2007/03/11/espana/1173591765.html.

[95]Sarah Gensburger, "Sens" ("Sense") in *The Sociological Chronicles of the 'Bataclan Neighborhood*,' (Blog) May 1, 2016. https://quartierdubataclan.wordpress.com/2016/05/01/sens-1052016.

[96]Kai Erikson, *New Species of Trouble: The Human Experience of Modern Disasters* (New York: Norton, 1995).

[97]David W. Dunlap, "At Battery Park City, 'Pioneers' Like Life," *New York Times*, July 22, 1983, p. B1.

[98]Iris Marion Young, "The Ideal of Community and the Politics of Difference," *Social Theory and Practice* 12 no. 1, Spring 1986, pp. 1–26. https://www.pdcnet.org

/pdc/bvdb.nsf/purchase?openform&fp=soctheorpract&id=soctheorpract_1986_0012 _0001_0001_0026.

[99]Kai Erikson, *Everything in Its Path: Destruction of Community in the Buffalo Creek Flood* (New York: Simon and Schuster, 1978), p. 47.

[100]Elizabeth Fussell, "Help from Family, Friends, and Strangers During Hurricane Katrina: Finding the Limits of Social Networks," in *Displaced: Life in the Katrina Diaspora*, eds. Lynn Weber and Lori Peek (Austin: University of Texas Press, 2012), pp. 150–166.

[101]Oscar Newman, *Defensible Space: Crime Prevention through Urban Design* (New York: Macmillan, 1972), p. 3. My italics.

[102]Nadia A. Mian, *Nehemiah Houses*, (New York: New York University Press, forthcoming).

[103]"Interim Assessment of the Hope VI Program Cross-Site Report," HUD 2003. Cited in "A Decade of Hope VI: Research Findings and Policy Challenges," p. 20. Urban Institute, 2004, p. 76. 4,119 units compared to 7,810. https://www.huduser.gov /Publications/pdf/HOPE_VI_Cross_Site.pdf.

[104]Sudhir Venkatesh, *Dislocation* (Documentary film) 2005.

[105]Bonnie Docherty and Tyler Giannini, "Confronting A Rising Tide: A Proposal For A Convention On Climate Change Refugees," *Harvard Environmental Law Review*, vol. 33, no. 2 (2009), pp. 349–403. www.law.harvard.edu/students/orgs/elr/vol33_2 /Docherty%20Giannini.pdf.

[106]Bureau of Labor Statistics, "Statistics at a Glance: Oil and Gas Extraction." http: //www.bls.gov/iag/tgs/iag211.htm.

[107]My father never forgave Nixon for lowering the speed limit nationwide to 55 miles an hour (to conserve gas during the fuel shortages of the 1970s), nor Reagan for giving in to diplomatic pressure and not more heavily arming the marines killed in the bombing of their barracks in Beirut.

[108]Center for Disease Control and Prevention, *National Diabetes Statistics Report 2014*. http://www.cdc.gov/diabetes/data/statistics/2014statisticsreport.html.

[109]Sabrina Tavernise, "Global Diabetes Rates Are Rising as Obesity Spreads," *New York Times*, June 8, 2015, http://www.nytimes.com/2015/06/08/health/research/global-diabetes-rates-are-rising-as-obesity-spreads.html?_r=0. According to the CDC, the rate of diabetes doubled between 1995 and 2010. CDC, "Increasing Prevalence of Diagnosed Diabetes—United States and Puerto Rico, 1995–2010," *Morbidity and Mortality Report Weekly*, November 16, 2012 / 61(45);918–921. http://www.cdc.gov/mmwr /preview/mmwrhtml/mm6145a4.htm.

[110]*Morbidity and Mortality Report Weekly*, CDC, 2012, p.918.

[111] Tavernise, 2015.

[112] Paul Zimmet, K.G.M.M. Alberti, and Jonathan Shaw, "Global And Societal Implications of the Diabetes Epidemic" *Nature* 414, no. 13 (December 2001), p. 782.

[113] Earl S. Ford, David F. Williamson, and Simin Liu, "Weight Change and Diabetes Incidence: Findings from a National Cohort of US Adults," *American Journal of Epidemiology*, Volume 146, Issue 3 (1997), pp. 214–222. http://aje.oxfordjournals.org /content/146/3/214.short.

[114] Jay Schulkin, ed., *Allostasis, Homeostasis, and the Cost of Physiological Adaptation* (New York: Cambridge University Press, 2004), p. 19.

[115] Peter Sterling, "Principles of Allostasis: Optimal Design, Predictive Regulation, Pathophysiology, and Rational Therapeutics," in Schulkin, 2004, p. 20.

[116] Sandeep Jauhar, "When Blood Pressure Is Political," *The New York Times*, August. 6, 2016. http://www.nytimes.com/2016/08/07/opinion/sunday/when-blood-pressure-is-political.html?_r=0.

[117] Bruce G. Link and Jo Phelan, "Social Conditions as Fundamental Causes of Disease," *Journal of Health and Social Behavior*, 1995 (extra issue), pp. 80–94. Jo C. Phelan, Bruce G. Link, and Parisa Tehranifar, "Social Conditions as Fundamental Causes of Health Inequalities: Theory, Evidence and Policy Implications," *Journal of Health and Social Behavior*, 2010, no. 51: p. S29.

[118] Editorial: "Understanding Sociodemographic Differences in Health—The Role of Fundamental Social Causes," *American Journal of Public Health* 86, no. 4, April 1996, p. 471.

[119] Sterling in Schulkin, p. 40.

[120] Robert O. Bonow, MD, Mihai Gheorghiade, MD, "The Diabetes Epidemic: A National And Global Crisis," *The American Journal of Medicine* Volume 116, Issue 5, Supplement 1, 8 March 2004, Pages 2–10. http://www.sciencedirect.com/science/article/pii /S0002934303006715 . On suggestive—but not conclusive—evidence regarding temperature and endocrine disruptors, see S. W. Keith 1, 2, D. T. Redden et al., *"Putative contributors to the secular increase in obesity: exploring the roads less traveled,"* International *Journal of Obesity* (2006) 30, 1585–1594. doi:10.1038/sj.ijo.0803326; published online 27 June 2006. http://www.nature.com/ijo/journal/v30/n11/full/0803326a.html.

[121] Katherine M. Flegal, Margaret D. Carroll, Cynthia L. Ogden, et al., "Prevalence and Trends in Obesity Among US Adults, 1999–2008, *Journal of the American Medical Association.* 2010;303(3):235–241 (doi:10.1001/jama.2009.2014), p. 240. https://carmen-wiki.osu.edu/download/attachments/26513653/JAMA+2008+Obesity+Trends.pdf.

[122] Richard Wilkinson and Kate Pickett, *The Spirit Level: Why Greater Equality Makes Societies Stronger* (New York: Bloomsbury Press, 2009), p. 73.

[123] Kimberly Richards, "Diabetes Rates Have Decreased, But A Narrow Group Primarily Benefits," *Huffington Post*, December 4, 2015. http://www.huffingtonpost.com/entry/us-diabetes-rates-decrease-narrow-group_565f06dae4b08e945fed7fd2.

[124] Dennis Thompson, "Diabetes Rates Leveling Off in U.S.," *Health Day*, September 23, 2014. http://consumer.healthday.com/diabetes-information-10/demographic-diabetes-news-177/diabetes-rates-leveling-off-in-u-s-691999.html.

[125] Note that the most significant changes in insurance brought by the Affordable Care Act occurred after this study period, and there is not more recent data on diabetes rates. Uninsured rates fell most for Blacks and Latinos, but diabetes dropped most for whites. The data, therefore, is suggestive but it is too early to untangle any definitive conclusions from this particular case. Richards, 2015. http://www.huffingtonpost.com/entry/us-diabetes-rates-decrease-narrow-group_565f06dae4b08e945fed7fd2. Stephanie Marken, "U.S. Uninsured Rate at 11.4% in Second Quarter," *Gallup*, July 10, 2015. http://www.gallup.com/poll/184064/uninsured-rate-second-quarter.aspx.

[126] "Got a Problem? Drop a Dime" *Philadelphia Daily News*, April 19, 2001, pp. 16 & 105.

[127] Elijah Anderson, *Streetwise: Race, Class, and Change in an Urban Community* (Chicago: University of Chicago Press, 1990), p. 112.

[128] Newman, Katherine, *No Shame in My Game: The Working Poor in the Inner City* (New York: Knopf, 1990).

[129] Kathryn Edin, Maria Kefalas, *Promises I Can Keep: Why Poor Women Put Motherhood Before Marriage* (Los Angeles: University of California Press, 2005), pp. 61, 74.

[130] David Ellwood, Elizabeth Ty Wilde, and Lily Batchelder, "The Mommy Track Divides: The Impact of Childbearing on Wages of Women of Differing Skill Levels," National Bureau Of Economic Research Working Papers Series, December 2010.

[131] Ta-Nehisi Coates, *Between the World and Me* (New York: Spiegel & Grau, 2015).

[132] Edin and Kefalas, 2005.

[133] Anderson, 1990, p. 113.

[134] For critical appraisals of oppositional culture, see Prudence L. Carter, *Keepin' It Real: School Success Beyond Black and White* (New York: Oxford University Press, 2005). Also, Garvey F. Lundy, "The Myths of Oppositional Culture," *Journal of Black Studies* 33, 4 (March 2003), pp. 450–467.

[135] CDC's National Center for Health Statistics (NCHS) "NCHS Data on Teen Pregnancy," Centers for Disease Control and Prevention, April 2014. http://www.cdc.gov/nchs/data/factsheets/factsheet_teenage_pregnancy.htm.

[136] Heather D. Boonstra, "What Is Behind the Declines in Teen Pregnancy Rates?" *Guttmacher Policy Review*, 17, no. 3 (Summer 2014). http://www.guttmacher.org/pubs/gpr/17/3/gpr170315.html#chart2.

[137] Centers for Disease Control and Prevention, "Birth Rates (Live Births) per 1,000 Females Aged 15–19 Years, by Race and Hispanic Ethnicity, Select Years," April 13, 2015.   http://www.cdc.gov/teenpregnancy/about/birth-rates-chart-2000-2011-text .htm.

[138] Heather D. Boonstra, "What Is Behind the Declines in Teen Pregnancy Rates?" *Guttmacher Policy Review*, 17, no. 3 (Summer 2014). https://www.guttmacher.org/gpr /2014/09/what-behind-declines-teen-pregnancy-rates.

[139] Centers for Disease Control and Prevention, "Birth Rates (Live Births) per 1,000 Females Aged 15–19 Years, by Race and Hispanic Ethnicity, Select Years," April 13, 2015. http://www.cdc.gov/teenpregnancy/about/birth-rates-chart-2000-2011-text.htm. "Teen Pregnancy Rates Have Declined Significantly among All Racial Groups," http: //www.familyfacts.org/charts/276/teen-pregnancy-rates-have-declined-significantly- among-all-racial-groups.

[140] Nadia Khomami, "Number of teenage births in England and Wales at lowest level in 70 years," *Guardian*, July 15, 2015. http://www.theguardian.com/lifeandstyle/2015 /jul/15/teenage-pregnancies-uk-drops-lowest-level-70-years. US rate, Boonstra 2014. http://www.guttmacher.org/pubs/gpr/17/3/gpr170315.html.

[141] Anderson, 1990, p. 112.

[142] Sarah Kliff, "The Mystery Of The Falling Teen Birth Rate," *Vox*. January 21, 2015. http://www.vox.com/2014/8/20/5987845/the-mystery-of-the-falling-teen-birth-rate.

[143] Kathrin F. Stanger-Hall and David W. Hall, "Abstinence-Only Education and Teen Pregnancy Rates: Why We Need Comprehensive Sex Education in the US," *PLoS One*. 2011; 6(10): e24658. http://www.ncbi.nlm.nih.gov/pmc/articles/PMC3194801/.

[144] Corrie MacLaggan, "In Texas, Less Progress on Reducing Teen Pregnancy," *Texas Tribune*, July 6, 2014. https://www.texastribune.org/2014/07/06/teen-births-texas.

[145] MacLaggan, 2014.

[146] Researchers found long-acting reversible contraceptives played at most a "modest role," although overall increases in the use of some form of birth control were more significant. The question, then, is what factors contributed to increased contraception use. Laura Lindberg, John Santelli, and Sheila Desai, "Understanding the Decline in Adolescent Fertility in the United States, 2007–2012," *Journal of Adolescent Health* 59 (2016), pp. 577–583.

[147] Rick Nevin, "How Lead Exposure Relates To Temporal Changes In IQ, Violent Crime, And Unwed Pregnancy," *Environmental Research*. May 2000; 83(1):1–22. http://www.ncbi.nlm.nih.gov/pubmed/10845777.

[148] Jamie Lincoln Kitman, "The Secret History of Lead," *The Nation*, March 2, 2000. http://www.thenation.com/article/secret-history-lead. On Nicander, H. A.

Waldon, "Lead Poisoning in the Ancient World," *Medical History* 17, 4 (October 1973), p. 395. https://www.ncbi.nlm.nih.gov/pmc/articles/PMC1081502.

[149] Nevin, 2000.

[150] Jessica Wolpaw Reyes, "Lead Exposure And Behavior: Effects On Antisocial And Risky Behavior Among Children And Adolescents," National Bureau of Economic Research Working Papers Series, August 2014, p. 26. http://www.nber.org/papers/w20366.

[151] Reyes, 2014, p. 22.

[152] Larry Johnson, "Iraqi Cancers, Birth Defects Blamed On U.S. Depleted Uranium," *Seattle Post-Intelligencer*, November 12, 2008.

[153] Sasha Abramsky, "Did Roe v. Wade Abort Crime?" *American Prospect*, December 19, 2001. http://prospect.org/article/did-roe-v-wade-abort-crime.

[154] See my critique of *Freakonomics* and discussion of the implications of the abortion-and-crime correlation: "Freak Out," *Dissent*, Spring 2006. https://www.dissentmagazine.org/article/freak-out.

[155] Jonathan Gruber, ed. *Risky Behavior Among Youths: An Economic Analysis* (Chicago: University of Chicago Press, 2001), p. 16. Cited in Reyes, 2014, p. 27.

[156] John J. Donohue III, Jeffrey Grogger, and Steven D. Levitt, "The Impact of Legalized Abortion on Teen Childbearing," White paper (Yale Law School Legal Scholarship Repository), May 5, 2009.

[157] Eileen Patten and Gretchen Livingston, "Why is the teen birth rate falling?," *Fact Tank*, Pew Research Center, April 29, 2016. http://www.pewresearch.org/fact-tank/2016/04/29/why-is-the-teen-birth-rate-falling/

[158] Quoted in Ehrenreich, *Blood Rites*, 1997, p. 4.

[159] Paul Krugman, "Inequality and the City," *New York Times*, November 30, 2015. http://nyti.ms/1IjbdF9.

[160] McFarland and Moore, 1957, p. 798.

[161] Gavin Francis, "Get the Placentas," *London Review of Books* 38, no. 11 (June 2, 2016). http://www.lrb.co.uk/v38/n11/gavin-francis/get-the-placentas.

[162] Katha Pollitt, "The Smurfette Principle," in *Reasonable Creatures: Essays on Women and Feminism* (New York: Knopf, 1994), pp. 154–155.

[163] Martha T. Moore and Dennis Cauchon, "Delay meant death on 9/11," *USA Today*, September 2, 2002. "If the boss left or told people to evacuate, workers usually got out. If the boss stayed, people were more likely to stay. Many who saw or felt nothing from the first jet's impact fled because of the fear they saw in colleagues who had. Well-compensated employees such as financial traders were less likely to leave their desks in time; lower-ranking employees were more likely to get out than top executives. Several executives and managers died because they spent crucial minutes making sure all their

subordinates were on the way out. Announcements that the building was 'secure' may have led to the deaths of hundreds of people. After American Airlines Flight 11 hit the north tower, fire safety officials for the Port Authority of New York and New Jersey, which operated the Trade Center, broadcast several announcements over the public-address system that the south tower was safe and that workers did not need to evacuate. Many who were leaving the south tower turned back when they heard them."

[164]Thomas Kaplan, "Cuomo Seeking Home Buyouts in Flood Zones," *The New York Times*, February 3, 2013.

[165]Christophe Boneuil and Jean-Baptiste Fressoz, *The Shock of the Anthropocene: The Earth, History, and Us* (New York: Verso, 2015).

[166]Douglas Massey and Nancy Denton, *American Apartheid: Segregation and the Making of the Underclass* (Cambridge, MA: Harvard University, 1993).

[167]See "Mapping Inequality" at https://dsl.richmond.edu/panorama/redlining. The accompanying report redlined my Brooklyn neighborhood in 1937 despite having "no Negros." The report noted a Jewish "infiltration."

[168]Douglas Massey, Nancy Denton, *American Apartheid: Segregation and the Making of the Underclass* (Cambridge, Ma: Harvard University Press, 1993), pp. 99–103.

[169]Mitchell Duneier, *Ghetto: The Invention of a Place, The History of an Idea* (New York: Farrar, Strauss and Giroux, 2016). Regarding the earlier origins of the Great Migration, see Isabel Wilkerson, *The Warmth of Other Suns: The Epic Story of America's Great Migration* (New York: Random House, 2010).

[170]Adrian Brune, "Tulsa's Shame: Race Riot Victims Still Wait For Promised Reparations," *The Nation*, February 28, 2002.

[171]Quoted in Weise, *A Place of Their Own*, p. 276.

[172]Richard G. Moye, Dawn X.Henderson, Michele K. Lewis, Andrea Lewis. "Moving On Up But Still Falling Down: A Framework For Understanding The Trayvon Martin's Of The World," *Race, Gender & Class*; vol. 22 issue 1/2, (2015), pp. 296-306. https://search.proquest.com/docview/1757047127?pq-origsite=gscholar .

[173]David Jacobs, Robert M. O'Brien, "The Determinants of Deadly Force: A Structural Analysis of Police Violence," *American Journal of Sociology*, vol. 103, no. 4 (January 1998), pp. 837–862. http://www.jstor.org/stable/10.1086/231291.

[174]US Department of Housing and Urban Development, *Moving to Opportunity for Fair Housing Demonstration Program: Final Impacts Evaluation*, 2011. https://www.huduser.gov/publications/pdf/mtofhd_fullreport_v2.pdf. For the $3,000 bump, see Raj Chetty, Nathaniel Hendren, and Lawrence F. Katz, "The Effects of Exposure to Better Neighborhoods on Children: New Evidence from the Moving to Opportunity Experiment," Harvard University and National Bureau of Economic Research, August 2015.

http://scholar.harvard.edu/files/hendren/files/mto_paper.pdf. Like the question of teen pregnancy, there is a puzzle here about effects: the MTO study, which, as a randomized study in which participants moved to different kinds of neighborhoods, appeared to be most rigorous, "found no detectable evidence on children's achievement test scores, on average, across the five program sites (Baltimore, Boston, Chicago, Los Angeles, and New York City)." Earlier long-term studies, particularly following the Gautreaux ruling in Chicago, had found there were differences in children's educational achievement when they moved to other neighborhoods. Overall, the effect appeared to be slight, and only occurred under certain contexts, and in some cities. Julia Burdick-Will, Jens Ludwig, Stephen W. Raudenbush, Robert J. Sampson, Lisa Sanbonmatsu, and Patrick Sharkey, "Converging Evidence for Neighborhood Effects on Children's Test Scores: An Experimental, Quasi-Experimental, and Observational Comparison," in *Whither Opportunity? Rising Inequality, Schools, and Children's Life Chances*, eds. Greg J. Duncan and Richard J. Murnane (New York: Russell Sage Foundation, 2011), pp. 255–276.

[175] Laurie Essig, *Queer in Russia: A Story of Sex, Self, and The Other* (Durham, NC: Duke University Press, 1999), p. 124.

[176] Essig, 1999, p. 150.

[177] Oliver Faye, « Le FN capte l'attention d'une partie de l'électorat gay, » Le Monde April 12, 2016. http://www.lemonde.fr/politique/article/2016/04/12/l-attraction-en-hausse-du-front-national-aupres-de-la-communaute-gay_4900269_823448.html.

[178] "I hear more and more testimony to the fact that, in certain neighborhoods, it's not good to be a woman, nor a homosexual, nor Jew, nor even French or white," said Le Pen. « J'entends de plus en plus de témoignages sur le fait que, dans certains quartiers, il ne fait pas bon être femme, ni homosexuel, ni juif, ni même Français ou blanc ». Faye, *Le Monde*, April 12, 2016.

[179] The term "punctuated equilibrium" is adapted from Stephen Jay Gould and Niles Eldredge, "Punctuated Equilibria; The Temps and Mode of Evolution Reconsidered,"*Paleontology* 3, no. 2 (Spring 1977) pp. 115–151.

[180] Miriam Greenberg, Kevin Fox Gotham, *Crisis Cities: Disaster and Redevlelopment in New York and New Orleans* (Oxford University Press, 2014).

[181] As Milton Friedman wrote, "Only a crisis—actual or perceived—produces real change. When that crisis occurs, the actions that are taken depend on the ideas that are lying around . . . Our basic function [is] to develop alternatives to existing policies, to keep them alive and available until the politically impossible." Quoted in Eric Klinenberg, "It Takes a Crisis" (review of Naomi Klein's *Shock Doctrine*), *Book Forum*, Fall 2007.

[182] For an example of a recent elaboration on Marx, see Thomas Picketty's observation

that Marx presumed a static rather than a growing economy, or postcolonialists noting his omission of the fundamental role of colonies in the European economy. Thomas Picketty, *Capital in the Twenty-First Century* (Cambridge, MA: Harvard University Press, 2014), p. 227.

[183] Adam Smith, *An Inquiry into the Nature and Causes of the Wealth of Nations* (Meta-Libri, 2007), p. 14. www.ibiblio.org/ml/libri/s/SmithA_WealthNations_p.pdf.

[184] Kertzer and Laslett, eds., *Aging in the Past: Demography, Society, and Old Age* (Berkeley, CA: University of California Press, 1995).

[185] While there are arguments on both sides of the "Great Standard of Living Debate," death from disease, malnutrition, reduced height, and the considerably diminished autonomy and independence of everyday people in England during industrialization would obligate Smith to do some research before presuming the superiority of his system.

[186] For more on definitions of class, see Michael Zweig, ed., *What's Class Got to Do with It? American Society in the Twenty-first Century* (Ithaca, NY: ILR Press/Cornell University Press, 2004).

[187] Adams, James Truslow, *The Epic of America* (Little, Brown, and Co., 1931).

[188] Bernadette D. Proctor, Jessica L. Semega, and Melissa A. Kollar, "Income and Poverty in the United States: 2015" (Population Reports) US Bureau of the Census, September 2016. www.census.gov/content/dam/Census/library/publications/2015/demo/p60-252.pdf.

[189] "A Peek Into Netflix Queues," *The New York Times*, January 8, 2010. http://www.nytimes.com/interactive/2010/01/10/nyregion/20100110-netflix-map.html?mcubz=1.

[190] Hofstadter, in his comprehensive essay on "The Paranoid Style in American Politics," notes that such theories do not lack for evidence, but that their critical weakness is in then jumping from abundant evidence (much of it true) to an unsubstantiated idea about causality—the conspiracy. Hofstadter, 1965, p. 37.

[191] Hofstadter, 1965, p, 36.

[192] Stuart Taylor, "Shootings By Hinckley Laid To Schizophrenia," *New York Times*, May 15, 1982. http://www.nytimes.com/1982/05/15/us/shootings-by-hinckley-laid-to-schizophrenia.html.

[193] One question that remains is the extent to which such assassins are a product of our time, as much mental illness manifests itself in socially specific ways. Given evidence that the incidence of schizophrenia, at least, is remarkably consistent across historical periods and cultural settings, have some fraction always been young men engaging in similar acts of violence against people in positions of authority? Or were they swept up by other social processes—war, work, everyday violence? Do guns and similar weapons make the expression of their anger different than it was in earlier eras?

[194] From Asia Booth Clarke, *John Wilkes Booth: A Sister's Memoir,* ed. Terry Alford, (Jackson: University Press of Mississippi, 1999). Quoted in Paige Williams, "The Closest Source We Have to Really Knowing John Wilkes Booth Is His Sister," *Smithsonian* March 2015. http://www.smithsonianmag.com/history/the-closest-source-we-have-knowing-john-wilkes-booth-is-his-sister-180954328/?no-ist.

[195] Although there are dangers in trying to apply contemporary definitions of mental illness to other historical periods, the temptation is irresistible. Booth shows some telling traits. At the time, it was recognized that mental illness ran in the family; Booth's father, himself a famous actor, was called the "Mad Tragedian," and a friend wrote that "the Booths had an inherited strain of darkness in them." Like Loughner, who was schizophrenic, Booth began ranting angrily in the months before the assassination. His sister Asia Booth Clarke later wrote in her biography of him that he raged against Lincoln and his delusion about an impending American monarchy. "A desperate turn towards the evil had come." Family described a change in John Wilkes Booth. The last time he saw his sister he left a packet of documents including a letter often called his manifesto; published in newspapers soon after his death. An actor who had known and performed with Booth said that "the signs of insanity are in this letter." See "The Murderer Of Mr. Lincoln; Extraordinary Letter of John Wilkes Booth Proof that He Meditated His Crime Months Ago His Excuses for the Contemplated Act His Participation in the Execution of John Brown," *New York Times*, reprinted from the *Philadelphia Inquirer*, April 21, 1865. http://www.nytimes.com/1865/04/21/news/murderer-mr-lincoln-extraordinary-letter-john-wilkes-booth-proof-that-he.html?pagewanted=allfo. Also Paige Williams, "The Assassination of Abraham Lincoln: The Closest Source We have to Really Knowing John Wilkes Booth is His Sister," *Smithsonian*, March 2015. http://www.smithsonianmag.com/history/the-closest-source-we-have-knowing-john-wilkes-booth-is-his-sister-180954328. Neil A. Grauer, "The Mad Booths of Maryland," *Baltimore Sun*, October 5, 1992. See Gene Smith, *American Gothic: The Story of America's Legendary Theatrical Family—Junius Edwin and John Wilkes Booth* (New York: Simon & Schuster).

[196] This is not to deny political meaning to the actions of young men (particularly when acting in concert, because a group of assassins are more likely to have a shared grievance than a shared mental health diagnosis).

[197] Editorial: "Adrian Fenty: The Jerk D.C. Needs Why you should vote for an unpopular mayor. And lots of other endorsements, too," *Washington City Paper*, September 10, 2010. http://www.washingtoncitypaper.com/articles/39709/2010-endorsements.

[198] Peter Jennings, "Reporting—Guantanamo," Air date: June 25, 2004. http://thedocumentarygroup.com/PJP/Transcripts%20Files/Script_Guantanamo.doc.

[199]John Simpson, "No Surprises In The War On Terror," BBC News, February 13, 2006. http://news.bbc.co.uk/2/hi/middle_east/4708946.stm .

[200]Incidentally, Jaurès's assassin was twenty-nine when he killed Jaurès; he was consumed by hatred for him, stalked him and scribbled incomprehensible notes about him before shooting him. Jaurès's speech comes from, Jean Jaurès, Conférence tenue à l'Alliance française, 1884, cited in Sandrine Lemaire, Nicolas Bancel, Pascal Blanchard, eds., *La Fracture Coloniale* (Paris: La Découverte, 2006), p. 39.

[201]Lemaire, Bancel, and Blanchard, 2006, pp. 117-118.

[202]For instance, after the November 13, 2015, terrorist attacks in Paris, Prime Minister Manuel Valls called for « une guerre de civilisation . . . contre la barbarie. » Former conservative President Nicolas Sarkozy spoke of «un combat pour la civilisation contre la barbarie. » See « Valls précise ses propos sur la « guerre de civilisation » et s'étonne qu'on lui fasse « un procès » » *Le Monde*, July 14, 2015. http://www.lemonde.fr/police-justice/article/2015/06/29/valls-precise-ses-propos-sur-la-guerre-de-civilisation-et-s-etonne-qu-on-lui-fasse-un-proces_4664161_1653578.html#XkM5BckEroDmiQBs.99. « Sarkozy à Tunis pour appuyer «le combat de la civilisation contre la barbarie» » *20 Minutes*, July 20, 2015. http://www.20minutes.fr/monde/1654591-20150720-sarkozy-tunis-appuyer-combat-civilisation-contre-barbarie.

[203]Lemaire, Bancel, and Blanchard, 2006.

[204]Paul Aussaresses, *Services Spéciaux, Algérie 1955–1957* (Paris: Perrin, 2001).

[205]« Mort du général Aussaresses, tortionnaire en Algérie, » *Libération*, December 4, 2013. http://www.liberation.fr/societe/2013/12/04/deces-du-general-paul-aussaresses_964056.

[206]Roger Trinquier, *La Guerre moderne* (Éditions Table Ronde, 1986).

[207]Marie-Monique Robin, « Les escadrons de la mort: L'École franco-algérienne. » *Lundi Investigation* (Canal +, 2003). https://www.youtube.com/watch?v=8IaA8rTeQRY.

[208]Robin, 2003. 29 minutes.

[209]Robin, 2003.

[210]Jane Mayer, "Whatever It Takes: The politics of the man behind '24.'" *The New Yorker*, February 19, 2007, http://www.newyorker.com/magazine/2007/02/19/whatever-it-takes.

[211]Sophia Raday, "David Petraeus Wants This French Novel Back in Print! Why Jean Lartéguy's The Centurions appeals to our generation's most influential military strategist," *Slate*, January 27, 2011. http://www.slate.com/articles/arts/culturebox/2011/01/david_petraeus_wants_this_french_novel_back_in_print.html.

[212]Sophia Raday, "David Petraeus Wants This French Novel Back in Print! Why Jean Larteguy's *The Centurions* appeals to our generation's most influential military strat-

egist." *Slate*, January 27, 2001. http://www.slate.com/articles/arts/culturebox/2011/01/david_petraeus_wants_this_french_novel_back_in_print.single.html.

[213]Jean Lartéguy, *Les Centurions* (Paris: Presses de la Cité, 1960), p. 397. My thanks to the EHESS Laboratoire de démographie historique for letting me borrow a copy from their collection.

[214]Lartéguy, 1960, p. 402.

[215]Lartéguy, 1960, p. 406.

[216]Mayer, 2007.

[217]Henry Shue, "Torture," Philosophy and Public Affairs vol. 7, no. 2 (1978), p. 141. Also cited in Yuval Ginbar, *Why Not Torture Terrorists? Moral, Practical, And Legal Aspects Of The "Ticking Bomb" Justification For Torture* (New York: Oxford University Press, 2008), p. 360.

[218]Association for the Prevention of Torture "Defusing the Ticking Time Bomb Scenario: Why We Must Say No To Torture, Always," 2007. http://www.apt.ch/content/files_res/tickingbombscenario.pdf.

[219]Denver Nicks, "Torture Debate Once Again Hinges on a 'Ticking Time Bomb'," Time, December 9, 2014. http://time.com/3626076/torture-report-ticking-time-bomb/.

[220]Senate Select Subcommittee on Intelligence, "Committee Study of the Central Intelligence Agency's Detention and Interrogation Program: Findings and Conclusions," Unclassified, December 4, 2014, p. 9.

[221]"Findings and Conclusions," 2014, p. 19

[222]Senate Select Subcommittee on Intelligence, "Committee Study of the Central Intelligence Agency's Detention and Interrogation Program: Findings and Conclusions," Unclassified, December 4, 2014, p. 3

[223]US Senate Select Committee, Committee Study of the Central Intelligence Agency's Detention and Interrogation Program (December 2014), p. 13. https://www.amnestyusa.org/pdfs/sscistudy1.pdf.

[224]Douglas Martin, "Paul Aussaresses, 95, Who Tortured Algerians, Dies," *The New York Times*, December 4, 2013. http://www.nytimes.com/2013/12/05/world/europe/paul-aussaresses-95-dies-confessed-to-torture.html?_r=0.

[225]On deviant engineers, see Diane Vaughn, *The Challenger Launch Decision: Risky Technology, Culture, and Deviance at NASA* (Chicago: University of Chicago, 1996).

[226]US Senate Select Committee 2014.

[227]David Denby, *Lit Up: One Reporter. Three Schools. Twenty-Four Books That Can Change Lives* (New York: Henry Holt & Company, 2016), pp. 52–53.

[228]R. B. Clayton, G. Leshner, and A. Almond, "The Extended iSelf: The Impact of iPhone Separation on Cognition, Emotion, and Physiology." *Journal of Computer-*

Mediated Communication, 20, 2014: 119–135. http://onlinelibrary.wiley.com/doi/10.1111/jcc4.12109/full.

[229]Cheever, N. A., Rosen, L. D., Carrier, L. M., and Chavez, A., "Out Of Sight Is Not Out Of Mind: The Impact Of Restricting Wireless Mobile Device Use On Anxiety Levels Among Low, Moderate And High Users." *Computers in Human Behavior,* 37 (2014), pp. 290–297. http://doi.org/10.1016/j.chb.2014.05.002. For a cautionary assessment of social media's effects, see Sherry Turkle, *Alone Together: Why We Expect More from Technology and Less from Each Other* (New York: Basic Books, 2011).

[230]In this version, it is comparable to what is sometimes called the Demonstration Effect.

[231]Incidentally, we don't worry about the ozone hole anymore, but it hasn't gone away. Scientists would count it as a victory if the ozone hole in the Antarctic stayed roughly the same size. In the North Pole, however, a new hole seems to be opening up. Aaron Sidder, "Remember the Ozone Hole? Now There's Proof It's Healing," *National Geographic,* June 30, 2016. http://news.nationalgeographic.com/2016/06/antarctic-ozone-hole-healing-fingerprints. Christine Dell'Ammore, "First North Pole Ozone Hole Forming?," *National Geographic News*, March 23, 2011. http://news.nationalgeographic.com/news/2011/03/110321-ozone-layer-hole-arctic-north-pole-science-environment-uv-sunscreen.

[232]In defense of my discipline, physics "predicts" things that already exist, like black holes. Sociology would have to predict a contingent outcome that have not yet occurred to think of itself as predictive.

[233]George Marshall, *Don't Even Think About It: Why our Brains Are Wired to Ignore Climate Change* (New York: Bloomsbury, 2014), p. 67.

[234]Michael Jensen and Erin Miller, "American Deaths in Terrorist Attacks, 1995-2015." National Consortium for the Study of Terrorism and Responses to Terrorism, (START), October 2015. http://www.start.umd.edu/publication/american-deaths-terrorist-attacks-1995-2015

[235]US in the 1960s: Ted Robert Gurr, "Some Characteristics of Political Terrorism in the 1960s," in Michael Stohl (ed.), *The Politics of Terrorism* (New York, 1979), pp. 23–50, cited in Martha Crenshaw, "The Causes of Terrorism," *Comparative Politics*, vol. 13, no. 4 (July 1981), pp. 379. http://www.jstor.org/stable/421717.

[236]Crenshaw defines the conventional idea of terrorism thus: "Terrorism occurs both in the context of violent resistance to the state as well as in the service of state interests. If we focus on terrorism directed against governments for purposes of political change, we are considering the premeditated use or threat of symbolic, low-level violence by conspiratorial organizations. Terrorist violence communicates a political message; its ends go beyond damaging an enemy's material resources. The victims or objects of terrorist attack have little intrinsic value to the terrorist group but represent a larger human au-

dience whose reaction the terrorists seek. Violence characterized by spontaneity, mass participation, or a primary intent of physical destruction can therefore be excluded from our investigation." Crenshaw 1981, p. 379.

[237]"Number of suicide attacks worldwide between 1982 and 2001," Statista. 2016. https://www.statista.com/statistics/251324/number-of-suicide-attacks-worldwide.

[238]According to US State Department data. Niall McCarthy, "The Countries With The Most Terrorist Attacks," Statista, June 7, 2016. https://www.statista.com/chart/4969/the-countries-with-the-most-terrorist-attacks.

[239]To the contrary, Bush suggested that this attack was worse than any US battle of the twentieth century (except Pearl Harbor) because it had taken place on US soil.

[240]Crenshaw, 1981, p. 383.

[241]Crenshaw, 1981, p. 384.

[242]Robert A. Pape, "The Strategic Logic of Suicide Terrorism," *American Political Science Review* vol. 97. no. 3, August 2003, pp. 343–361.

[243]"Myth Busting: Robert Pape on ISIS, suicide terrorism, and U.S. Foreign Policy." *Chicago Policy Review*, May 5, 2015. http://chicagopolicyreview.org/2015/05/05/myth-busting-robert-pape-on-isis-suicide-terrorism-and-u-s-foreign-policy.

[244]Cited in Naomi Klein, "Let Them Drown: The Violence of Othering in a Warming World," *London Review of Books* 38, no. 11, June 2, 2016, pp. 11–14. http://www.lrb.co.uk/v38/n11/naomi-klein/let-them-drown.

[245]Marshall, 2014, p. 63.

[246]Bonneuil and Fressoz, 2015, p. 5. If you were expecting carbon dioxide should be measured as a percentage rather than the tiny *parts per million*, remember that 10 percent CO_2 can cause death. Our atmosphere is mostly nitrogen (80%) and oxygen (20%).

[247]Marshall, 2014, p. 63.

[248]Marshall, 2014.

[249]Marshall, 2014, p. 106.

[250]Intergovernmental Panel on Climate Change, Climate Change 2014: Synthesis Report. Contribution of Working Groups I, II and III to the Fifth Assessment Report of the Intergovernmental Panel on Climate Change [Core Writing Team, R.K. Pachauri and L.A. Meyer (eds.)]. (Geneva, Switzerland: WMO, UNEP, 2014.) From low pollution to high pollution, the climate predictions have the non-catchy names of RPG 2.6, RPG 4.5, RPG 6.0, and RPG 8.5.

[251]David Bello, "10 Solutions for Climate Change: Ten Possibilities For Staving Off Catastrophic Climate Change," *Scientific American*, November 26, 2007. https://www.scientificamerican.com/article/10-solutions-for-climate-change.

[252]Office of Hilary Clinton, "Climate Change," https://www.hillaryclinton.com/issues/cli-

mate/. "Hillary Clinton Pledges Half A Billion Solar Panels For US If She Wins Office," *The Guardian*, July 26, 2015. https://www.theguardian.com/us-news/2015/jul/27/hillary-clinton-pledges-half-a-billion-solar-panels-for-us-if-she-wins-office. Accessed November 21, 2017.

[253]The sources that make these calculations do not do very sophisticated calculations, typically multiplying energy-per panel ratings until they reach total US energy production. My use of this example is not to suggest these back-of-the-envelope calculations are ready to be field tested, but to suggest that, as with other strategies, alternative energy sources could make a meaningful dent in atmospheric carbon. Gabriel Reilich Jordan Crucchiola, "The Amount Of Land Required To Run America On Solar Power Is Shockingly Small," *Good*, April 22, 2016. https://www.good.is/infographics/solar-power-all-of-america.

[254]See Liz Koslov, "The Case for Retreat," *Public Culture* vol. 28 no. 8 (2016), pp. 373–401, and Katrina Kuh, "Agnostic Adaptation," in "A Response to the IPCC Fifth Assessment," by Sarah Adams-Schoen et al., *Environmental Law Reporter* 45, no. 1, pp. 10027–28.

[255]84 percent of whites in 2013 supported interracial marriage. Frank Newport, "In U.S., 87% Approve of Black-White Marriage, vs. 4% in 1958," Gallup.com, July 25, 2013. http://www.gallup.com/poll/163697/approve-marriage-blacks-whites.aspx.

[256]Taeku Lee, "2014 Midterms: Patterns and Paradoxes in Voting Among Asian Americans," Brookings Institute, October 29, 2014. https://www.brookings.edu/blog/fixgov/2014/10/29/2014-midterms-patterns-and-paradoxes-in-voting-among-asian-americans. On Asian voting patterns in the Clinton/Trump election, Asma Khalid, "Fueled By Young Voters, Asian-Americans Increasingly Identify As Democrats," WNYC (NPR), May 24, 2016. http://www.npr.org/2016/05/24/479192873/fueled-by-young-voters-asian-americans-increasingly-identify-as-democrats.

[257]For exit-poll data on voting by race, see Jon Huang, Samuel Jacoby, Michael Strickland, and K.K. Rebecca Lai, "Election 2016: Exit Polls," *The New York Times*, November 8, 2016 (and updated). http://www.nytimes.com/interactive/2016/11/08/us/politics/election-exit-polls.html."Hispanic voters and the 2016 election," *Pew Research Center*, July 6 2016. http://www.people-press.org/2016/07/07/6-hispanic-voters-and-the-2016-election.

index